SACRAMENTO PUBLIC LIBRARY

3 3029 04950 9631

CENTRAL LIBRARY
828 "I" STREET
SACRAMENTO, CA 95814

OCT - - 2003

D1015455

GOD'S
DEFENDERS

GOD'S
DEFENDERS

What they Believe and Why They Are Wrong

WILLIAM JAMES • G.K. CHESTERTON

T.S. ELIOT • WILLIAM F. BUCKLEY

JERRY FALLWELL • ANNIE DILLARD

C. S. LEWIS

S.T. JOSHI

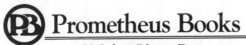 **Prometheus Books**

59 John Glenn Drive
Amherst, New York 14228–2197

Published 2003 by Prometheus Books

God's Defenders: What They Believe and Why They Are Wrong. Copyright © 2003 by S. T. Joshi. All rights reserved. No part of this publication may be reproduced, stored in a retrieval system, or transmitted in any form or by any means, digital, electronic, mechanical, photocopying, recording, or otherwise, or conveyed via the Internet or a Web site without prior written permission of the publisher, except in the case of brief quotations embodied in critical articles and reviews.

Inquiries should be addressed to
Prometheus Books
59 John Glenn Drive
Amherst, New York 14228–2197

716–691–0133 (x207). FAX: 716–564–2711.
WWW.PROMETHEUSBOOKS.COM

07 06 05 04 03   5 4 3 2 1

Library of Congress Cataloging-in-Publication Data

Joshi, S. T., 1958–
   God's defenders : what they believe and why they are wrong / by S. T. Joshi.
      p. cm.
   Includes bibliographical references (p.   ) and index.
   ISBN 1–59102–080–8
   1. Religion—Controversial literature. 2. Christianity—Controversial literature. I. Title.

BL2775.3.J67 2003
200—dc21

                                                                2003008112

Printed in Canada on acid-free paper

To

Robert M. Price

If there be an infinite Being, he does not need our help—
we need not waste our energies in his defence.

—Robert G. Ingersoll, "God in the Constitution" (1890)

One does not kill by anger but by laughter.

—Friedrich Nietzsche, *Thus Spake Zarathustra*

CONTENTS

INTRODUCTION

Either there is one god, multiple gods, or none. Either there is such a thing called the human soul or there isn't, and, if there is, it either can or cannot survive the death of the body. Either Jesus Christ, if he existed, was the son of God or he wasn't. Either Mohammed, if he existed, was God's prophet or he wasn't.

That the essential doctrines of many of the world's major religions—especially Christianity, Judaism, and Islam—are matters of *truth or falsity* is itself a fact around which no amount of sophistry or special pleading can get. Unfortunately for them, evidence has been steadily accumulating for at least the last half-millennium to suggest that these doctrines are false. What has saved religions from completely collapsing of their own absurdity is, of course, the difficulty—

indeed, the impossibility—of *definitively* determining the truth or falsity of these doctrines. The impossibility allows the pious to maintain, as a slim and ever-decreasing hope, that the tenets of their religion *might* somehow still be true, or at least not clearly false. No amount of negative evidence can ever conclusively put any given religious dogmas out of court (aside from those that can be shown to be self-inconsistent), because there will always remain the remote possibility that they are true. The notion that truth or falsity is somehow not involved in the analysis of religious doctrine—a view fostered not only by many modern theologians but by some recent philosophers of language who maintain that religious principles are merely "language games" that do not commit their exponents to any truth-claims—has now, I trust, been shown to be a dodge and an evasion. The great majority of the faithful would certainly be astounded and offended if someone were to tell them that when they say "God created the universe," they are merely expressing some kind of "attitude of piety" rather than making an assertion about the nature of entity.

What the religious ignore in all this, of course, are two basic facts: (1) although *no* "truth" about the empirical world is other than provisional—and, in theory, falsifiable—or based upon anything but statistical probabilities, certain propositions are, nevertheless, far more likely to be "true" than others; and (2) the advance of knowledge over the past five hundred years has demonstrated with as near an approach to certainty as it may be possible to get that every single religious doctrine ever propounded is not only overwhelmingly improbable and implausible but entirely at variance with all other "truths" that have subsequently been ascertained.

I do not have the space here to write a full-scale history of this advance of knowledge, but some notes may be in order. Since Copernicus, natural science has been making startling strides in the explication of terrestrial and cosmic phenomena, and Darwin's *Origin of Species* destroyed one of the last remaining intellectual props of religion—the "argument from design," or the notion that all things in the universe were benevolently designed by God for the advantage of the human race (an argument, however, that David Hume had already shattered on logical grounds a century earlier). All these discoveries meant more than merely the collecting of isolated facts; as John William Draper stressed in his pioneering and still valuable *History of the Conflict Between Religion and Science* (1874), what was at stake were *two differing worldviews*, the religious and the scientific (or secular). The former maintained—on no evidence but that of the various sacred texts of the world, all of which differed in significant particulars—that all phenomena were caused, at least in an ultimate sense, by God. The latter established by the immense accumulation of evidence that the postulation of a god was *unnecessary* to the explanation of visible phenomena. In other words, the advance of human knowledge represented the definitive replacement of *supernatural by natural causation.* To be sure, the nineteenth-century scientists may have been a bit cocksure about the extent to which human knowledge could extend, but they were sound in their fundamental attitude. Even if all phenomena could not be (and perhaps never will be) explained, the *presumption* of a natural explanation of these phenomena ought to be paramount. The inveterate human tendency to leap to the supernatural when faced with some inexplicable occurrence should be restrained. A god or gods might still conceivably exist, but one could not be postulated to explain the existence of any object or event within the radius of human knowledge. God had become supernumerary.

But in some ways more important than the advances in natural sciences were discoveries in history, psychology, sociology, and anthropology: these sciences made it eminently clear that religious belief was an entirely natural product of primitive humanity's bewilderment in the face of natural phenomena whose causation it did not understand. Here again Hume was a pioneer, with his *Dialogues Concerning Natural Religion* (1779), although the work was carried forward by such monumental works as Edward Burnett Tylor's *Primitive Culture* (1871) and Sir James George Frazer's *The Golden Bough* (1890–1915). Whatever else religion may have been, it was preeminently a means of *explaining* (and, secondarily, controlling) the natural world to a human species that could not account for it otherwise.[1] This religious sensibility, it was discovered, far antedated the establishment of organized religions in human history; indeed, the latter were, in their various ways, mere condensations and systematizations of the former, and it was seen that these religious were perpetuated not through the accumulation of additional evidence that validated their tenets, but through the systematic indoctrination of peoples into religious dogma from infancy onward, generation after generation. It was this natural *accounting* for the origin and continuance of religious belief that shattered another favorite "proof" of theism—that religion must be true because the great majority of human beings believed it to be. Long before the advent of democracy as a political system, the notion of determining truth by majority vote—what I call the democratic fallacy—was a well-established principle of religious orthodoxy.

The dominant question thus becomes not why religion has not died away but why it continues to persist in the face of monumental evidence to the contrary. To my mind, the answer can be summed up in one straightforward sentence: People are stupid.

The fundamental fact of human history is that people in the mass are irremediably ignorant. Even a cursory examination of such phenomena as network television, politicians, astrology, best-selling novels, the *Weekly World News,* psychic hotlines, horoscopes, alien abduction theories, professional wrestling, and fashion magazines proves the point with overwhelming emphasis. The great majority of genuinely intelligent thinkers in human history has endorsed the notion.

Consider John Stuart Mill: "on any matter not self-evident there are ninety-nine persons totally incapable of judging of it for one who is capable; and the capacity of the hundredth person is only comparative."[2]

Consider H. L. Mencken: "independent thought, to a good many men, is quite impossible, and to the overwhelming majority of men, extremely painful."[3]

Consider Bertrand Russell: ". . . nine-tenths of the beliefs of nine-tenths of mankind are totally irrational."[4]

Perhaps the most pungent, and most relevant in this context, is from George Santayana, in a letter to Bertrand Russell: "People are not intelligent. It is very unreasonable to expect them to be so, and that is a fate my philosophy reconciled me to long ago. How else could I have lived for forty years in America?"[5]

Lest I be accused of making exactly the kind of "appeal to authority" that elsewhere in this book I accuse others of making, let me state that I cite these remarks—which could be multiplied so as to fill this entire volume—only as illustrations. In our age of democratic tyranny it has become, at the very least, tactless to point out the stupidity of the common people, but the evidence does not seem to admit of any other conclusion.

It may also be objected that I am putting forth an excessively simple—even simple-minded—account of the persistence of religious belief. Stupidity is, however, a phenomenon of wondrous, ineffable complexity, and its effects and ramifications are well-nigh infinite. One of the leading scholars on this crucial subject, Walter B. Pitkin, wrote as follows in his seminal treatise, *A Short Introduction to the History of Human Stupidity* (1932):

> Stupidity can easily be proved the supreme Social Evil. Three factors combine to establish it as such. First and foremost, the number of stupid people is legion. Secondly, most of the power in business, finance, diplomacy and politics is in the hands of more or less stupid individuals. Finally, high abilities are often linked with serious stupidity, and in such a manner that the abilities shine before all the world while the stupid trait lurks in deep shadow and is discerned only by intimates or by prying newspaper reporters.[6]

Certain other clarifications are necessary. When I declare that religion is so widespread because people in the mass are stupid, I assert that they lack the information needed to make a well-informed evaluation of the truth-claims of religion. Such an evaluation requires at least a surface knowledge of physics, biology, chemistry, geology, history (particularly the history of religions), psychology, anthropology, and philosophy (or, more generally, the ability to fashion reasoned arguments or to detect fallacious arguments). It is plain that the great majority of people can claim knowledge in no more than one or two of these disciplines, and most lack knowledge of them all. Indeed, so far as I can tell, only a single individual in the entire twentieth century *did* possess a passing acquaintance with all these fields: Bertrand Russell, whose antireligious views are too well known for citation.

I will go further and state that even if the mass of people had the concrete information (in science and philosophy) required for an assessment of the truth-claims of religion, they would be unable to process it; their brains simply cannot digest this kind of information. Even those who are intelligent or accomplished in other fields— authors, artists, composers, even some scientists and philosophers—are insufficiently acquainted with the many other intellectual disciplines relevant to the issue. Some scientists who have a prodigious expertise in one field of scientific inquiry frequently lack even the rudiments of knowledge in others—which is why so many physicists, for example, have lapsed into religious mysticism when approaching the edges of their subject. Knowledge is very inequitably divided—not only in the people at large, but in any given individual. I will happily maintain that all the thinkers whom I berate so lustily in this book were or are intelligent or accomplished in various ways—C. S. Lewis as a literary critic, William F. Buckley as a political commentator, Reynolds Price as a novelist—but not one of them had the all-encompassing knowledge in fields that are vital to gauging the truth or falsity of religion.

What has clearly happened in the case of many otherwise intelligent people, is that childhood crippling of their brains and emotions in favor of some dogmatic religion has for all practical purposes made their theistic views impervious to logical analysis. It is an area they simply will not investigate objectively or impartially, because it has become so deeply fused with their entire self-image that it is beyond their psychological powers to question it. My own view is that this infantile brainwashing is one of the great crimes against humanity— and it has been practiced for countless millennia (well before the advent of organized religion) and continues to be practiced to this day. Religious leaders would no doubt react with horror at the recommendation that children actually be allowed to make up their own minds about the adoption of a given religion, or any religion at all, until they are intellectually and emotionally ready to do so, without the prejudicial influence of parents, clerics, and the society at large. (No exception need be made for communist societies, for in such societies the people are brainwashed into atheism just as vigorously—and perniciously—as people in other societies are brainwashed into theism.) H. P. Lovecraft laid bare the matter long ago:

> We all know that *any* emotional bias—irrespective of truth or falsity—can be implanted by suggestion in the emotions of the young, hence the inherited traditions of an orthodox community are absolutely without evidential value regarding the real "is-or-isn't-ness" of things. Only the exceptional individual reared in the nineteenth century or before has any chance of holding any genuine opinion of value regarding the universe—except by a slow and painful process of courageous disillusionment. If religion were true, its followers would not try to bludgeon their young into an artificial conformity; but would merely insist on their unbending quest for *truth*, irrespective of artificial backgrounds or practical consequences. With such an honest and inflexible *openness to evidence*, they could not fail to receive any *real truth* which might be manifesting itself around them. The fact that religionists do *not* follow this honorable course, but cheat at their game by invoking juvenile quasi-hypnosis, is enough to destroy their pretensions in my eyes even if their absurdity were not manifest in every other direction.[7]

The great majority of the world's governments have found it politically advantageous to support religion as a means of keeping the populace suitably docile, so no help is likely to come from them. Indeed, the pervasiveness of religiosity in virtually every society ever known to exist is overwhelming and difficult for all but the most intellectually and psychologically fortified to resist.

Interestingly enough, religious leaders have grudgingly acknowledged some of the views I have just outlined. Guenter Lewy, a writer who could hardly be accused of being unsympathetic to religion, has forthrightly expounded the role of education as a determinant in religious belief:

Over the last fifty years, the number of Americans who graduate from high school and go on to college has increased sharply, and this fact, too, has ramifications for the role of religion in American society. On the whole, it appears, religious commitment decreases as the educational level increases. For example, . . . those with more education consider religion to have less importance in their lives, while those with less education place more importance on religion.

There are other areas in which increased education correlates with decreased religious activity or belief:

- 40 percent of those who did not graduate from high school read the Bible at least once a week; only 28 percent of those with education beyond high school do so.
- 45 percent of those who did not graduate from high school see the Bible as the literal word of God; only 11 percent of college graduates hold this view.
- 90 percent of those with a high-school degree or less believe that Jesus is God or the son of God; only 66 percent of college graduates hold this belief.
- 40 percent of those who did not graduate from high school describe themselves as born-again Christians; only 22 percent of college graduates so describe themselves.

After these and other data are brought forth, Lewy's contention that a correlation between intelligence and religious belief is merely a sign of "intellectual arrogance" is not likely to disturb the atheist's equanimity.[8]

The standard "proofs" for the existence of God—arguments that held sway throughout the medieval period and well into the nineteenth century—have all been destroyed and are now discarded even by most theologians. Most of these "proofs" can be refuted in approximately thirty seconds. Consider the most popular of them:

The First Cause. This is the idea that since every event is assumed to have an antecedent cause, there must have been a First Cause (i.e., God), or a cause that did not itself have an antecedent cause, to get the whole show moving. This argument is subject to numerous philosophical and scientific objections. Firstly, there is no reason to postulate a *single* First Cause; given the multiplicity of phenomena throughout the universe, there is no logical reason for assuming that there could not be two, three, or many First Causes. Indeed, it is logically possible that every event in the universe could have had its own First Cause. In any event, the Big Bang theory seems to be exactly what the medieval First Cause was thought to have been. It could always be asserted that God himself caused the Big Bang, but God's existence must be established independently before one can assume that he triggered the Big Bang.

The "Consensus of Mankind." The fact that the overwhelming majority of individuals throughout human history, in widely different cultures, have believed in God was once thought to be a decisive argument in favor of theism. The argument is much weaker now, given the widespread prevalence of atheism and agnosticism among the intelligent classes of many societies. Piety is still strong in the United States, with polls showing anywhere between 92 percent to 97 percent of the public attesting belief in God, but that still leaves 3 percent to 8 percent who do not believe (or anywhere from 8 million to 22 million unbelievers). It would be begging the question—or, at any rate, extremely implausible—to assert that all these individuals are either depraved or insane, as religious thinkers used to maintain when faced with the existence of infidelity. In any event, as I have suggested, psychology and anthropology have demonstrated that religious belief is chiefly fostered by fear (fear of the unknown, fear of death), hope (the flip side of fear—hope that God will somehow iron out the massive inequities of human life, usually in the next world where disproof is impossible), and the systematic indoctrination of children into a given religious dogma at a time before they have the intelligence and strength of character to resist the commands of parents or other authority figures. And comparative religion has shown that conceptions of godhead differ so widely from culture to culture—even from individual to individual within a given culture—that it becomes preposterous to assume that all these people are believing in the same or even an approximately similar god.

The Argument from Design. This argument remained popular for a much longer period than the others, because the scientific evidence overturning it did not emerge until a relatively late date. This argument contends that the earth (there is little thought given to the rest of the universe) and everything in it is so well designed for the continuance of life—hands designed for grasping objects, eyes designed for seeing, noses designed for smelling, etc.—that it must have been the conscious work of a god. Even if this argument is not extended to the absurdity of assuming that all things on the earth are specifically designed for the benefit of human beings, it is very weak. The very notion of "design" may be a purely human conception, and probably any kind of "design" exhibited by phenomena would have been sufficient to convince the pious of a beneficent deity. Moreover, there is the plain fact that many things do *not* seem well designed: if the divine purpose of existence is the fostering of life, then the exact function of diseases, earthquakes, typhoons, and other such embarrassments is, to put it mildly, problematical. But the theory of evolution definitively shattered this argument.

The Argument from Feelings. This argument also remained popular long after the others had fallen by the wayside, as the work of William James attests. This assumes that the profound feelings that many people have of some divine force or entity in the universe constitute evidence that there actually is such a force or entity. This argument is also very weak. Once again it can be demonstrated that in the great majority of cases these "feelings" are the result of prior religious indoctrination. The assumption that those who do not have such feelings are corrupt or insensible to perceptions of deity is, like the assumptions in regard to infidelity in the "consensus of mankind" argument, both question-begging and insulting. The fact that certain people are entirely convinced, from their "feelings," that they are Napoleon or Julius Caesar is sufficient to refute this argument; to assume that these individuals are simply "insane" whereas the pious are sane is again to beg the question.

The Moral Argument. This assumes that religious belief is necessary to good morals (i.e., to socially acceptable behavior) and that people will "run amok" if they are not restrained by belief in a powerful deity who will punish moral derelictions. This argument is probably the weakest of all, for it does not even seek to prove that a god exists but merely that it is socially beneficial for the people to believe in a god — and specifically the kind of god who will punish malefactors. The argument is simply refuted by elementary observations of history, which establish (1) that nonreligious people have behaved in a moral way (thereby destroying the belief that religion is *necessary* to good morals), (2) that religious people have frequently behaved in nonmoral ways (thereby establishing — as many social scientists have demonstrated in study after study — that religion has a minimal role in moral behavior), and (3) that many of the moral precepts actually propounded by most religions, being largely the products of barbarism, are unsuited for a civilized society (e.g., condoning of slavery, denigration of women, killing of heretics and witches, severe punishments for violations of religious ritual, absurd restrictions on sexual behavior, unquestioning acceptance of "divine" political authority, etc.).

A vague notion has developed that it is bad form to criticize someone's religion, and, by extension, religion in general. To be sure, those well informed in history can only look with bemused horror at how the devotees of one religion, for hundreds or thousands of years, persecuted the devotees of other religions, or even "heretics" within their own religion; and it certainly does seem absurd nowadays to engage in this kind of disputation, especially given that one religion is no more likely to be true than another. We are in an age of "toleration" and ecumenicalism — a somewhat paradoxical development, at least in the West, given that the scriptures of each of the major religions of Europe and the Middle East (Christianity, Judaism, and Islam) clearly and unequivocally declares that it and it alone possesses the truth about God and the universe. But surely it is still a valid procedure to assess the truth-claims of any given religion or all religions, and to determine whether their scriptures do or do not provide accurate information about human beings, human society, or the universe at large. Religions themselves have craftily put forth this hands-off principle precisely in order to shield themselves from scrutiny by pestiferous critics. Listen again to H. L. Mencken:

. . . even a superstitious man has certain inalienable rights. He has a right to harbor and indulge his imbecilities as long as he pleases, provided only he does not try to inflict them upon other men by force. He has a right to argue for them as eloquently as he can, in season and out of season. He has a right to teach them to his children. But certainly he has no right to be protected against the free criticism of those who do not hold them. He has no right to demand that they be treated as sacred. He has no right to preach them without challenge. . . .

The meaning of religious freedom, I fear, is sometimes greatly misapprehended. It is taken to be a sort of immunity, not merely from governmental control but also from public opinion. A dunderhead gets himself a long-tailed coat, rises behind the sacred desk, and emits such bilge as would gag a Hottentot. Is it to pass unchallenged? If so, then what we have is not religious freedom at all, but the most intolerable and outrageous variety of religious despotism. Any fool, once he is admitted to holy orders, becomes infallible. Any half-wit, by the simple device of ascribing his delusions to revelation, takes on an authority that is denied to all the rest of us.[9]

In some senses it appears that religious belief is now regarded as somehow equivalent to racial identity, so that it becomes a kind of "religious racism" for anyone outside of a given religion to criticize it. The history of actual race prejudice is certainly such that one would do almost anything to avoid repeating its errors and injustices. But even the most cursory examination of this analogy of religion to race shows it to be fatally flawed. Even assuming, for the sake of argument, that there are such things as clear and distinct races—a highly problematical assertion in itself—one surely cannot plausibly maintain that one is "born" with a specific religious outlook as one is presumably born into a given racial or ethnic group. There are few people today who would follow Jung in believing that the human race has some sort of inborn predisposition to seek a higher power; religion—and, a fortiori, any given religious dogma—is so clearly inbred by socialization that the analogy breaks down at once. One cannot change one's race, but many people have changed their religion, or gone from being religious to being irreligious or from being irreligious to being religious. There is no intellectual factor involved in one's race (that is, one does not choose to belong to a given race by a conscious intellectual decision), whereas there are numerous intellectual factors involved in the choice of one's religion.

It is still less plausible to assert that religion is a kind of preference—a matter of taste for which there are no grounds for disputation. Indeed, even if such an analogy were true, it would be far more harmful to religion than otherwise. One surely cannot dispute over genuine matters of taste—say, my preference for chocolate ice cream over your preference for vanilla ice cream—but it is plainly evident that religion is not one of these matters. If it were, the depth and bitterness of the arguments that have gone on over the centuries would be incomprehensible. Even more importantly, the notion that one's religion is merely a preference would shatter the truth-claims that every religion seeks to make. Surely it cannot be declared that my preference for chocolate ice cream is "truer" than your preference for vanilla ice cream: truth—in the sense of an accurate conception of the nature of the universe—does not enter into this matter. But every religion wishes to claim (although, because of the "toleration" specified above, it now does so in a rather muted way) that it is indeed "truer" than every other religion, and certainly truer than irreligion. This notion of religion as a preference is merely another way in which members of various religions seek to protect themselves from intellectual examination of their doctrines and dogmas.

I would now like to say a few words about the nature and scope of this book.

My aim here is to subject the arguments of a wide variety of religious thinkers of the twentieth century to close scrutiny and analysis. I have made every effort to eschew technical philosophical language that many readers might find confusing or baffling. As should be evident by now, my perspective is that of an atheist—but that is only because, for reasons found throughout this book, I regard atheism as the worldview most in accordance with the facts of the universe as we now know them. In other words, I am an atheist not by *presupposition*; rather, my atheism is the *culmination* of a long series of inquiries into the nature of entity. In any event, the logical and other fallacies I claim to have found in the works under analysis would persist even if I were writing from some other perspective; in other words, my arguments cannot be refuted merely on the ground that I am an atheist, but only by a demonstration that those arguments are in themselves faulty.

I am aware that atheism in its literal sense is unprovable; that is, it is impossible to maintain definitively that a god does *not* exist. All my atheism asserts is that (a) all the gods propounded by all the religions known to humanity are monumentally unlikely to exist, and (b) the reasoned belief that there is no god in the universe is the best *working hypothesis* that we have. I am not an agnostic because there appears to be an unsatisfactory fence-sitting quality to agnosticism as conventionally understood: if agnostics declare (as they are bound to do by the etymology of the word) that they simply "do not know" whether or not a god exists, the underlying assumption is that the chances are fairly even that a god exists or that a god doesn't exist. I regard this to be plain folly; there is in fact such overwhelming evidence against theism that atheism is left as the only viable option. As Lovecraft declared, in defending his stance as an actual atheist instead of an agnostic:

> All I say is that I think it is *damned unlikely* that anything like a central cosmic will, a spirit world, or an eternal survival of personality exist. They are the most preposterous and unjustified of all the guesses which can be made about the universe, and I am not enough of a hair-splitter to pretend that I don't regard them as arrant and negligible moonshine. In theory I am an *agnostic*, but pending the appearance of rational evidence I must be classed, practically and provisionally, as an *atheist*. The chances of theism's truth being to my mind so microscopically small, I would be a pedant and a hypocrite to call myself anything else.[10]

It will quickly be observed that this book makes more than occasional use of satire, repartee, persiflage, and other rhetorical devices not generally found in sober discussions of religion. I make no apology for such usages. I am not seeking to ridicule an argument simply for the sake of ridiculing it but because I regard it as so plainly nonsensical that it deserves to be ridiculed. I find it rather disheartening that the long tradition of poking fun at religion—a tradition that can be traced at least as far back as Aristophanes, and on through Juvenal, Jonathan Swift, Voltaire, Denis Diderot, Mark Twain, Ambrose Bierce, H. L. Mencken, and many others—appears to have suffered a decline in our overly polite and deferential age, with the solitary but monumental exception of Gore Vidal. A healthy dose of laughter would do more to shatter the pretensions of many religious tenets than any amount of reasoned argument. If my opponents claim that I am merely heaping indiscriminate abuse and billingsgate upon my pious enemies, then they stand self-convicted of a failure to take note of the reasoned arguments that augment and, indeed, serve as the basis of my ridicule. And if they assert that by the use of this kind of mockery I am treating a serious subject with unconscionable levity, I can only raise one eyebrow in the manner of Mr. Spock and declare with due humility that the buffoonery originates largely—and unwittingly—from the other side.

I will no doubt be criticized for belaboring my pious opponents in this book without offering anything "positive" or "constructive" to appease them. I find it difficult to be patient with such a complaint. In the first place, it would take another book of at least this size to put forth a thorough and comprehensive "atheist way of life" (I presume even the pious can get beyond the moronic idea that atheists "don't believe in anything" and therefore have no social, political, or moral ideals), and I for one admit to a temperamental disinclination to make such a case. Sharp readers of this book might perhaps pick up a few incidental hints along the way. But since religion and all it stands for comprises, to my mind, so large a proportion of what Bertrand Russell called "intellectual rubbish," it seems to me that a certain cleaning of the Augean stables is in order before a positive system can be advocated. Ambrose Bierce wrote on this very point in defending the agnostic Robert G. Ingersoll:

A respectable contemporary gets afoul of Colonel Bob Ingersoll and drubs hum stoutly because, he as what we may call a practicing infidel, "would leave us without a light or guide, to grope in entire darkness. He should not attempt," says this mindless parrot, "to tear down unless he can build up for us something better—but he has nothing better to offer." I fatigue and fall ill of this hoary, decrepit, and doddering protest of brainless imbecility; it is the first, last, intermediate and only argument of mental vacuity. In the mouth of a Christian it is an unconscious, but unconditional surrender, for it distinctly implies that there may be something better than Christianity—that Christianity is a make-shift. . . .

No man of sane intelligence will plead for religion on the ground that it is better than nothing. It is not better than nothing if it is not true. Truth is better than anything or all things; the next best thing to truth is absence of error. When you are in the dark, stand still; when you do not know what to do, do nothing. To say "don't take away my faith unless you can give me another" is to beg the question—to assume the very point in dispute for the taker-away denies that you need a faith. If you think you do that is your affair.[11]

This book should not be taken as a comprehensive analysis of theories in support of religion. Not only is my focus chiefly on Christian thinkers (since it is they who have most vigorously engaged in purportedly intellectual defenses of their dogma), but it is possible that I have chosen what might be termed "lightweight" thinkers to dissect. And yet, I cannot see that more learned theologians have made any more cogent arguments on the points in question. Many of the writers I discuss have attracted a very wide following among the pious, and in most cases their religious arguments have not been subject to careful analysis, so I think I am justified in treating them at length and in detail. There will inevitably be a certain element of repetition in some of my discussions, as several writers return obsessively to the same cruxes (especially the "problem of evil") that have dogged religious thinkers for millennia, but I have found that a study of individual theists is more fruitful than a thematic study of individual theological issues.

I do, however, regret not treating the subject of religion and science, but this topic is so complex and multifaceted that discussion in anything short of a separate book would be fruitless.[12] I can at best offer only a few notes here. Many scientists throughout the twentieth century engaged in a furious attempt to "reconcile" science and religion, asserting implausibly that there was no fundamental conflict between the two disciplines. Chief among them was Nobel Prize–winning physicist Robert Andrews Millikan, in such works as *Science and Life* (1924), *Evolution in Science and Religion* (1927), and *Time, Matter and Values* (1932). Not far behind were British astrophysicists James Jeans and Arthur S. Eddington; even Albert Einstein propounded a vague "cosmic religion" that seems to have been nothing more than wonder at the grandeur of the universe. Several recent works leave themselves wide open for pungent rebuttal, ranging from the relatively sane but nonetheless fallacy-ridden treatises of John Polkinghorne (*Belief in God in an Age of Science*, 1998; *The God of Hope and the End of the World*, 2002) to such crackpot works of "neuro-theology" as *Why God Won't Go Away* (2001), by Andrew B. Newberg et al., which purports to "prove" that a need for God is hardwired into our brains (in which case it would appear that atheists or any others who are not aware of such a need are either mentally aberrant or perhaps not even fully human). Even the otherwise sensible Stephen J. Gould, in *Rocks of Ages: Science and Religion in the Fullness of Life* (1999), utters much foolishness, contending on no legitimate grounds that science and religion should occupy separate domains of authority, but regrettably failing to specify what religion has done to deserve its domain— chiefly that of morals—and why it should be shielded from criticism by science or any other discipline.

Then, of course, there is the richly absurd and ever-growing literature on the subject of "intelligent design," that half-baked mix of bad theology and bad science that maintains that organisms on this planet are too complex to have evolved by mere "chance" and that some "designer" must have fashioned them.[13] This minimally refashioned version of the old and exploded "argument from design," even if provisionally accepted, only pushes back the inquiry further: *How* did such a "designer" fashion the entities he is supposed to have fashioned? Did the designer himself evolve from some simpler state? What independent evidence do we have, aside from the purely abstract concern about the purportedly excessive complexity of earthly entities, that such a designer actually exists? The unspoken assumption behind many of these works is that because science cannot (yet) explain *everything*, it can't explain *anything;* that God can somehow be inserted into the gaps in our current knowledge regarding the origin and development of the universe. But this is dangerous ground for any theologian to stand on, for there is a perennial risk that these "gaps" will be increasingly and inexorably filled by exact knowledge (as in fact they have been filled over the past half-millennium), leaving only the slimmest toehold for the pious. The work of Nobel Prize–winning physicist Steven Weinberg is rapidly eliminating even this toehold, and his several trenchant works—notably *God and the New Physics* (1983) and *The Mind of God: The Scientific Basis for a Rational World* (1992)—go far in presenting a compelling account of the universe without dragging in the Big Guy to explain anything.

So it is plain that the battle against religious obscurantism must and will continue. The moment one folly is snuffed out, another and still greater folly seems to emerge to take its place. The greatest harm that religion has done, and continues to do—well beyond such malfeasances as the killing of witches and heretics, the suppression of civil liberties, the disastrous uniting of religion with morality, and the terrorizing of its own adherents with thoughts of hellfire and eternal damnation—is *the subversion of clear thinking.* This subversion, in my judgment, corrupts even the social benefits that religion has on occasion provided. My only plea, therefore, is that atheists, agnostics, and secularists speak out a bit more vociferously, even tartly and pungently, against their foes—for foes they certainly are, not only to human freedom and dignity, but to the advance of all human knowledge and civilization.

A NOTE ON CITATIONS

In referring to the Bible, I generally cite the King James version, only because all other versions seem to me so literarily inferior that they become aesthetically repulsive. In instances where the King James translation has been shown to be faulty or otherwise dubious, I have consulted the Revised English Bible (1989) and, of course, the original texts in Greek and Hebrew. My citations from the Koran are taken from the translation by J. M. Rodwell.

NOTES

1. "Religion as such . . . is primarily *a recognition of a sacred order of reality which transcends the ordinary and commonplace and is responsive to human needs.* To enable man to gain some measure of control over the unpredictable and inexplicable elements in his everyday experience, a technique has been devised with which certain beliefs have become associated, to establish an efficacious relationship with the sacred." E. O. James, *Comparative Religion* (London: Methuen, 1938, rev. 1961), p. 39. "Recognition" is a bit problematical here, since it begs the question by assuming that there is a "sacred order of reality," which is the very point at issue, but no doubt Professor James (D.Litt., Ph.D., F.S.A., Hon.D.D., Professor Emeritus of the History and Philosophy of Religion at the University of London) was a pious fellow. A remark by James's contemporary, the religious scholar E. O. Kellett, seems to me more pertinent: "while not every philosophy is a religion, every religion is a philosophy. Religion, to be worth anything, must cast out fears, allay bewilderment, solve perplexities: and this cannot be done without the formation of theories, that is, without philosophizing." E. O. Kellett, *A Short History of Religions* (1933; reprint Harmondsworth, England: Penguin, 1962), p. 12.

2. John Stuart Mill, *On Liberty* (1859; reprint Harmondsworth, England: Penguin, 1974), p. 79.

3. H. L. Mencken, "The Genealogy of Etiquette," *Smart Set* 47, no. 1 (September 1915): 309.

4. Bertrand Russell, "Is There a God?" (1952), in *The Collected Papers of Bertrand Russell,* ed. John G. Slater and Peter Köllner (London: Routledge, 1997), vol. 11, p. 548.

5. George Santayana, letter to Bertrand Russell (c. December 1917), *The Autobiography of Bertrand Russell* (Boston: Little, Brown, 1968), vol. 1, p. 57.

6. Walter B. Pitkin, *A Short Introduction to the History of Human Stupidity* (New York: Simon & Schuster, 1932), p. 6.

7. H. P. Lovecraft, letter to Maurice W. Moe (August 3, 1931), *Selected Letters 1929–1931,* ed. August Derleth and Donald Wandrei (Sauk City, Wisc.: Arkham House, 1971), pp. 390–91.

8. Guenter Lewy, *Why America Needs Religion* (Grand Rapids, Mich.: William B. Eerdmans, 1996), pp. 77–78, 82.

9. H. L. Mencken, "Aftermath," *Baltimore Evening Sun,* September 14, 1925, p. 1.

10. H. P. Lovecraft, letter to Robert E. Howard (August 16, 1932), *Selected Letters 1932–1934,* ed. August Derleth and James Turner (Sauk City, Wisc.: Arkham House, 1976), p. 57.

11. Ambrose Bierce, "Prattle," *Argonaut* 3, no. 24 (December 21, 1878): 17.

12. For a good discussion see Tad S. Clements, *Science versus Religion* (Amherst, N.Y.: Prometheus Books, 1990).

13. See now Frederick Crews, "Saving Us from Darwin," *New York Review of Books* 48, no. 15 (October 4, 2001): 24–27; 48, no. 16 (October 16, 2001): 51–55.

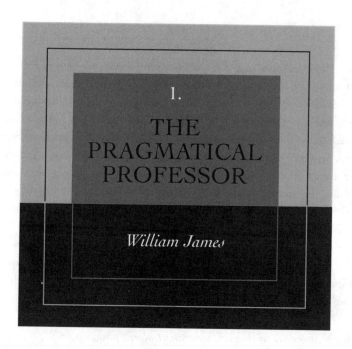

1.

THE PRAGMATICAL PROFESSOR

William James

In 1919 H. L. Mencken, reflecting upon the intellectual culture of the United States over the previous decade, especially as reflected in the magazines of the period, wrote:

> The periodicals that I then gave an eye to, setting aside newspapers, were chiefly the familiar American imitations of the English weeklies of opinion, and in these the dominant Great Thinker was, first, the late Prof. Dr. William James, and, after his decease, Prof. Dr. John Dewey. The reign of James, as the illuminated will recall, was long and glorious. For three or four years running he was mentioned in every one of those warmed-over *Spectators* and *Saturday Reviews* at least once a week, and often a dozen times.... Now and then, perhaps, Jane Addams had a month of vogue, and during one

winter there was a rage for Bergson, and for a short space German spies tried to set up Eucken (now damned with Wagner, Nietzsche and Ludendorff), but taking one day with another James held his own against the field. His ideas, immediately they were stated, became the ideas of every pedagogue from Harvard to Leland Stanford, and the pedagogues, laboring furiously at space rates, rammed them into the skulls of the lesser *intelligentsia*. To have called James an ass, during the year 1909, would have been as fatal as to have written a sentence like this one without so many *haves*. He died a year or so later, but his ghost went marching on: it took three or four years to interpret and pigeon-hole his philosophical remains and to take down and redact his messages (via Sir Oliver Lodge, Little Brighteyes, Wah-Wah the Indian Chief, and other gifted psychics) from the spirit world.[1]

To which one can only say: *Sic transit gloria philosophi!*

William James (1842–1910) was the first philosopher in America to gain universal celebrity. The hardheaded practical wisdom of Benjamin Franklin could hardly be termed a philosophy; from an entirely different perspective, the obfuscatory maunderings of Emerson did not count as such, either. Something with a bit more intellectual rigor of the English or German sort was needed if Americans were not to feel that they were anything but the ruthless money-grubbing barbarians they in fact were and are. James filled the bill. His younger contemporary George Santayana (1863–1952) was considerably more brilliant and scintillating, but for regular, 100 percent Americans he had considerable drawbacks. In the first place, he was a foreigner, born in Spain, even though his Boston upbringing and Harvard professorship would otherwise have given him the stamp of approval. Moreover, he was not merely suspiciously interested in art and poetry (*The Sense of Beauty* [1896], *Three Philosophical Poets* [1910]), but he actually wrote poetry himself! No, he would never do.

James, on the other hand, was just the sort of philosopher suited to the American bourgeoisie. His chief mission, expressed from one book to the next, was to protect their piety from the hostile forces of science and skepticism—an eminently laudable and American goal.

Bertrand Russell, in a devastating early critique, notes the distinctly American cast of pragmatism:

> The influence of democracy in promoting pragmatism is visible in almost every page of William James's writing. There is an impatience of authority, a tendency to decide philosophical questions by putting them to the vote, which contrast curiously with the usual dictatorial tone of philosophic writings. . . . William James claims for the pragmatist temper 'the open air and possibilities of nature, as against dogma, artificiality, and the pretence of finality in truth'. A thing which simply *is* true, whether you like it or not, is to him as hateful as a Russian autocracy; he feels that he is escaping from a prison, made not by stone walls but by 'hard facts', when he has humanized truth, and made it, like the police force in a democracy, the servant of the people instead of their master. The democratic temper pervades even the religion of the pragmatists: they have the religion they have chosen, and the traditional reverence is changed into satisfaction with their own handiwork. 'The prince of darkness', James says, 'may be a gentleman, as we are told he is, but whatever the God of earth and heaven is, he can surely be no gentleman.' He is rather, we should say, conceived by pragmatists as an elected president, to whom we give a respect which is really a tribute to the wisdom of our own choice.[2]

Unfortunately for James, however, he grew up at the exactly the most inopportune moment for someone devoted to religion, even of an unorthodox variety. The latter half of the nineteenth century saw an ever mounting array of leading intellectuals, mostly in England and France, either shedding religious belief altogether or, at the very least, expressing grave doubts about the authority of orthodox theism. Charles Darwin, Thomas Henry Huxley, John Stuart Mill, Leslie Stephen, Herbert Spencer, George Eliot, Charles Bradlaugh, Samuel Butler, Ernest Renan, Anatole France, W. K. Clifford, J. M. Robertson, Ernst Haeckel, and the early Bertrand Russell (whose "Free Man's Worship" dates to 1903) — the list goes on and on. There was even an entire subgenre of novels — of which Mrs. Humphry Ward's *Robert Elsmere* (1888) is the most celebrated example — in which formerly pious Victorians wrestle with the loss of their faith. In America it was somewhat riskier to be irreligious, where such a practice was usually restricted to those whom it was easy to dismiss (like the anarchist Emma Goldman) or those who were themselves obscure enough to be ignored (like Ambrose Bierce, poking vicious fun at clerics from the editorial page of William Randolph Hearst's *San Francisco Examiner*). However the thunderous agnostic orator Robert G. Ingersoll defied these risks and caused considerable agitation, becoming the most popular public speaker of the later nineteenth century. Mark Twain would have raised some ruckus with such impious specimens as *The Mysterious Stranger* and *Letters from the Earth*, but even he was too timorous to allow them to be published in his lifetime.

It was against this entire trend of intellectual advance that James resolutely stood, arms waving like Canute commanding the waves. James's father, Henry James Sr., was a pious gent who had a "religious experience" of exactly the sort that his son would later outline, but this experience plunged him into despondency and despair until his adoption of the genial mummery of Swedenborgianism cheered him up. William, like his father, may not ever have been orthodox, but religion was in his very marrow. His entire philosophical enterprise, including his advocacy of pragmatism, had as its chief goal the reconciliation of science and religion, given his belief that the "common layman . . . wants facts; he wants science; but he also wants a religion" (P 14–15). One of the most poignant documents in his entire corpus — not for its philosophical arguments, which are feeble at best, but for its revelation of James's own tortured temperament — is the essay "Is Life Worth Living?" (1895), one of the numerous flatulent defenses of religion in *The Will to Believe* (1897). It becomes rapidly obvious that the question posed by the title is one James had put to himself. What are pious folk to do when the course of human thought is so resolutely turning against conventional religion? What can they do when, starting out with the belief in a benevolent God, they find that nature is in fact utterly indifferent to human — and all other — life? James laments: "Beauty and hideousness, love and cruelty, life and death keep house together in indissoluble partnership; and there gradually steals over us, instead of the old warm notion of a man-loving Deity, that of an awful power that neither hates nor loves, but rolls all things together meaninglessly to a common doom" (W 41–42). James explicitly calls this "an uncanny, a sinister, a nightmare view of life" (W 42)!

He was, of course, not alone in this reaction. It was a mental transition that many thinking individuals of the later nineteenth century had to pass through. The comment of W. K. Clifford, writing in 1877, is only one of many that could be cited:

> It cannot be doubted that theistic belief is a comfort and a solace to those who hold it, and that the loss of it is a very painful loss. It cannot be doubted, at least, by many of us in this generation, who either profess it now, or received it in our childhood and have parted from it since with such searching trouble as only cradle-faiths can cause. We have seen the spring sun shine out of an empty heaven, to light up a soulless earth; we have felt with utter loneliness that the Great Companion is dead.[3]

Very touching, indeed! But whereas people like Clifford faced the new revelation courageously and became atheists or agnostics (a more prudent choice at a time when speaking out against the church still carried a heavy burden of social disapproval), James engaged in a rearguard action to shore up what remnants of faith could, in his view, be preserved.

James of course was too intelligent not to be aware that the advance of science had made naive religious belief impossible, and yet he was still convinced that "something deep down in . . . us tells us that there *is* a Spirit in things to which we owe allegiance" (W 43). But, typically, James does not pause to wonder what that "something" might be, or where it originated. What is it but Clifford's "cradle-faith"—the infantile brainwashing that has led so many, from refined philosophers like James to the most ignorant backwoods fundamentalist, to hope for some alternative to the "soulless" world they lament? Not once in all his copious writing on religion does James examine the *origin* of religious belief, either in the individual or in society at large. It is beyond his powers of imagination to conceive these beliefs as anything but innate in human beings; he cannot bring himself even to consider the possibility that they may have been induced by countless millennia of indoctrination and wish fulfillment.

James presents no evidence for the existence of this "Spirit"; the best he can do is to attack science by demonstrating that scientific knowledge is not yet, and never will be, complete enough to rule out the possibility entirely: "What, in short, has authority to debar us from trusting our religious demands? Science as such assuredly has no authority, for she can only say what is, not what is not" (W 56). This is only a restatement of the truism that one cannot prove a negative. One assuredly cannot prove that God does *not* exist. One also cannot prove that unicorns do not exist—but does that mean that there is any good reason for believing in unicorns? James goes on to say: "We are free to trust at our own risks anything that is not impossible" (W 57)! In other words, whatever science cannot definitively *disprove* is acceptable to believe. I am, for example, on James's principles permitted to believe that all the events of the universe are caused by thought waves sent out by little bug-eyed monsters dwelling in the Andromeda nebula. Certainly, no one can disprove that! I have no positive evidence for it, but it is certainly "not impossible"! What James is overlooking, of course, is the notion of *probability*. Even if definitive knowledge one way or the other is lacking, there are many indicators that will point pretty strongly in one direction or another. Religious apologists throughout the twentieth century carried this notion of the "uncertainty" of science far beyond even James's limits, using it as a ready excuse to return to naive faith in formerly outmoded religious conceptions, but it was James who started the ball rolling.

And yet the matter was actually one of life and death—for James, at any rate. After all, his "final appeal" as to whether life is worth living or not "is to nothing more recondite than religious faith" (W 39). It is, therefore, permissible to accept "an unseen spiritual order which we assume on trust, if only thereby life may seem to us better worth living again" (W 52). I will postpone comment on whether this idea of a "soulless" universe is as "nightmarish" as James maintains; certainly it appears to have been to him.

But James is correct on one point: one must really take a stand on this issue, since the scientific "suspension of judgment" (preserving doubt until definitive evidence is in) is itself a decision that will affect many actions of our daily lives:

> Belief and doubt are living attitudes, and involve conduct on our part. Our only way, for example, of doubting, or refusing to believe, that a certain thing *is*, is continuing to act as if it were *not*. If, for instance, I refuse to believe that the room is getting cold, I leave the windows open and light no fire just as if it still were warm. If I doubt that you are worthy of my confidence, I keep you uninformed of all my secrets just as if you were *un*worthy of the same. . . . And so if I must not believe that the world is divine, I can only express that refusal by declining ever to act distinctively as if it were so, which can only mean acting on certain critical occasions as if it were *not* so, or in an irreligious way. (W 55)

There are some troubling conceptions here also—the idea that one's views on these matters are unchangeable ("declining ever to act") rather than mere working hypotheses; the suggestion that behaving in an "irreligious way" is necessarily morally inferior to behaving in a religious way (a point James elaborates in a later essay, "The Sentiment of Rationality")—but I will bypass these matters for now. James himself, of course, overlooks the degree to which even avowedly religious people behave, on the whole, "irreligiously" in the great majority of the mundane actions in their daily lives except when some event—usually of a traumatic or melancholy nature—impels them to appeal to the God that otherwise seems quite absent from their thoughts and actions.

Clearly, this issue of *action* was critical to James, for it served as the basis of another defense of religious belief as expressed in his celebrated essay "The Will to Believe" (1896). Here we have many of the same notions as in "Is Life Worth Living?" He enunciates the core notion in imposing italics:

Our passional nature not only lawfully may, but must, decide an option between propositions, whenever it is a genuine option that cannot by its nature be decided on intellectual grounds; for to say, under such circumstances, "Do not decide, but leave the question open," is itself a passional decision, —just like deciding yes or no, —and is attended with the same risk of losing the truth. (W 11)

But are religious hypotheses of this sort? Is the idea of God's existence a "genuine option"—a proposition whose truth or falsity is legitimately in doubt? Certainly it was to James, and he peremptorily dismisses those who do not find it so: "If we are to discuss the question at all, it must involve a living option. If for any of you religion be a hypothesis that cannot, by any living possibility be true, then you need go no farther" (W 26). The point is that James's "will to believe" in one proposition or its opposite can only apply when the likelihood of a proposition's truth or falsity is approximately equal. It is difficult to see how in the face of overwhelming negative evidence the existence of God—or even of James's attenuated idea of an "unseen spiritual order" (W 52)—can fall into that paradigm.

In *Pragmatism* (1907) James comes up with yet another defense of religion—this time on the ground that religious beliefs might somehow be "useful." The point is emphasized over and over again: "If theological ideas prove to have a value for concrete life, they will be true, for pragmatism, in the sense of being good for so much" (P 40); "On pragmatic principles we cannot reject any hypothesis if consequences useful to life flow from it" (P 131); "On pragmatistic principles, if the hypothesis of God works satisfactorily in the widest sense of the word, it is true" (P 143). But this conception is fatally compromised by a lack of specificity as to what "useful" really means. Useful in what sense? On occasion James appears to maintain that a belief is "useful" merely if it provides some kind of emotional satisfaction; at other times he seems to indicate that "useful" beliefs are those that directly affect one's actions (presumably "good" actions, since actions that are "bad"—i.e., socially unacceptable—cannot possibly be said to validate the beliefs inspiring them). Both senses of "useful" are seriously flawed, for the first merely endorses wishful thinking (i.e., any belief that one may happen to have and which has not been absolutely disproven by science can be accepted if it makes one feel good) and the second quickly leads to grotesque absurdity. If I open a soup kitchen for the poor (an action conventionally regarded as "good," both morally and socially) because (so I maintain) the Martian god Lxqzsby whispered in my ear to do so, does that act by itself verify the existence of Lxqzsby?

Possibly James did not feel satisfied with these merely verbal attempts to shore up religious belief. Accordingly he undertook a voluminous analysis of actual religious sentiments, mingling psychology, anthropology, and his brand of pragmatism. The result was *The Varieties of Religious Experience* (1902), originally the Gifford Lectures on Natural Religion delivered in Edinburgh in 1901–1902. When this book appeared, it was immediately hailed by the devout as a validation of religious belief from a scientific, "empirical" perspective. It was endlessly reprinted (I myself own a thirty-sixth impression issued in 1928) and inspired much further "research" of the same sort. Under the guise of an apparently objective, scientific study of the psychology of religious sentiment, James in fact writes a polemic whose purpose is to vindicate the truth-value (or what he calls the "revelation-value" [5]) of religious feeling. James is fully aware that the higher criticism of the preceding half-century had significantly shattered the illusion of the Bible as a direct revelation from God — that it was, in fact, an historical document whose origin, sources, revision, and internal contradictions were exhaustively chronicled. Nevertheless, he regards it as axiomatic that the Bible can still be regarded as "a revelation in spite of errors and passions and deliberate human composition, if only it be a true record of the inner experiences of great-souled persons wrestling with the crises of their fate" (5). Whether the authors of the Bible really were "great-souled" is not of any interest to me here; what is of relevance is James's deceitful use of language — something that vitiates his entire work — in suggesting that the "record of inner experiences" are "true." James is really using the word *true* in two senses; that is, that the "inner experiences" are *true* both as psychological phenomena (which no one denies) and as reflections of some ontological reality (which, to say the least, is highly open to question). As the atheist psychologist Chapman Cohen pointed out long ago:

> How religious visionaries have felt, or what has been their experiences, can only furnish the mere data of an enquiry, and *their explanation of the cause of their experiences is a part of the data.* This, apparently, Professor James overlooked; and it will be noted by critical readers of his book that it proceeds on the assumption that the statements of religious visionaries are to be taken, not only as true concerning their subjective experiences at a given time, but also as approximately true as to the causes of their mental states. This, of course, by no means follows.[4]

At the outset James warns that impugning the *sources* for religious psychological states is not sufficient to prove them false. He is, to be sure, correct, but the matter is more complex than his superficial remarks indicate. James dismisses to his satisfaction certain crude attempts by his contemporaries to account naturalistically for a religious experience—that it is, for example, merely the symptoms of a bad liver or epilepsy—and thereby thinks he has taken care of the difficulty. He also thinks he now has the license to disregard entirely the origin of the experiences he treats so copiously. But there is much more to it than that. The psychological and anthropological accounting for religious sentiment is now so overwhelmingly satisfactory that it can be overlooked only by the rash or the desperate. Surely even James does not believe that an individual is innately endowed with some specific religious dogma; it is (to use the language of genetics) an acquired characteristic. If someone had a "religious experience" of Jesus Christ without having the least knowledge of the Christian religion, then certainly that experience could well be regarded as validating Christianity. But there has never been any such experience, and although James thinks he may have found a few to approximate it, he has clearly done nothing of the sort. The fact that James almost never considers any "experiences" outside the Christian tradition also allows him a convenient escape from this dilemma. If, for example, James was forced to consider Thutmose IV's dream of Horus, or (assuming for the nonce that it was an actual event) the vision that Venus induces in Aeneas (in Virgil's *Aeneid*) of the Olympian gods assisting the Greeks in destroying Troy, he would either have to regard these visions as delusions or maintain that they point to the truth of the Egyptian and Greek mythologies.

In the chapter "The Reality of the Unseen," James provides a rather tedious array of examples of religious visions from a variety of contemporary sources. He prefaces the account by declaring flatly: "It is as if there were in the human consciousness a *sense of reality, a feeling of objective presence, a perception* of what we may call *'something there,'* more deep and more general than any of the special and particular 'senses' by which the current psychology supposes existent realities to be originally revealed" (58; emphasis in original). Note the pseudo-scientific language here: religious feelings really are a kind of sense-perception and, in fact, are superior to them ("more deep and more general"). A "sense of reality" is for James sufficient indication of the actual reality of the object so perceived.

Curiously enough, James initially refers to such visions as "hallucination[s]" (58); but this is only a rhetorical ploy to allay the skepticism of his audience, for by the end of his account his interpretation of such visions will be very different. Unfortunately for James, the advance of psychology makes all his accounts so self-evidently delusional that they betray themselves in their very utterance.

Occasionally James reveals himself as astonishingly credulous. He blandly quotes from the charlatanic *Journal of the Society for Psychical Research* (James was a willing dupe of psychical research of all kinds, seizing upon it as an antidote to science and positivism), and actually cites a fellow professor's account of the sensations of a woman who (in James's words) "has the gift of automatic or involuntary writing": "Whenever I practice automatic writing, what makes me feel that it is not due to a subconscious self is the feeling I always have of a foreign presence, external to my body" (62). Evidently that "feeling" is sufficient for James to discount the delusional origin of the "gift."

Even some of the less obviously irrational accounts eventually collapse of their own absurdity. Perhaps the most interesting one is the account of a woman who was "the daughter of a man well known in his time as a writer against Christianity" (69). James cleverly assumes that such a person could not possibly be predisposed to religious mania or hallucination, but his subsequent description of her shows clearly that she was:

> The suddenness of her conversion shows well how native the sense of God's presence must be to certain minds. She relates that she was brought up in entire ignorance of Christian doctrine, but, when in Germany, after being talked to by Christian friends, she read the Bible and prayed, and finally the plan of salvation flashed upon her like a stream of light. (69)

Is it not obvious that this woman's fears and hopes had led her to rebel against her father's teaching and snatch greedily at the "comfort" of religion the moment it was offered her? Atheist leader Madalyn Murray O'Hair's son became a born-again Christian in exactly the same manner.

Another visionary—a clergyman, no less—asserts that his perception of deity was such that "I could not any more have doubted that *He* was there than that I was" (66–67). The mere utterance of this assertion seems to James sufficient to guarantee its metaphysical truth. Still another fellow admits that without a belief in God's presence "life would be a blank, a desert, a shoreless, trackless waste" (71)—as if the comfort provided by a delusion is adequate warrant for its validity.

In many accounts, God actually talks to the victim of the hallucination. In a Swiss account, translated from French, we learn that God made a "reply" (no doubt in French) to the words this individual addressed to him. Another fellow, a twenty-seven-year-old Englishman, states blandly that "I talk to [God]"—no doubt in English. God is the preeminent linguist.

James betrays a staggering lack of awareness of the degree to which the societal forces of his time—the relentless indoctrination of all citizens, from infancy onward, into religious belief; the immense social disapproval and ostracism inflicted upon anyone deviating from orthodoxy; the role that government has always taken in endorsing religious belief as a tool to control its citizenry—led even the intelligent to toe the line in religious matters and induced a few of the more unbalanced to hallucinations.

At the end of his array of accounts James launches a predictable attack on rationalism: this kind of logic-chopping (so termed by James) will never convince the true devotee that the visions he has experienced are merely delusional.

> If you have intuitions at all, they come from a deeper level of your nature than the loquacious level which rationalism inhabits. Your whole subconscious life, your impulses, your faiths, your needs, your divinations, have prepared the premises, of which your consciousness now feels the weight of the result; and something in you absolutely *knows* that that result must be truer than any logic-chopping rationalistic talk, however clever, that may contradict it. (73)

James's real agenda could hardly be more openly displayed. Religious visions are now a form of "knowledge"—they are not merely "true," but actually "truer" than weak, feeble, superficial rationalism. We have gone from hallucinations to knowledge—not through any marshaling of evidence, but rather through the repetitive accumulation of accounts of religious epiphanies, every one of which can easily be accounted for naturalistically. James is hoping that the *depth* or *intensity* of a belief or sentiment will somehow guarantee its truth-value, but a quick glance at history is sufficient to refute this naive view. Several centuries ago, the average citizen would no doubt have felt in his bones that the sun revolved around the earth, and would have been outraged at any suggestion so contrary to his innermost feelings as the possibility that the earth revolves around the sun.

Throughout his account James is eager to stress that religious "experiences" are somehow instinctive, "natural," and therefore must somehow have arisen out of the most fundamental sources of our being, but his own accounts repeatedly put the lie to this assertion.

The chapter on "Conversion" makes this eminently clear. Here we find one individual who speaks of his conversion as follows: "My heart increased in its beating, which soon convinced me that it was the Holy Spirit from the effect it had on me" (191). The remark is prototypical: in the first half a (presumably real) physiological experience is related, but James fails to note that the second half is an *intellectual inference* (very likely false) from that experience; in other words, it is no longer pure experience but experience plus an analysis of it. A later account makes this still clearer, as a former alcoholic testifies to his reformation:

> One Tuesday evening I sat in a saloon in Harlem, a homeless, friendless, dying drunkard. . . . I had often said, 'I will never be a tramp. I will never be cornered, for when that time comes, if it ever comes, I will find a home in the bottom of the river.' But the Lord so ordered it that when that time did come I was not able to walk one quarter of the way to the river. As I sat there thinking, I seemed to feel some great and mighty presence. I did not know then what it was. I did learn afterwards that it was Jesus, the sinner's friend. (201–202)

James remarks that "there is little doctrinal theology in such an experience" (203)—but if so, why did this person not feel the presence of Allah or Apollo or Thoth rather than Jesus? How else could he have "learned" that it was Jesus unless he had been previously exposed to Christian doctrine, as opposed to the doctrines of Islam or the Greek or Egyptian mythology?

James declares that these sudden conversions are "in no need of doctrinal apparatus or propitiary machinery" (211)—in other words, he wants us to believe that these conversions are a kind of "pure," untainted psychological experience not dependent upon doctrine or dogma, since he is well aware that the actual dogmas of most religions are preposterous and not likely to be credited by intelligent people— to say nothing of the fact that the dogmas of different religions are so varied that it is difficult to reconcile them all to some direct perception of the nature of entity. But James is stymied by the recalcitrance of his actual testimonials, which are one and all in the direction of a specific religious doctrine. Consider the account of one David Brainerd, an Englishman living in the middle of the eighteenth century, to which James apparently attaches great importance (I mercifully abridge the long quotation printed by James):

> One morning, while I was walking in a solitary place as usual, I at once saw that all my contrivances and projects to effect or procure deliverance and salvation for myself were utterly in vain; I was brought quite to a stand, as finding myself totally lost. . . . I saw that there was no necessary connection between my prayers and the bestowment of divine mercy; that they laid not the least obligation upon God to bestow his grace upon me . . . then, as I was walking in a thick grove, unspeakable glory seemed to open to the apprehension of my soul. . . . I had no particular apprehension of any one person in the Trinity, either the Father, the Son, or the Holy Ghost; but it appeared to be Divine glory. . . . At this time, the way of salvation opened to me with such infinite wisdom, suitableness, and excellency, that I wondered I should ever think of any other way of salvation . . . I wondered that all the world did not see and comply with this way of salvation, entirely by the righteousness of Christ. (212–14)

How is there no "doctrinal apparatus" here? How can these notions of "salvation" and "divine mercy" be anything but Christian? Brainerd's remark about not seeing "any one person in the Trinity" might suggest to a credulous or desperate analyst like James that Brainerd's experience is somehow free of dogma, but Brainerd's very formulation—as well as the rest of his account—suggests that he is clearly working within a Christian tradition so deeply implanted within his psyche that even his hallucinations took a Christian form.

At the end of his long and tiresome account, James finally has to face the origin of these conversions. More pages of psychological mumbo jumbo pass, but James cannot hold off the conclusion any further:

> If, abstracting altogether from the question of their value for the future spiritual life of the individual, we take them on their psychological side exclusively, so many peculiarities in them remind us of what we find outside of conversion that we are tempted to class them along with other automatisms, and to suspect that what makes the difference between a sudden and a gradual convert is not necessarily the presence of divine miracle in the case of one and of something less divine in that of the other, but rather a simple psychological peculiarity, the fact, namely, that in the recipient of the more instantaneous grace we have one of those subjects who are in possession of a large region in which mental work can go on subliminally, and from which invasive experiences, abruptly upsetting the equilibrium of the primary consciousness, may come. (237)

Whittled down to plain English, all this means is that these sudden conversions can be entirely accounted for on psychological grounds. One can only imagine the scowls on the faces of the dour Scots Presbyterians in James's audience as they heard these words. But not to worry! A few pages onward James, like a shamed sinner, recants: "But if you, being orthodox Christians, ask me as a psychologist whether the reference of a phenomenon to a subliminal self does not exclude the notion of the direct presence of the Deity altogether, I have to say frankly that as a psychologist I do not see why it necessarily should" (242). Do I hear the grunts of grudging approval from those Scotsmen?

Very well, Professor. What do you make of the following? Here is a bit from H. P. Lovecraft:

> When about seven or eight I was a genuine pagan, so intoxicated with the beauty of Greece that I acquired a half-sincere belief in the old gods and nature-spirits. I have in literal truth built altars to Pan, Apollo, Diana, and Athena, and have watched for dryads and satyrs in the woods and fields at dusk. Once I firmly thought I beheld some of these sylvan creatures dancing under autumnal oaks; a kind of "religious experience" as true in its way as the subjective ecstasies of any Christian. If a Christian tell me he has *felt* the reality of his Jesus or Jahveh, I can reply that I have *seen* the hoofed Pan and the sisters of the Hesperian Phaëthusa.[5]

Now one can always conclude that Lovecraft was lying (but then, James displays no skepticism whatever as to the particulars or sincerity of any of the accounts he cites). But if the "experience" is gauged to have actually occurred, what conclusions can we draw from it? Can we say (trivially) that the incident is real in the sense that it did indeed occur, or can we go on and say (absurdly) that it is real in the sense of indicating the actual existence of Pan and, by extension, the rest of the Greek pantheon? Shall we follow Lovecraft in building altars to Pan, Apollo, Diana, and Athena? James of course wants to claim that these conversions, however mundane their origin, do still have value, since in his view we are to gauge them solely on their "effects" (243)—a point I shall return to later.

Throughout James's book there is a consistent denigration of rational states of mind and a blunt assertion of the superiority (both moral and even intellectual) of religious sentiment. James is particularly impressed by the *solemnity* of religious emotions, as if this were another guarantee of the validity of the emotions. Any failure to regard life as a suitably serious affair brings down his lofty condescension. And, of course, James cannot help pointing out that one of his visionaries had once actually been "agnostic and irreligious" (64)—hence, presumably, not the usual sort of dupe given to religious hysterics. James allows this person to add that "I cannot say that I ever lost that 'indefinite consciousness' . . . of an Absolute Reality behind phenomena" (64), but does not make the obvious conclusion that this person was nonetheless predisposed to hallucinations of deity in spite of his avowed irreligion.

Part and parcel with this is a denigration of science—or, rather, an assertion that science is itself imbued with religious sentiment: "'Science' in many minds is genuinely taking the place of a religion. Where this is so, the scientist treats the 'Laws of Nature' as objective facts to be revered" (57). This is so appalling a misconstrual of the scientific mentality, even of James's time, that it seems inconceivable that he could have written it with a straight face. No scientist "reveres" the "Laws of Nature"; and all scientists know that those "Laws" are merely a human attempt to catalog the phenomena of nature for our own understanding. The "Laws of Nature" are *not* conceived to be "objective facts" but rather abstractions derived from the observation of similar events and occurrences.

The irony of all this, of course, is that James's very procedure in analyzing the psychology of religion is scientific—or, at any rate, a manipulation of the language and principles of science. He was writing at a time when science had already become the arbiter of truth, and he had no option but to use its methodology—or its outward rhetoric—to convince a skeptical audience. James's strategy is unwittingly laid bare in an early passage, when, as part of his scorn of rationalism, he notes: "That vast literature of proofs of God's existence drawn from the order of nature, which a century ago seemed so overwhelmingly convincing, to-day does little more than gather dust in libraries, for the simple reason that our generation has ceased to believe in the kind of God it argued for" (73–74).

James is correct in the first part of this utterance but completely wrong in the second part. He is alluding, preeminently, to such works as William Paley's *Evidences of Christianity* (1794) and *Natural Theology* (1802), which put forth what was then considered a strong argument for the existence of God based on the "argument from design." James fails to note, however, that Paley's notion was discredited chiefly because Darwin's theory of evolution satisfactorily explained this "order of nature" as an inevitable, natural, and non-divine result of the gradual evolution of species. It was only the advances of science on many fronts throughout the nineteenth century that caused the intelligent people of James's time to abandon credence in "the kind of God" Paley and other orthodox religionists had argued for.

Accordingly, James can no longer appeal to rationalistic arguments for the existence of God, since these arguments have been shown to be utterly at variance with the facts of the universe as then understood, as well as being intellectually shabby, paradoxical, and internally self-contradictory. All that was left to James was to appeal to the brute fact of religious *sentiment*—those personal "revelations" he chronicles at fatiguing length in the early parts of his treatise—and then to perform the rhetorical legerdemain of demonstrating that the mere *existence* of these sentiments somehow validates their *content*.

James carries on his polemic against science in the chapter "The Religion of the Healthy-Minded." Here James stresses the role of religion in making people happy, as if that were any indication of the metaphysical truth of the religion. We find James making the following breathtaking utterance:

> With such relations between religion and happiness, it is perhaps not surprising that men come to regard the happiness which a religious belief affords as a proof of its truth. If a creed makes a man feel happy, he almost inevitably adopts it. Such a belief ought to be true; therefore it is true—such, rightly or wrongly, is one of the 'immediate inferences' of the religious logic used by ordinary men. (78–79)

Rightly or wrongly? Come now, Willie. If a person's happiness is based upon his belief that he is the reincarnation of Julius Caesar, does that mean that he actually *is* the reincarnation of Julius Caesar? No doubt many people have been cheered by religion (perhaps just as many as those who have been terrified by the thought of hell, sin, a vengeful God, and the like), but what possible inferences as to the actual *truth* of religion can we derive from this cheerfulness?

But most of James's chapter is a long and wearisome disquisition on New Thought, that feeble amalgam of mysticism, self-help, and pop psychology that proved fatally attractive to superficial minds at the turn of the twentieth century. James himself, expressing an irony of which he is blissfully unaware, actually refers to the movement as America's "only decidedly original contribution to the systematic philosophy of life" (96) and rightly sees its logical culmination in Christian Science (106). Essentially, New Thought stressed mind over matter and advocated a variety of mental or "spiritual" exercises for the cure of various ailments, usually of a psychological order. It was, however, distinctly religious in tone: "The first underlying cause of all sickness, weakness, or depression is the *human sense of separateness* from that Divine Energy which we call God," as James quotes from the letter of a personal friend (102). James's polemic against science is a bit slow in emerging, but it finally raises its head rather shyly toward the end. Pointing to the unquestioned physical and mental benefit some individuals have received by the practice of New Thought, James imagines that these results somehow vindicate the beliefs (such as Edward Everett Hale's "I always knew God loved me" [82] and so forth) held by these individuals. But James had already noted (rather hastily and covertly, possibly in the hope that no one would notice) that such results could be accounted for by "medical-materialistic" means (111). He concludes: "Science gives to all of us telegraphy, electric lighting, and diagnosis, and succeeds in preventing or curing a certain amount of disease. Religion in the shape of mind-cure gives to some of us serenity, moral poise, and happiness and prevents certain forms of disease as well as science does, or even better in a certain class of persons" (122). Science has now been reduced to technology, and religion is now superior to it "in a certain class of persons."

As a counterweight to his argument that religion is cheering, James is obliged to claim that atheism or agnosticism is the reverse. In a throwaway line in the chapter "The Sick Soul" (the title is itself significant), dealing with the sense of gloom and futility that overwhelms certain individuals, James makes the outrageous utterance: "This sadness lies at the heart of every merely positivistic, agnostic, or naturalistic scheme of philosophy" (140). Oddly, he does not develop his argument on this point here, but another salvo in the chapter on "Conversion" gets more to the heart of the matter. He notes that certain people are incapable of the kind of maniacal religious conversion so pungently found in some of our fundamentalist friends, especially of the Pentecostal variety, and he attempts to account for this regrettable failing:

> Such inaptitude for religious faith may in some cases be intellectual in its origin. Their religious faculties may be checked in their natural tendency to expand, by beliefs about the world that are inhibitive, the pessimistic and materialistic beliefs, for example, within which so many good souls, who in former times would have freely

indulged their religious propensities, find themselves nowadays, as
it were, frozen; or the agnostic vetoes upon faith as something weak
and shameful, under which so many of us to-day lie cowering, afraid
to use our instincts. (204)

I hardly know how to respond to this farrago of nonsense. Religious
feeling is now deemed a "natural tendency," even an "instinct," rather
than a product of indoctrination from infancy onward; and of course
James cannot bring himself to acknowledge that the growth of agnosticism has anything to do with the advance of human knowledge that
renders so many religious conceptions absurd and contemptible.

But let us examine this entire matter a bit more closely. In order
to prove his case, James needs to establish not merely (a) that religious people are, as a whole, more cheerful than nonreligious people
(which several surveys have indeed approximately established), but
also (b) that the *reasons* for the sadness of nonreligious people are
directly attributable to their lack of religious belief (which no survey,
to my knowledge, has adequately established). Since James is
unwilling to provide testimony that runs counter to his dogma, let us
ourselves call up some examples of cheerful atheists.

Take David Hume: "I was . . . a man of mild dispositions, of command of temper, of an open, social, and cheerful humour, capable of
attachment, but little susceptible of enmity, and of great moderation
in all my passions. Even my love of literary fame, my ruling passion,
never soured my temper, notwithstanding my frequent disappoint-
ments."[6]

And how about the always jovial H. L. Mencken: "I speak as one
who has had what must be regarded, speaking statistically, as a happy
life. I work a great deal, but working is more agreeable to me than
anything else I can imagine. I am conscious of no vast, overwhelming
and unattainabled desires. I want nothing that I can't get."[7]

Even Nietzsche, often ignorantly branded a pessimist, can be
brought forward: "Life was easy for me—easiest when it made the
hardest demands on me. Whoever saw me during the seventy days
this fall . . . will not have noticed any trace of tension in me; but rather

an overflowing freshness and cheerfulness. I never ate with more pleasant feelings; I never slept better."[8]

Throughout his work James commits the elementary fallacy of assuming that since the adoption of an atheistic or agnostic worldview would reduce *him* to pessimism and futility it would reduce *everyone* to this state. The idea that freedom from religious mummery could actually be liberating, exhilarating, and even reassuring, is foreign to James's temperament. As a matter of fact, the great majority of leading atheistic, agnostic, and secular philosophers throughout human history have been pretty jovial fellows, and the same appears to be true even among average citizens, if my own wide acquaintance with atheists is any gauge.

The awkward thing about James's "Sick Soul" chapter, however, is that the testimonials he brings forth in regard to depressed, pessimistic mentalities are all religious in nature! Hence a patient in a French asylum writes in a letter: "I am afraid of God as much as of the devil" (148), and yet James remarks, with incredible fatuity, "how the querulous temper of his misery keeps his mind from taking a religious direction" (149)!

James's two chief witnesses in this bizarre chapter are John Bunyan and Leo Tolstoy. Bunyan initially felt the terrors habitually associated with the bleaker side of the Christian religion—"I thought none but the Devil himself could equal me for inward wickedness and pollution of mind. . . . Now I blessed the condition of the dog and toad, yea, gladly would I have been in the condition of the dog or horse, for I knew they had no soul to perish under the everlasting weight of Hell or Sin, as mine was like to do" (158). Tolstoy, sensing the futility of existence, finds that "my heart kept languishing with another pining emotion. I can call this by no other name than that of a thirst for God" (156). The result, in both cases, is inevitable. Bunyan gains his peace of mind by convincing himself that God loved him: "Now I could see myself in Heaven and Earth at once; in Heaven by my Christ, by my Head, by my Righteousness and Life, though on Earth by my body or person" (187). Tolstoy, who opines that "the idea of an infinite God, of the divinity of the soul, of the union of men's actions with Gods—these are ideas . . . without which there would be no life" (184), manages to persuade himself that "He [God] is there: he, without whom one cannot love. To acknowledge God and to live are one and the same thing. God is what life is. . . . After this, things cleared up with me" (185). So Bunyan and Tolstoy have, it would appear, exchanged a gloomy fantasy for a cheerful one.

Where all this leads is made evident in the chapter on "Saintliness," which for James means the "practical fruits of life" (259) resulting from religious conversions. James remarks smugly, "The highest flights of charity, devotion, trust, patience, bravery to which the wings of human nature have spread themselves have been flown for religious ideals" (259–60), and he goes on to relate how people have become glowingly happy and have cured themselves of a variety of psychological ailments as a result of faith. He puts particular stress on reformed alcoholics. But James, so fixated as he is upon *results* as opposed to *processes*, fails to realize that he can only make his case *if these results could only have been produced by religious belief*. Whatever the "practical fruits" of religion, is it really better for someone to achieve these effects by means of probable delusion and intellectual error? Taking two individuals—an alcoholic who reforms himself by strength of will alone, and an alcoholic who reforms himself by convincing himself that Jesus loves him or something of the sort—is the latter more admirable than the former? The various wholesome attitudes that James quotes from James Starbuck's *Psychology of Religion*: "I began to work for others"; "I had more tender feeling for my family and friends"; "I spoke at once to a person with whom I had been angry"; "I felt for every one, and loved my friends better"; "I felt every one to be my friend" (280) are surely not specific to the religious mentality. What does it say about the average run of people that they need to be duped by a religious fantasy before they can adopt these sane and self-evident ethical maxims?

But what, specifically, are the "practical fruits" that James believes to be the product of religious belief? In the chapter "The Value of Saintliness," he states flatly and pragmatically that

> What I then propose to do is, briefly stated, to test saintliness by
> common sense, to use human standards to help us decide how far
> the religious life commends itself as an ideal kind of human activity.
> If it commends itself, then any theological beliefs that may inspire it,
> in so far forth will stand accredited. If not, then they will be discred-
> ited, and all without reference to anything but human working prin-
> ciples. (331)

I am not at the moment concerned with the obvious fallacy of this
utterance—if the religious life of an ancient Egyptian were somehow
established as "an ideal kind of human activity," would that suddenly
validate the existence of Isis, Osiris, Thoth, and the rest? What James
sees as the "virtues" of religion are "devout love of God, purity,
charity, [and] asceticism" (340). James is willing to acknowledge that
each of these "virtues" can be carried to excess, and in fact much of
his account is devoted to a mild reproof of these excesses; but he
appears to maintain that in their normal essence they are entirely beneficial. What is more, James concludes that all these attributes, in
combination, can be found only in the religious:

> Single attributes of saintliness may, it is true, be temperamental
> endowments, found in non-religious individuals. But the whole
> group of them forms a combination which, as such, is religious, for
> it seems to flow from the sense of the divine as from its psycholog-
> ical centre. Whoever possesses strongly this sense comes naturally
> to think that the smallest details of this world derive infinite signifi-
> cance from their relation to an unseen divine order. The thought of
> this order yields him a superior denomination of happiness, and a
> steadfastness of soul with which no other can compare. (369)

Here is the crux of the matter. James is so keen on the (purportedly
wholesome) *effects* of religion that he fails to consider whether those
effects are intellectually well-founded. What if, as is extremely likely,
"this world" does *not* have a "relation to an unseen divine order"? What
if there is no unseen divine order? Does truth count for nothing? How
can effects be truly beneficial if they are founded upon fallacies?

James finally comes around to the study of this question—the actual truth of religious beliefs or conceptions—toward the end of his treatise. He begins his discussion by actually apologizing to his Scotsmen for his previous analysis of religion based solely upon its "fruits":

> How, you say, can religion, which believes in two worlds and an invisible order, be estimated by the adaptation of its fruits to this world's order alone? It is its *truth*, not its utility, you insist, upon which our verdict ought to depend. If religion is true, its fruits are good fruits, even though in this world they should prove uniformly ill adapted and full of naught but pathos. (377)

It is typical that James does not mention the converse of this proposition, i.e., that if religion is false, its "fruits" may be bad even though they appear to be good to its adherents.

It is in his chapter "Mysticism" that James hopes to establish some kind of "truth" in religion, but his analysis is subject to the same logical fallacies as his earlier accounts. In remarking that mystical states and experiences are on the whole ineffable and also "more like states of feeling than like states of intellect" (380), James maintains that these states nonetheless do "*seem* to those who experience them to be also states of knowledge" (380) [my italics]. No doubt, but does this mean that they actully *are?* And is the "knowledge" they purportedly experience true knowledge or false knowledge? James argues in this chapter that a mystical experience "resembles the knowledge given to us in sensations more than that given by conceptual thought" (405); this, really, is the crux of his entire argument here. But in the very enunciation of this assertion lies his downfall. Even if one can accept this view—even if one can believe that the "sensations" of mystics are not ones that prior religious exposure, or their own hopes and wishes, would have led them to have—an awkward question raises itself: Are not sensations, or, rather, the assumptions one makes based upon them, on occasion false? Is someone who sees a mirage in the desert seeing something that is there, or not there? Once again, James's entire account of mystical states is vitiated by the idea that their mere *existence*—their "reality" as psychological states—somehow vindicates their *content*. James adduces no evidence for the ontological truth of mystical states, but merely asserts it and augments his case by the rhetorical sleight of hand of gradually inserting the word *truth* into his analysis of the accounts without first establishing that there is any truth to be had ("Mystical truth exists for the individual who has the transport, but for no one else" [405]; "The kinds of truth communicable in mystical ways . . . are various" [410]). James reaches the height of absurdity when he claims some truth-value to the "consciousness produced by intoxicants and anaesthetics, especially by alcohol": drunkenness "makes him for the moment one with truth" (387)! No doubt many a toper has received some brilliant flash of insight when under the influence, only to find it dissipating into nothingness when he regretfully lapses into sobriety.

It is in this chapter in particular that James's credulity in regard to the testimonials he cites—or, rather, his complete lack of interest in the *origin* of these mystical experiences—betrays him into folly. Does James think that these mystical visions come out of nowhere? The fact that a manifestly Christian God is at the heart of many of the accounts upon which James places greatest weight does not, apparently, cause him to question why these mystics should envision just such a deity rather than some other. J. A. Symonds states: "I thought that I was near death; when, suddenly, my soul became aware of God, who was manifestly dealing with me, handling me, so to speak, in an intense personal present reality" (391). Henri Frédéric Amiel asserts that "The vestiges they [his mystical experiences] leave behind are enough to fill us with belief and enthusiasm, as if they were visits of the Holy Ghost" (395). It is safe to assume that Muslim, Hindi, or Buddhist mystics would not be inclined to compare their mystical visions to the Holy Ghost.

The account in which James puts the most value, apparently, is that of St. Teresa. One passage is worth citing:

> Thus does God, when he raises a soul to union with himself, suspend the natural action of all her faculties. . . . God establishes him-

self in the interior of this soul in such a way, that when she returns
to herself, it is wholly impossible for her to doubt that she has been
in God, and God in her. This truth remains so strongly impressed on
her that, even though many years should pass without the condition
returning, she can neither forget the favor she received, nor doubt
of its reality. If you, nevertheless, ask how it is possible that the soul
can see and understand that she has been in God, since during the
union she has neither sight nor understanding, I reply that she does
not see it then, but that she sees it clearly later, after she has
returned to herself, not by any vision, but by a certitude which
abides with her and which God alone can give her. (409)

I am not interested in the rhetorical ingenuity with which St.
Teresa incorporates such words as *truth*, *certitude*, and the like into her
account; it is merely her way of convincing herself. The likelihood
that St. Teresa had the vision she describes only because of her prior
indoctrination into Christian belief is of course quite strong; but the
fact that she "later" rationalized that vision with Christian dogma is a
telltale sign that many mystics, whatever the origin of their visions, do
much more than receive them as mere "sensations": after the experience is over, they harmonize them with the religion in which they
happen to believe. As for the "certitude" she cites: no doubt this is the
case, and no doubt it would be impossible to convince her or other
mystics that she is in error. But no doubt it would be equally impossible for someone to convince our friend in the loony bin that he is not
the reincarnation of Julius Caesar.

James of course scorns the rationalistic interpretation of these
mystical experiences as merely the result of psychological aberration
("To the medical mind these ecstasies signify nothing but suggested
and imitated hypnoid states, on an intellectual basis of superstition,
and a corporeal one of degeneration and hysteria" [413]); he claims,
in his pragmatic way, that "we must not content ourselves with superficial medical talk, but inquire into their fruits for life" (413). What
are those fruits? James sees two in particular, "optimism" and
"monism" (416). The first is nothing more than James's previous
assertion of the cheering nature of religious belief—it makes one

happy! James carries this idea so far that he even maintains that any mystical states that result in pessimism must be the result of insanity!

> In delusional insanity, paranoia, as they sometimes call it, we may have a *diabolical* mysticism, a sort of religious mysticism turned upside down. The same sense of ineffable importance in the smallest events, the same texts and words coming with new meanings, the same voices and visions and leadings and missions, the same controlling by extraneous powers; only this time the emotion is pessimistic: instead of consolations we have desolations; the meanings are dreadful; and the powers are enemies to life. (426)

It is as if optimism is in itself a sign of mental health, not to mention the "truth" of one's mystical experiences!

By "monism" James means the mystic's perception of the unity of all nature, usually summed up by the notion that everything is God. James actually asserts in one passage that the uniformity of mystical visions as to this point may be an indication of the truth of the experiences (419), although he quickly retracts the remark:

> Even religious mysticism itself, the kind that accumulates traditions and makes schools, is much less unanimous than I have allowed. It has been both ascetic and antinomianly self-indulgent within the Christian church. It is dualistic in Sankhya, and monistic in Vedantic philosophy. I called it pantheistic; but the great Spanish mystics are anything but pantheists. . . . How different again, apart from the happiness common to all, is the mysticism of Walt Whitman, Edward Carpenter, Richard Jefferies, and other naturalistic pantheists, from the more distinctively Christian sort. (425)

But even if mystical experiences did have any kind of uniformity (which they don't), that might be an indication of nothing more than a uniform kind of wish fulfillment inbred in human beings through countless generations of religious indoctrination.

James nevertheless concludes magisterially that "the existence of mystical states absolutely overthrows the pretension of non-mystical states to be the sole and ultimate dictators of what we may believe" (427). How does James think he has established this principle? It is by his old fallacy that the "reality" of these experiences as psychological phenomena ensure their ontological "truth." As James stated earlier, "The cognitive aspects of them, their value in the way of revelation, is what we are directly concerned with" (408). *Revelation* is the key word. James was writing at a period of intellectual history in which appeals to *external nature* to confirm religious belief were no longer possible: too much knowledge had been gained about the actual workings of the universe to make any conventional religious conception of the world even remotely plausible to an intelligent human being. This is made abundantly evident in James's penultimate chapter "Philosophy," in which he systematically destroys many of the previous "proofs" of the existence of God—the argument from design (refuted by Darwin), the "consensus of mankind" (very likely a product of brainwashing and/or wishful thinking), and the like—as intellectually worthless. James must therefore fall back on *internal* sources, the "sensations" of the religious believer, specifically the mystic. To him, these "sensations" cannot be disputed: they are flashes of "revelation," and of course the fact that the mystics themselves have a "certitude" in regard to them is conclusive proof of their "truth." But sensations can be misleading; mystical visions may be nothing more than hallucinations or delusions.

James, incredibly enough, grudgingly acknowledges this, although in a typically backhanded manner: "It must always remain an open question whether mystical states may not possibly be such superior points of view, windows through which the mind looks out upon a more extensive and inclusive world" (428). To be sure, it would be an error for a rationalistic critic to maintain that *all* mystical experiences, by their very nature, are merely the results of aberrant psychological states. They *may* be true. But to assert that they *are* true, merely because they exist, is an even grosser philosophical mistake. And it is exactly this mistake that James makes. He goes on to state: "As a rule, mystical states merely add a supersensuous meaning to the outward data of consciousness" (427), but he ignores the numerous mystical states that definitively *contradict* not only our ordinary sense-perceptions but our knowledge of how the universe is actually set up. Without an analysis of *why* and *how* mystics came to have the visions that they do, and whether some prior religious influence may have influenced the visions, a blithe acceptance of these experiences merely because the mystics themselves are "certain" of their truth is mere credulousness.

In his concluding chapters James returns to the notion that "feelings" are at the heart of religious belief, and indeed are also vindicators of its truth. But in order to lay the groundwork for this conclusion, James must wage an all-out warfare on science, specifically the sciences of psychology and anthropology that had, in the course of the later nineteenth century, established conclusively that religion is merely an anachronism, a survival from primitive thought and primitive misconstruals of natural phenomena. His purported refutation is encapsulated in the following self-important italics:

> In spite of the appeal which this impersonality of the scientific attitude makes to a certain magnanimity of temper, I believe it to be shallow, and I can now state my reason in comparatively few words. That reason is that, so long as we deal with the cosmic and the general, we deal only with the symbols of reality, but *as soon as we deal with private and personal phenomena as such, we deal with realities in the completest sense of the term.* (498)

What this means, evidently, is that science overlooks the "subjective" aspect of human experience, or, as James says a little earlier, "It is the terror and beauty of phenomena, the 'promise' of the dawn and of the rainbow, the 'voice' of the thunder, the 'gentleness' of the summer rain, the 'sublimity' of the stars, and not the physical laws which these things follow, by which the religious mind still continues to be most impressed" (498). But in the analysis of phenomena, what possible role can these subjective impressions have, especially given that people of widely differing temperaments will have widely differing subjective impressions of the same phenomenon? What James is really trying to do is to exalt "feeling" above intellectual analysis, but the end result is merely a license for the subjective mind to believe whatever it feels like believing. James concludes his polemic against science with the pitiable whine, "It does not follow, because our ancestors made so many errors of fact and mixed them with their religion, that we should therefore leave off being religious at all" (500) — but nothing in his account justifies this belief.

But what, exactly, are the "feelings" that distinguish the religious believer? James identifies two facets, "an uneasiness" and "a solution":

1. The uneasiness, reduced to its simplest terms, is a sense that there is *something wrong about us* as we naturally stand.
2. The solution is a sense that *we are saved from the wrongness* by making proper connection with the higher powers. (508)

He goes on to state (with more pompous italics):

The individual, so far as he suffers from his wrongness and criticises it, is to that extent consciously beyond it, and in at least possible touch with something higher, if anything higher exist. Along with the wrong part there is thus a better part of him, even though it may be but a most helpless germ. With which part he should identify his real being is by no means obvious at this stage; but when stage 2 (the stage of solution or salvation) arrives, the man identifies his real being with the germinal higher part of himself; and does so in the following way. *He becomes conscious that this higher part is conterminous and continuous with a* MORE *of the same quality, which is operative in the universe outside of him, and which he can keep in working touch with, and in a fashion get on board of and save himself when all his lower being has gone to pieces in the wreck.* (508)

This, really, is the core of James's entire treatise. I am not at the moment concerned with the multifarious, and on occasion contradictory, senses in which different religions have conceived of what exactly is "wrong about us" and how its correction is to be effected. The root conception is the notion that something "more" exists in the universe that is outside of ourselves. James does not hesitate to declare that "God is the natural appellation, for us Christians at least, for the supreme reality" (516). Once again, I will overlook the plain fact that nothing remotely approaching this attenuated conception can be found in the Bible, where God is manifestly personal and anthropomorphic. James is quite prepared to acknowledge that the above formulation may, in the religious individual, be entirely subjective ("this may be nothing but his subjective way of feeling things, a mood of his own fancy" [509]), but he goes on to maintain that this "MORE" is actually *true.*

James begins by stating that all religions "agree that the 'more' really exists; though some of them hold it to exist in the shape of a personal god or gods, while others are satisfied to conceive it as a stream of ideal tendency embedded in the eternal structure of the world" (510). This is not very helpful. If a random group of people all believe that the earth is flat, it does not prove that the earth *is* flat. Even if the entire human race believed that the earth is flat, it would not constitute any kind of proof. This is simply another version of the old argument from the "consensus of humanity," which James himself had already discredited. If all religions are uniform on this point, it may indicate nothing more than the universal tendency in human beings toward this particular type of fantasy and wish fulfillment. And the fact that different religions are in total disagreement as to the nature of this something "more" does not suggest that all, or any, of them are deriving this belief from a neutral and objective analysis of phenomena.

James is compelled to fall back upon his notion of "feelings." His notion that feelings and "private and personal phenomena" are somehow more real than intellectual analysis circles back to his earlier notion that these feelings are sensations, and as such are some kind of direct perception of phenomena. But they are plainly nothing of the sort. All such religious beliefs are sensations *plus* intellectual deductions from those sensations. If a man says, "I saw a blinding flash of light and knew that it was God," he is expressing, first, a sensation (whether internal or external, subjective or objective) *plus* an interpretation of that sensation. It is the latter that is most vulnerable to criticism, even though James wants to invest the entire process with the immediacy of someone's perception of a cow or a slap in the face.

James then fancies that he has found the missing link that con-
nects the subjective self with the something "more"—the subconscious. Exactly how James comes to this conclusion is a wonder, and
his rationalization must be quoted at length:

> Let me then propose, as an hypothesis, that whatever it may be on
> its *farther* side, the 'more' with which in religious experience we feel
> ourselves connected is on its *hither* side the subconscious continua-
> tion of our conscious life. Starting thus with a recognized psycho-
> logical fact as our basis, we seem to preserve a contact with 'science'
> which the ordinary theologian lacks. At the same time the theolo-
> gian's contention that the religious man is moved by an external
> power is vindicated, for it is one of the peculiarities of invasions
> from the subconscious region to take on objective appearances, and
> to suggest to the Subject an external control. In the religious life the
> control is felt as 'higher'; but since on our hypothesis it is primarily
> the higher faculties of our own hidden mind which are controlling,
> the sense of union with the power beyond us is a sense of something,
> not merely apparently, but literally true. (512–13)

I am completely at a loss to see how James thinks he has proven his
point. There is nothing in this entire passage that is not capable of a
psychological explanation—indeed, that is not more probable as a
psychological explanation. If these "invasions from the subconscious
region . . . take on objective *appearances* [my italics]," does that mean
that they actually *are* objective? If these "invasions" "suggest" to the
subject that they are external, does that mean that they *are* external?
The totality of James's argument amounts to this: If the subject *feels*
that these perceptions of a "higher" reality are external to him, then
they must, in the absence of definitive proof otherwise, *be* external.
James totally ignores the rationalization that is constantly going on in
the religious subject while he is having these "feelings" (even though
these rationalizations themselves may be partially subconscious), as
well as the hopes, fears, wishful thinking, and prior indoctrination
into religious dogma that led the subject to come to this conclusion in
the first place. And yet, James thinks that he has now found the magic

talisman that vindicates religious experience: "we have in *the fact that the conscious person is continuous with a wider self through which saving experiences come,* a positive content of religious experience which, it seems to me, *is literally and objectively true as far as it goes*" (515).

At the very end of his treatise James resurrects his pragmatism: "God is real since he produces real effects" (517). What exactly are these effects? I am unable to ascertain them from James's utterly vague and nebulous maunderings. He begins by saying: "The real effects in question . . . are exerted on the personal centres of energy of the various subjects" (517). But this is nothing more than the assertion that religious beliefs cause people to behave in certain ways, and nothing in those behavior-patterns can possibly validate the beliefs themselves. James, however, goes on and lists some further "effects":

> Most religious men believe (or 'know,' if they be mystical) that not only they themselves, but the whole universe of beings to whom the God is present, are secure in his parental hands. There is a sense, a dimension, they are sure, in which we are *all* saved, in spite of the gates of hell and all adverse terrestrial appearances. God's existence is the guarantee of an ideal order that shall be permanently preserved. This world may indeed, as science assures us, some day burn up or freeze; but if it is part of his order, the old ideals are sure to be brought elsewhere to fruition, so that where God is, tragedy is only provisional and partial, and shipwreck and dissolution are not the absolutely final things. (517)

Let it pass that it would be next to impossible to harmonize all the various and conflicting religions with even this core doctrine. The basic problem is this: How can these things be termed "effects"? They are surely *beliefs*. To be sure, many individuals act upon them and thereby produce effects, but these things, in themselves, are *not* effects, and as beliefs they are surely liable to error. It is plain that James, now confident that religion of some kind is "literally and objectively true," is in a blinding hurry to establish a religion that at least vaguely approximates the Christianity to which he himself is accostumed, even if it includes such unorthodox notions as universal salvation and, still more fantastically, the idea that human life will survive on some other planet once the earth is destroyed!

Throughout the latter parts of his book James flirts with science, materialism, and even atheism, almost as if he is aware that they have really become the arbiters of truth and are now formidable opponents. Indeed, his very proposal of a "science of religions" (455) and the pseudoscientific language he adopts throughout his treatise make it evident that James himself is aware that he needs to be—or seem— "scientific" in order to convince a wider public. And yet, he cannot embrace the scientific worldview. "The whole drift of my education goes to persuade me that the world of our present consciousness is only one out of many worlds of consciousness that exist, and that those other worlds must contain experiences which have a meaning for our life also" (519), an utterance that unwittingly reveals the degree to which prior religious indoctrination and wishful thinking have colored James's own mentality. His final salvo is not long in coming:

> I *can*, of course, put myself into the sectarian scientist's attitude, and imagine vividly that the world of sensations and of scientific laws and objects may be all. But whenever I do this, I hear that inward monitor of which W. K. Clifford once wrote, whispering the word 'bosh!' Humbug is humbug, even though it bear the scientific name, and the total expression of human experience, as I view it objectively, invincibly urges me beyond the narrow 'scientific' bounds. (519)

In other words, James rejects the scientific worldview not because it is false, but because he believes it to be unpleasant. And the refutation is effected not by adducing evidence, but by a peremptory dismissal that only testifies to his refusal to countenance a set of facts that runs counter to the religious brainwashing to which he has subjected himself over the course of a lifetime, as a bulwark against what he mistakenly fancies to be the hopelessness and pessimism that atheism would bring.

Why have I left poor Willie James writhing on the dust like this when he's not around to defend himself? I can think of three reasons. First, it appears that James still has a small army of devotees, including a few pious sycophants and special pleaders who continue to find value in his religious speculations.[9] Second, it appears that *Varieties of Religious Experience* is widely regarded, even by psychologists of religion, as some kind of objective, impartial, "scientific" study, when it is manifestly nothing of the sort. It is instead a sly, tendentious, fallacy-ridden brief in support of continued religious belief, however attenuated, in the face of massive evidence to the contrary. Third, and most important, the problem James was facing—continued belief in some kind of god in an age of science and religious skepticism—is one that has been faced throughout the twentieth century by many liberal theologians, from Harry Emerson Fosdick to Paul Tillich to Hans Küng, all of whom preserved their faith only by the desperate expedient of ignoring or denying the many intellectually embarrassing portions of the scriptures in which they professed belief. All these thinkers have sought to preserve the husk of religious belief without the kernel inside: they have discarded many absurd specifics of their religious dogmas in the hope that some "spiritual" essence can survive the onslaughts of science, especially if it is vague and imprecise enough to withstand definitive disproof. James opted for a supremely nondoctrinal and nondogmatic religion that he claimed to find satisfying; as he stated in "Is Life Worth Living?": "It is a fact of human nature, that men can live and die by the help of a sort of faith that goes without a single dogma or definition" (W 56). But who are these men? To what degree can this kind of intellectualized belief be genuinely satisfying to the religious public at large? Walter Lippmann broached this point in *A Preface to Morals* (1929). Alluding to Alfred North Whitehead's opaque definition of God ("God is not concrete, but He is the ground for concrete actuality"), Lippmann noted:

> For while this God may satisfy a metaphysical need in the thinker, he does not satisfy the passions of the believer. This God does not govern the world like a king nor watch over his children like a father. He offers them no purposes to which they can consecrate themselves; he exhibits no image of holiness they can imitate. He does not chastise them in sin nor console them in sorrow. He is a principle with which to explain the facts, if you can understand the

explanation. He is not himself a personality who deals with the facts. For the purposes of religion he is no God at all; his universe remains stonily unaware of man.[10]

And yet, James not only professed to find this juiceless god (the "unseen spritual order" to which "we owe allegiance") satisfying but claimed that it was the only kind of god that could now be believed in. At the same time he continued to maintain that he himself was still a Protestant (W 6), which he manifestly was not, if that means accepting the central metaphysical and ethical doctrines of the Old and New Testaments. James had no particular sympathy with religious fundamentalists, scorning their ostrich-act of ignoring or denying facts merely to preserve their faith, but one may wonder whether the fundamentalist position is now the only possible one to salvage religious belief, even if it ends up making fools of its adherents. "Religious fermentation is always a symptom of the intellectual vigor of a society," says James, "and it is only when they forget that they are hypotheses and put on rationalistic and authoritative pretensions, that our faiths do harm" (W xiii). But the great majority of the pious would not find religion efficacious unless it *was* authoritative—unless it claimed full possession of the complete truth. On James's own pragmatic principles, any other kind of religion would be "useless."

NOTES

References to William James's works occur in the text as follows: P = *Pragmatism* (1907; reprint Cambridge: Harvard University Press, 1975); W = *The Will to Believe and Other Essays in Popular Philosophy* (London: Longmans, Green & Co., 1897); page citations without a letter abbreviation refer to *The Varieties of Religious Experience* (London: Longmans, Green & Co., 1902).

1. H. L. Mencken, "Prof. Veblen and the Cow," *Smart Set* 59, no. 1 (May 1919): 138–39.
2. Bertrand Russell, "Pragmatism," *Philosophical Essays* (1910; reprint London: George Allen & Unwin, 1966), pp. 106–107.

3. W. K. Clifford, "The Influence upon Morality of a Decline in Religious Belief," *Nineteenth Century*, no. 2 (April 1877): 355.

4. Chapman Cohen, *Religion and Sex: Studies in the Pathology of Religious Development* (London: T. N. Foulis, 1919), p. 272.

5. H. P. Lovecraft, "A Confession of Unfaith" (1922), in *Miscellaneous Writings*, ed. S. T. Joshi (Sauk City, Wisc.: Arkham House, 1995), pp. 534–35.

6. David Hume, "My Own Life," *Essays: Moral, Political, and Literary* (Indianapolis: Liberty Classics, 1985), p. xl.

7. H. L. Mencken, "On Suicide" (1926), in *A Mencken Chrestomathy* (New York: Alfred A. Knopf, 1949), p. 132.

8. Friedrich Nietzsche, *Ecce Homo* (1888), in *On the Genealogy of Morals and Ecce Homo*, trans. Walter Kaufmann (New York: Vintage, 1969), pp. 257–58.

9. See, e.g., Ellen Kappy Suckiel, *Heaven's Champion: William James's Philosophy of Religion* (Notre Dame, Ind.: University of Notre Dame Press, 1996). See also *Pragmatism, Neo-Pragmatism and Religion*, ed. Charley D. Hartwick and Donald A. Crosby (New York: Peter Lang, 1997), although this book is not quite so sycophantic.

10. Walter Lippmann, *A Preface to Morals* (New York: Macmillan, 1929), p. 26.

2.

THE BULLDOG AND THE PATRICIAN

G. K. Chesterton and T. S. Eliot

here are few more irritating writers than G. K. Chesterton (1874–1936). No doubt his supporters would argue that he is considered irritating because he scores telling blows in defense of religion against agnosticism, secularism, and atheism, but in fact the reverse is the case. There is a unique combination of ignorance and smugness that cripples nearly the whole of his literary work. Chesterton's only gift is a facile pen, but this very gift proves to be a double-edged sword, since it effectively conceals both from his readers and from Chesterton himself how little he knows about the subjects—and specifically his chief subject, Christianity—he treats in his multitudinous works. To anyone well informed on the issues, it becomes a mildly amusing sport to detect the fallacies and errors with which his work abounds. Chesterton may have thought himself—by analogy with Thomas Henry Huxley, nicknamed "Darwin's bulldog" for his vigorous support of the theory of evolution—a kind of Catholic bulldog, but all he can accomplish is a querulous snapping at the heels of his intellectual betters.

Chesterton's writings are worth investigating, not for any great intrinsic merits but because they embody a mode of argumentation still popular among theologians and religious apologists: the mode of reasoning with *words* rather than *facts*. Chesterton became celebrated, even notorious, in his day for his paradoxes; in this sense he was a kind of poor relation to his older contemporary, Oscar Wilde, both of whom are merely clever without being in any sense profound. But what these paradoxes reveal is the degree to which Chesterton allows himself to fall into nearly every possible logical fallacy simply in order to strike a blow against his hated enemies and, in his estimation, win a battle for Mother Church. With unintentional but pungent irony, he himself states: "Mere light sophistry is the thing that I happen to despise most of all things, and it is perhaps a wholesome fact that this is the thing of which I am generally accused" (O 213). Chesterton's paradoxes, his argumentation based upon words, metaphors, and analogies rather than facts and observation, all serve to throw a smoke screen in front of the awkward points of Christian doctrine upon which science has cast such grave doubts. It is again ironic that in one of his numerous attacks upon Nietzsche, an incalculably greater philosopher whom he systematically and deliberately misconstrued, Chesterton remarks: "Had he faced his thought without metaphors, he would have seen that it was nonsense" (O 309). A more succinct encapsulation of Chesterton's own arguments would be difficult to find.

Chesterton is in today's intellectual culture totally and irrevocably dead. His Christian apologetics have been forgotten by all but a dwindling handful of fervent Catholics. Although the pious Ignatius Press began, in 1986, an ambitious project of publishing his collected works—a project that may ultimately fill as many as forty volumes—the edition is destined to be fossilized only in a small number of university libraries and theological seminaries. Chesterton lives, if at all, on a popular level with his Father Brown detective stories—and even these would probably be more read than they are if they were not weighted down with the heavy hand of Christian theologizing and moralizing.

Chesterton's prodigally bountiful work is so massively repetitious, especially in his journalism, that a few works will reveal the little that he has to say. Among the earliest of his religious polemics is a series of essays that the editors of his collected works call "The Blatchford Controversies" (1904), written in response to the antireligious attacks of Robert Blatchford, editor of the *New Age*. This was followed by *Heretics* (1905), in which Chesterton rapped such contemporaries as Shaw, Wells, and Kipling on the knuckles for their purported lapses in morality and piety; then by *Orthodoxy* (1908), which Chesterton claims is not a work of apologetics, even though it is exactly that. Of the works he wrote after his conversion to Roman Catholicism in 1922—*The Everlasting Man* (1925), *The Catholic Church and Conversion* (1927), *The Thing: Why I Am a Catholic* (1929), and *The Well and the Shallows* (1935)—I shall have much less to say, not only because they largely repeat arguments stated earlier but because they are chiefly concerned with distinctions between Catholicism and Protestantism, a distinction I consider about as meaningful as the distinction between believing in Peter Pan and the tooth fairy.

Chesterton's method is perfectly exhibited in *Orthodoxy*. In this treatise he claims to have "attempted in a vague and personal way, in a set of mental pictures rather than a series of deductions, to state the philosophy in which I have come to believe" (O 211). In this sense it anticipates William F. Buckley's "autobiography of faith," written nine decades later. Chesterton states that he developed skepticism at an early age but then renounced it: "I was a pagan at the age of twelve, and a complete agnostic by the age of sixteen" (O 288). And yet, he "retain[ed] a cloudy reverence for a cosmic deity and a great historical interest in the Founder of Christianity" (O 288). Certainly a strange kind of "complete agnostic"! But he goes on to say that although he read a multitude of agnostic and atheistic attacks on Christianity he eventually found these to be filled with paradoxes and contradictions, and so his faith was reaffirmed.

What first strikes us about Chesterton is that what he calls Christianity is something very largely his own invention: it is as much a literary creation as Father Brown or the Man Who Was Thursday. He almost never quotes anything out of the Bible to prove a point; one begins, indeed, to wonder how familiar Chesterton was with the scripture in which he professed belief. For example, early in *Orthodoxy* he makes the startling claim that the doctrine of original sin "is the only part of Christian theology which can really be proved" (O 217). It takes him a long time to explain or justify this utterance, but he appears to provide his rationale for it in a later passage:

> Christianity spoke again and said: "I have always maintained that men were naturally backsliders; that human virtue tended of its own nature to rust or to rot; I have always said that human beings as such go wrong, especially happy human beings, especially proud and prosperpous human beings. This eternal revolution, this suspicion sustained through centuries, you (being a vague modern) call the doctrine of progress. If you were a philosopher you would call it, as I do, the doctrine of original sin. You may call it the cosmic advance as much as you like; I call it what it is—the Fall." (O 321)

But surely this is nothing more than the commonplace that all human beings are morally imperfect—a truism that is at the basis of every religious and secular ethic ever devised but manifestly *not* identical to the specific theological doctrine of original sin. Even if it could be asserted that the essential kernel of original sin is the notion of human moral imperfection, it is only the supernatural framework in which this kernel is expressed—the eating of the fruit by Adam and Eve and their expulsion from Eden—that distinguishes this idea from every other embodiment of it, and it is exactly that framework that is open to criticism.

It is inevitable that Chesterton would take aim at science and rationalism, since these had, for the previous century or more, been destroying the foundations of his faith. But his arguments rarely show, or even purport to show, that science is false; rather, they demonstrate instead that the *results* of scientific inquiry are morally and psychologically unwelcome. In attacking materialism, Chesterton writes: "you may explain the order of the universe by saying that all things, even the souls of men, are leaves inevitably unfolding on an utterly unconscious tree—the blind destiny of matter," but he objects to this explanation because the "normal human mind" (O 226) revolts against it! In other words, those minds bred on the cheering fancies of religion dislike the materialist cosmos because it is cold and impersonal—as if that were some valid argument against its truth. This cosmos "has more restrictions" (O 227) than a cosmos in which we are allowed to believe in the existence of fairies (an example Chesterton explicitly cites here). Well, I suppose I can accustom myself to such a cosmos. To be sure, it is more "restrictive" to believe that two plus two always equals four rather than that, at various times as my fancy dictates, it equals five or seven or a billion, but what is one to do?

Then Chesterton draws out the hoary objection that "it is the charge against the main deductions of the materialist that, right or wrong, they gradually destroy his humanity; I do not mean only kindness, I mean hope, courage, poetry, initiative, all that is human" (O 227). Chesterton does not elaborate upon this idea—apparently he regards it as self-evident. It is the old idea that without a belief in a benevolent god, there is no reason to be moral. In fact, the very opposite could be asserted. The secularist's reasons for behaving in a moral manner may well be said to be *purer* than those of the religionist. The former expresses kindness to another human being because he genuinely cares for that human being or thinks kindness a good thing to practice in civilized society. The latter expresses kindness because he thinks it commanded by a god—in other words, he is merely being obedient. The object of one's benevolence becomes one step removed from oneself: the bulky presence of God intervenes awkwardly. George Eliot well expressed the secondhand nature of this attitude in criticizing the assertion of the evangelical preacher John Cumming that all actions ought to be done "for the greater glory of God":

> God, then, in Dr. Cumming's conception, is a Being who has no pleasure in the exercise of love and truthfulness and justice, considered as affecting the well-being of His creatures; He has satisfaction

in us only in so far as we exhaust our motives and dispositions of all relation to our fellow beings, and replace sympathy with men by anxiety for the "glory of God." The deed of Grace Darling, when she took a boat in the storm to rescue drowning men and women, was not good if it was only compassion that nerved her arm and impelled her to brave death for the chance of saving others; it was only good if she asked herself—Will this redound to the glory of God? The man who endures tortures rather than betray a trust, the man who spends years in toil in order to discharge an obligation from which the law declares him free, must be animated not by the spirit of fidelity to his fellow man, but by a desire to make "the name of God more known." The sweet charities of domestic life—the ready hand and the soothing word in sickness, the forbearance towards frailties, the prompt helpfulness in all efforts and sympathy in all joys—are simply evil if they result from a "constitutional ten-dency," or from dispositions disciplined by the experience of suf-fering and the perception of moral loveliness. A wife is not to devote herself to her husband out of love to him and a sense of the duties implied by a close relation—she is to be a faithful wife for the glory of God; if she feels her natural affections welling up too strongly, she is to repress them; it would not do to act from natural affection—she must think of the glory of God. A man is to guide his affairs with energy and discretion, not from an honest desire to fulfil his respon-sibilities as a member of society and a father, but—that "God's praise may be sung." Dr. Cumming's Christian pays his debts for the glory of God: were it not for the coercion of that supreme motive, it would be evil to pay them. A man is not to be just from a feeling of justice; he is not to help his fellow men out of good will to his fellow men; he is not to be a tender husband and father out of affection: all his natural muscles and fibres are to be torn away and replaced by a patent steel-spring—anxiety for the "glory of God."[1]

When Chesterton finally gets around to an examination of whether the scientific account of the universe is actually true or not, he falls entirely on his face. He first begins with an appeal to tradition, presumably because it embodies the accumulated wisdom of the human race, and since tradition has for so long endorsed Christian and other religious beliefs, these beliefs must be true. Indeed, tradition is intimately related to democracy: "Tradition means giving votes to the most obscure of all classes, our ancestors. It is the democracy of the dead. Tradition refuses to submit to the small and arrogant oligarchy of those who merely happen to be walking about" (O 251). This is merely a version of what I call the democratic fallacy: that truth can and should be determined by a vote of the majority. But in cases where scientific discoveries have overthrown long-held beliefs—such as the belief that the earth is flat, or that the sun revolves around the earth—how can tradition help us? As H. P. Lovecraft pointed out in reference to another traditionalist who was lamenting the increasing irreligion of the age: "He weeps vainly for departed values, and pleads weakly for *continuity* in what he calls 'spiritual evolution'. Alas! he does not see that the 'spiritual' is exploded, and that *continuity* is never possible in matters of *discovery*. Before America was discovered it was unknown—then suddenly it *was* known! And so with the facts overturning religion."[2] Elsewhere Chesterton declares: "The general existence of a world of spirits and of strange mental powers is a part of the common sense of all mankind" (B 389). Note the deceitful use of language here: the root idea is that such beliefs have been "common" (i.e., nearly universal) in human beings, but there is also a duplicitous subtext suggesting that such beliefs are to be regarded as "common sense."

Chesterton tries to combat the findings of science by maintaining that the truths are merely provisional and tentative, and not inexorably true. Oddly enough, he is here anticipating the arguments of the religious apologists of the next several generations, who asserted that the "uncertainty" of science did not entirely rule out the dogmas they wished to believe. Chesterton writes: "We cannot say why an egg can turn into a chicken any more than we can say why a bear could turn into a fairy prince. As *ideas*, the egg and the chicken are further off from each other than the bear and the prince; for no egg in itself suggests a chicken, whereas some princes do suggest bears" (O 255). I fear this argument is not likely to win many converts. If Chesterton thinks a hen's egg, even though it has invariably yielded a chicken, might one day yield a pony, he will be waiting a long time. The argument really rests upon Chesterton's own ignorance of biology: because *he* cannot explain why a chicken comes from an egg, therefore *no one* can. Chesterton cannot conceive of any kind of biological or chemical analysis of the egg that shows why it will hatch a chicken instead of a pony; he fancies that we all think chickens come from eggs only because we have habitually seen the phenomenon come about and never seen it otherwise. Here Chesterton is, whether consciously or not, adapting Hume's argument against causality: the mere fact that one event occurs after another does not necessarily mean that the first event was the cause of the second. But Hume went on to add that in many cases the assumption of causality is a sound and plausible inference. Chesterton, on the contrary, believes that the repetitions and regularities that we find in nature could be the work of God:

> It may not be automatic necessity that makes all daisies alike; it may be that God makes every daisy separately, but has never got tired of making them. . . . The repetition in Nature may not be a mere recurrence; it may be a theatrical *encore.* Heaven may *encore* the bird who laid an egg. If the human being conceives and brings forth a human child instead of bringing forth a fish, or a bat, or a griffin, the reason may not be that we are fixed in an animal fate without life or purpose. It may be that our little tragedy has touched the gods, that they admire it from their starry galleries, and that at the end of every human drama man is called again and again before the curtain. (O 264)

It "may be," indeed, but the probabilities are against it. In the first place, God's existence needs to be established independently before he can be brought in to account for causation; it cannot be assumed at the start. In the second place, Chesterton has fallen into an error that Percy Bysshe Shelley (following Hume) long ago pointed out in refuting the argument from design: "We can only infer from effects causes exactly adequate to those effects."[3] In other words, if the scientific explanations for the regularities of nature are adequate to account for the phenomena (and they surely are), then the assumption that God brought about or allowed these results to occur is logically supernumerary: it is supplying a cause *in excess* of what needs to be explained.

In truth, Chesterton objects to science not on factual but on moral or psychological grounds. In replying to secularists who asserted that the size of the cosmos makes it unlikely that God singled out this small world for his benevolence, Chesterton retorts merely that this huge cosmos of science is not "interesting" and that it does not have "forgiveness or free will"—in fact, it is "empty of all that is divine" (O 265)! Evidently the cosmos can only be interesting if a god were in it.

In this connection it is interesting to observe another favorite rhetorical tactic of Chesterton's: the perversion of his opponent's position. Chesterton frequently sets up straw men so that he can gain the satisfaction of knocking them down. Consider his criticism of Darwinian evolution:

> Evolution is a good example of that modern intelligence which, if it destroys anything, destroys itself. Evolution is either an innocent scientific description of how certain earthly things came about; or, if it is anything more than this, it is an attack upon thought itself. If evolution destroys anything, it does not destroy religion but rationalism. If evolution simply means that a positive thing called an ape turned very slowly into a positive thing called a man, then it is stingless for the most orthodox; for a personal God might just as well do things slowly as quickly, especially if, like the Christian God, he were outside time. But if it means anything more, it means that there is no such thing as an ape to change, and no such thing as a man for him to change into. It means that there is no such thing as a thing. At best, there is only one thing, and that is a flux of everything and anything. This is an attack not upon the faith, but upon the mind; you cannot think if there are no things to think about. You cannot think if you are not separate from the subject of thought. Descartes said, "I think; therefore I am." The philosophic evolutionist reverses and negatives the epigram. He says, "I am not; therefore I cannot think." (O 237–38)

I have quoted this passage at such excruciating length because it is so typical of Chesterton's mode of argumentation. Let us bypass the fallacy of assuming that God somehow brought about evolution: this falls into the same error that Shelley pointed out, for it is exactly the claim of evolutionists that the transition from ape to human being was brought about by natural causes and does not require the intervention of a deity. But it is when Chesterton makes the argument for the "philosophic evolutionist" that he lapses into the nadir of grotesque absurdity: the views expressed are so nonsensical that no one could possibly hold them (and, indeed, no one ever has), so that it is easy for Chesterton to show that they are nonsensical. And when, in *The Everlasting Man,* Chesterton seeks to refute evolution by the following piece of idiocy—"Nobody can imagine how nothing could turn into something. Nobody can get an inch nearer to it by explaining how something could turn into something else" (E 156)—one begins to sense the truth of H. L. Mencken's harsh remark, written at exactly this time, that hostility to the theory of evolution and other scientific doctrines is the result of pure ignorance:

> The popularity of Fundamentalism among the inferior orders of men is explicable in exactly the same way. The cosmogonies that educated men toy with are all inordinately complex. To comprehend their veriest outlines requires an immense stock of knowledge, and a habit of thought. It would be as vain to try to teach to peasants or to the city proletariat as it would be to try to teach them to streptococci. But the cosmogony of Genesis is so simple that even a yokel can grasp it. It is set forth in a few phrases. It offers, to an ignorant man, the irresistible reasonableness of the nonsensical. So he accepts it with loud hosannas, and has one more excuse for hating his betters.[4]

Another rhetorical trick is found in Chesterton's criticism of those secularist pamphlets he admits to having read as a youth. He states that he eventually found them unconvincing because they made contradictory assertions about Christianity:

> As I read and re-read all the non-Christian or anti-Christian accounts of the faith, from Huxley to Bradlaugh, a slow and awful

impression grew gradually but graphically upon my mind—the impression that Christianity must be a most extraordinary thing. For not only (as I understood) had Christianity the most flaming vices, but it had apparently a mystical talent for combining vices which seemed inconsistent with each other. It was attacked on all sides and for all contradictory reasons. (O 289)

As an example Chesterton adduces the following:

I felt that a strong case against Christianity lay in the charge that there is something timid, monkish, and unmanly about all that is called "Christian," especially in its attitude towards resistance and fighting. . . . it did seem tenable that there was something weak and over patient about Christian counsels. The Gospel paradox about the other cheek, the fact that priests never fought, a hundred things made plausible the accusation that Christianity was an attempt to make a man too like a sheep. I read it and believed it, and if I had read nothing different, I should have gone on believing it. But I read something very different. I turned the next page in my agnostic manual, and my brain turned upside down. Now I found that I was to hate Christianity not for fighting too little, but for fighting too much. Christianity, it seemed, was the mother of wars. Christianity had deluged the world with blood. (O 291)

The paradox is only in Chesterton's manner of exposition. He has quietly assumed, for the purpose of this argument, that Christianity is a kind of monolithic entity that cannot in itself harbor contradictory tendencies, and so he is able to maintain that any secularist attacks that reveal such contradictory tendencies betray not the weaknesses of Christianity but the weaknesses of the attacks. Clearly there is a side of Christianity that tends toward retreat from the world, but just as clearly there is another side that demands the aggressive promulgation of the faith, by force if necessary. That both sides at various times—or at the same time in various individuals—have been displayed is an historical fact, and that both can be criticized is certainly within the bounds of argument. Chesterton is, in any case, perfectly happy to consider Christianity a multifaceted phenomenon when it suits his purposes to do so: "The Church is a house with a hundred gates; and no two men enter at exactly the same angle" (C 72).

The lengths to which Chesterton will go in falsifying history become evident in another of his attempted refutations—that religion in general emerged in the "darkness and terror" (O 349) of primitive times, and that Christianity in particular laid a heavy hand on the Dark Ages. Chesterton first maintains that there is no "direct evidence" for the former part of the assertion: "Science knows nothing whatever about pre-historic man; for the excellent reason that he is pre-historic" (O 349). Here is another argument based solely on *words*; the overwhelming bulk of anthropological scholarship is against Chesterton, for it is plain that rudimentary religious instincts were part and parcel of the development of early man. As for the origin of Christianity, Chesterton exclaims: "If any one says that the faith arose in ignorance and savagery the answer is simple: it didn't. It arose in the Mediterranean civilization in the full summer of the Roman Empire. The world was swarming with sceptics, and pantheism was as plain as the sun, when Constantine nailed the cross to the mast" (O 352). He repeats the claim even more egregiously elsewhere: "Christianity arose and spread in a very cultured and very cynical world—in a modern world" (B 381). Because a few of the Roman intelligentsia of the first centuries B.C.E. and C.E.—an infinitesimally tiny proportion of the general populace—were skeptics in religion, Chesterton feels at liberty to affirm that the entire Roman world was "swarming with sceptics." It is a plain fact of history that the populace at this time was grotesquely ignorant and credulous and seeking all manner of spiritual solace from the political and cultural turbulence of the period, so that the emergence of Christianity and other mystery religions was only to be expected. Surely Chesterton does not fancy that Lucretius, Virgil, Horace, or Ovid could have originated Christianity, or would have joined it? Even a sympathetic historian of Christianity, Kurt Aland, commenting on Paul's remark that "not many wise men after the flesh, not many mighty, not many noble, are called; but God hath chosen the foolish things of the world to confound the wise" (1 Cor. 1:26–27), admits:

Christianity in the earliest period was found among the lower—we can almost say the "lowest"—classes of society. Here is where Christianity had its chief influence and from where most of its adherents came. Yet we must not interpret this one-sidedly in the sense of a proletarian Christianity . . . for what Paul says is that not many wise according to worldly standards, not many powerful, not many of noble birth were called—not many, but still a few of the wise, powerful, and those of noble birth. Besides the large number of simple Christians, representatives of the middle and upper classes were found in the early churches. . . . But the majority of churches appeared just the way Paul described them in the first chapter of 1 Corinthians far into the third century.[5]

But Chesterton becomes even bolder and asserts fearlessly that far from bringing about or perpetuating the long twilight of medievalism Christianity "was a shining bridge connecting two shining civilizations" (O 352). Indeed, the Middle Ages were in fact superior to classical antiquity: "there was more cosmic contentment in the narrow and bloody streets of Florence than in the theatre of Athens or the open garden of Epicurus. Giotto lived in a gloomier town than Euripides, but he lived in a gayer universe" (O 364). This rosy picture of medievalism is very popular with Catholics, for it was the last time that the Church held undisputed sway over all Western civilization—politically, socially, and culturally. But let us see how an impartial authority views the period:

This world was held to be a vale of blood and tears preparatory to the next, which was, for the majority, to be one of eternal torture and damnation. It was, indeed, a culpable heresy to hold that more than a tiny minority were likely ever to escape hell fires. "How shall I laugh, how shall I rejoice?" asked Tertullian, and orthodoxy agreed that such behaviour was inviting the fires of Eternity. . . . The body was an ass, and too conscious care of it was another short cut to hell. Roman hygiene gave way to pious dirt, and it was with a strong sense of the miraculous that Christians learnt that St Bridget had been vouchsafed a vision that they might without offence wash twice a month. . . . The followers of St Thomas à Becket—even the less

initiated—were able to extol his grime and the number of lice to
which he was host. Fasting, flagellation, and maceration of every
kind were sought willingly. The end of the world might come at any
moment, and preparation for it was the only useful occupation of a
mankind driven desperate in search of salvation.[6]

And as for the suggestion that it was actually Christendom that
brought medievalism to an end (see O 352), it is too contemptibly
false even for argument. After a thousand years of intellectual stagnation, the Renaissance only occurred through the revival of classical
(i.e., pre-Christian) literature, and the scientific renaissance of the fifteenth through the nineteenth centuries, although frequently carried
on by devout Christians, had the manifest result of systematically
destroying many of the intellectual foundations of religious belief. If
Chesterton is ignorant of these plain facts, then he is simply a fool; if
he is (as I suspect) quite aware of them but deliberately perverting
them, then he is a disingenuous hypocrite.

In this same light, Chesterton casually dismisses the horrors of
Christian tyranny and persecution in the medieval period. In *Heretics*
he casually notes that killing heretics "was done very frequently in the
last decadence of the Middle Ages" (H 39–40), as if it were not done
at any other period; and in "The Blatchford Controversies" he writes:

> The Secularist says that Christianity produced tumult and cruelty.
> He seems to suppose that this proves it to be bad. But it might prove
> it to be very good. For men commit crimes not only for bad things,
> far more often for good things. For no bad things can be desired
> quite so passionately and persistently as good things can be desired,
> and only very exceptional men desire very bad and unnatural
> things. (B 377)

At the risk of repeating myself, I must once again point out that this
is an argument of words, not facts. The most egregious of its fallacies
is the implicit notion that "good" and "bad" things can be clearly and
unequivocally defined, and are universally valid for everyone. Let us
consider only a single example. In 1633 the Catholic Church com-

pelled Galileo to recant his assertion that the earth moved around the sun. No doubt the church thought it "good" that the dogma of the sun's revolution around the earth be maintained, since it bolstered the notion that the earth was the center of the universe and therefore the object of God's special benevolence; the church did not in fact reverse itself on this point of doctrine until 1822. I presume we are in agreement that this doctrine is now and has always been "bad," because it is false.

In speaking of the historical benefits of Christianity, Chesterton avers: "Christianity, which is a very mystical religion, has nevertheless been the religion of the most practical section of mankind. It has far more paradoxes than the Eastern philosophies, but it also builds far better roads" (B 382). The comparison is a most unfortunate one, for it would suggest that the Roman religion was superior to early Christianity. Who, after all, built better roads (some still in use today) than the Romans? But Chesterton, undeterred, forges ahead:

> The Moslem has a pure and logical conception of God, the one Monistic Allah. But he remains a barbarian in Europe, and the grass will not grow where he sets his foot. The Christian has a Triune God, "a tangled trinity," which seems a mere capricious contradiction in terms. But in action he bestrides the earth, and even the cleverest Eastern can only fight him by imitating him first. The East has logic and lives on rice. Christendom has mysteries—and motor cars. (B 382)

This goes from bad to worse. Basing a religion's superiority on its prowess in war produces some awkward consequences, as Bertrand Russell pointed out in 1952:

> If the truth of a religion is to be judged by its worldly success, the argument in favour of monotheism is a very strong one, since it possessed the largest armies, the largest navies, and the greatest accumulation of wealth. In our own day this argument is growing less decisive. It is true that the un-Christian menace of Japan was defeated. But the Christian is now faced with the menace of atheistic Muscovite

hordes, and it is not so certain as one could wish that atomic bombs will provide a conclusive argument on the side of theism.[7]

In this entire argument, Chesterton is falling into the elementary fallacy of assuming that since technological progress was largely produced in the West by a predominantly Christian civilization and by predominantly Christian inventors, it was therefore produced *as a result* of Christianity. But I have my doubts whether Henry Ford was wishing to give thanks to God when he began mass-producing the automobile. And Chesterton would have an awkward time explaining the tremendous advance of technology in the past two and a half centuries—exactly the time when Christianity was systematically losing its hold upon the educated population in the West. After all, there were no motor cars in the Middle Ages! It would, I suppose, be a cruel kind of overkill to point out that, elsewhere, Chesterton excoriates the "modern industrial monotony and herding" (E 215) that his beloved Christian technology has inexorably engendered. But I cannot resist adding that the logical extension of Chesterton's argument is that the very rise of disbelief is a direct product of Christian civilization.

In the matter of miracles, Chesterton similarly adopts a number of fallacies. Predictably, he first asserts that denial of miracles on the part of skeptics is itself a dogma: "In their doubt of miracles there was a faith in a fixed and godless fate; a deep and sincere faith in the incurable routine of the cosmos" (O 332). This argument is too palpably absurd for much discussion: doubt of miracles came about because of repeated observances of the regularities in nature, so that the burden of proof for the miracles fell upon those asserting them—proof that was never forthcoming. Chesterton goes on to assert that the skeptical position is not even consistent, since "miracles" in science are happening all the time: "Things that the old science at least would frankly have rejected as miracles are hourly being asserted by the new science" (O 331). But if Chesterton is here referring to new advances in science, then once again he is guilty, at the very least, of a careless use of language: such advances do not validate the existence of "miracles" but in fact present a stronger case against them, since the new advance, e.g., the curing of some forms of mental illness by drugs or therapy, has shown that what was once taken as a supernatural phenomenon (madness as an affliction from God) is in fact within the domain of the natural.

Chesterton now appeals to the democratic fallacy, and also claims a greater degree of open-mindedness than the secularist:

> The believers in miracles accept them (rightly or wrongly) because they have evidence for them. The disbelievers in miracles deny them (rightly or wrongly) because they have a doctrine against them. The open, obvious, democratic thing is to believe an old apple-woman when she bears testimony to a miracle, just as you believe an old apple-woman when she bears testimony to a murder. The plain, popular course is to trust the peasant's word about the ghost exactly as far as you trust the peasant's word about the landlord. Being a peasant he will probably have a great deal of healthy agnosticism about both. Still, you could fill the British Museum with evidence uttered by the peasant, and given in favour of the ghost. If it comes to human testimony there is a choking cataract of human testimony in favour of the supernatural. (O 355)

Evidently, what is attested by a great many people must be true, just as the assertion that witches with supernatural powers existed was attested by many people (and the church) for centuries. But the plain fact is that such "peasants" (i.e., the uneducated) do *not* have a "healthy agnosticism" regarding ghosts or miracles. Chesterton is in fact appealing to a stereotype: the uneducated are assumed to have a hard-headed realism when dealing with mundane features of their ordinary lives. But it is plain that they are, because of the religious indoctrination to which they were exposed from childhood onward and because of their generally weak grasp of the facts of science, far more inclined to regard the supernatural without the skepticism that knowledge of natural causation brings; in fact, to such people, "miracles" are really not very miraculous, only a little out of the ordinary. It is exactly they who leap to the supernatural whenever anything unusual occurs. Their testimony, accordingly, is valueless unless it can be independently corroborated. Chesterton predictably expresses quick disdain of skeptics' demands for authoritative proof, specifically in the case of spiritual manifestations: surely no spirit of a dead person would choose to communicate with the living under "scientific conditions," given such an "unsympathetic atmosphere" (O 357)! How many times have we heard charlatanic mediums make this same claim. . . . Chesterton in fact addresses the possibility of fraud, only to discount it with an analogy that is itself fraudulent: "For I hope we may dismiss the argument against wonders attempted in the mere recapitulation of frauds, of swindling mediums or trick miracles. That is not an argument at all, good or bad. A false ghost disproves the reality of ghosts exactly as much as a forged banknote disproves the existence of the Bank of England—if anything, it proves its existence" (O 357–58). No one asserts that frauds of this kind *in themselves* disprove the existence of miracles, but the obvious fact that there have been *so many frauds* in the matter of miracles (whereas forged banknotes are quite uncommon), and that *no single miracle has ever been authenticated by sound evidence* (whereas genuine banknotes are widely available), causes the analogy to break into pieces.

It becomes apparent that Chesterton espouses Christianity not because it is true but because it is pleasant, and, conversely, he scorns secularism not because it is false but because it is, in his judgment, productive of unhappiness. Toward the end of *Orthodoxy* he makes a celebrated formulation: "Christianity satisfies suddenly and perfectly man's ancestral instinct for being the right way up; satisfies it supremely in this; that by its creed joy becomes something gigantic and sadness something special and small. The vault above us is not deaf because the universe is an idiot; the silence is not the heartless silence of an endless and aimless world" (O 365). Translated into plain English, all this means is that Chesterton cannot face what seems to him the bleak, cold world of modern science: unless he can think that the universe is not "deaf" (even though it probably is), then his own happiness would be shattered. The notion of "joy" seems particularly important to Chesterton; in "The Blatchford Controversies" he goes so far as to say: "Nowhere in history has there ever been any popular brightness and gaiety without religion" (B 374). Nothing can be clearer than that Chesterton was seeking to avoid the "despair" of secularism:

> And its despair is this, that it does not really believe that there is any meaning in the universe; therefore it cannot hope to find any romance; its romances have no plots. A man cannot expect any adventures in the land of anarchy. But a man can expect any number of adventures if he goes travelling in the land of authority. (O 362)

Chesterton has reached the pinnacle of special pleading and self-contradiction. In the first place, it is only *he*, putting himself in the place of the secularist, who finds "despair" in a meaningless universe—it is beyond his powers to find a meaning in his own life independently of the meaning a sacred text commands him to find. In the second place, even if the assertion that secularism produces despair were sound (which it is not), it would not be equivalent to an assertion that secularism is *untrue*. There are, after all, unpleasant truths that must be faced. And that secular "anarchy" does not harmonize very well with the "cosmic prison" (O 265) he complained of earlier—the prison of natural law that did not allow his precious miracles and other irregularities, God-willed or otherwise, to take place! But after all, what can one expect of him? "Having found the moral atmosphere of the Incarnation to be common sense, I then looked at the established intellectual arguments against the Incarnation and found them to be common nonsense" (O 347). To one who has indoctrinated himself into believing that there is some common sense in the world being flat, the notion that the world is round will naturally appear to be nonsense.

Chesterton has, manifestly, not addressed the most serious and cogent secularist attacks on his religion. Although he claims to have read many such attacks in his youth, he discusses in his writings only the most superficial of these—or, rather, distorts them so that they come to seem shallow or erroneous. There is no evidence that he ever wrestled seriously with such things as John Stuart Mill's skepticism regarding the immortality of the soul, the trenchant agnosticism of

Thomas Henry Huxley and Leslie Stephen, and exposés of religious intolerance extending back to Spinoza, Hume, and Voltaire.

A related, if unanswerable, question is whether Chesterton really believed that the fallacies, evasions, question-beggings, and outright errors in his own arguments in support of Christianity could really be convincing to anyone whose mind was not already made up—indeed, whether they were convincing even to himself. It is true that England had no such dramatic conflict of secularism vs. religion as the Scopes trial of 1925, and it is also true that English religious history does not feature the kind of repeated recrudescence of religious fundamentalism and evangelicalism that has made America such a laughingstock to the civilized world: the last such movement of any consequence in England, the Methodism of the Wesleys, dates to the late eighteenth century. At the same time, as indicated in the previous chapter, England had a far more vigorous tradition of anticlericalism and secularism than the United States, and Chesterton was clearly battling the latest such tradition, launched by Darwin's theory of evolution in the later nineteenth century and continuing through World War II. By the 1920s the kind of orthodox religiosity that Chesterton espoused had become a minority opinion among the English intelligentsia, and he could hardly have avoided feeling like a kind of fossil—as someone left behind by history. The relentlessly hostile, and even condescending, reviews that Chesterton received in the secular press made it clear that after the initial impress of his clever rhetorical tricks had worn off he was regarded less as an intellectual force in modern England than as a kind of unwitting joke or self-parody. No one but Catholics took Chesterton seriously after about 1920. As early as 1909, H. L. Mencken, in reviewing *Orthodoxy,* dismissed it in short order:

> The book pretends to describe the author's gradual conversion to Christianity, and it is written with all his accustomed wit, ingenuity and vivacity. It is, indeed, the best argument for Christianity I have ever read—and I have gone through, I suppose, fully a hundred. But after you lay it down you suddenly realize that Chesterton has been trying to prove, not only that Christianity is reasonable, but

> also that supernaturalism is truth. His argument, indeed, crossing the bounds of merely sectarian apologetics, passes on to the fundamental problem of philosophy: what is true? The materialists answer that anything man can prove is true. Chesterton answers that anything man can believe with comfort is true. Going further, he maintains that anything which gives disquiet is, *ipso facto,* false.
>
> Here we have pragmatism gone to seed, and here we have, too, a loud "No" to all human progress. As a matter of fact, the world gets ahead by losing its illusions, and not by fostering them. Nothing, perhaps, is more painful than disillusion, but all the same, nothing is more necessary. Because there were men willing to suffer painful doubts hundreds of years ago, we civilized white men of today were born without our ancestors' harassing belief in witches. Because a horde of impious critics hang upon the flanks of our dearest beliefs today, our children, five hundred years hence, will be free from our present firm faith in political panaceas, unlucky days, dreams, hunches and the influence of mind over matter. Disillusion is like quinine. Its taste is abominable—but it cures. Not even Chesterton, with all his skill at writing, and with all his general cleverness—and he is the cleverest man, I believe, in the world today, though also one of the most ignorant—can turn that truth into anything else.[8]

❊ ❊ ❊

T. S. Eliot (1888–1965) is a very different kettle of fish. This scion of Boston Brahmins became the highest of highbrow writers in his time, and he continues to be the subject of an appalling tidal wave of criticism, biography, and dissertations. It is true that his reputation has taken a bit of a beating of late, especially in light of Anthony Julius's trenchant monograph *T. S. Eliot, Anti-Semitism, and Literary Form* (1996), which exposed the bland anti-Semitism that colored Eliot's thought and poetry for much of his career, but he remains an icon of modernism. And yet, his various screeds on religion live today—if indeed they do—only because they are the products of his pen: if anyone else had written them, they would have met their deserved fate in the dustbin of intellectual history. Eliot exhibited a quiet but inexorably increasing religiosity from his earliest days—although until the late 1920s he managed to keep it well hidden in essays and poems alike—but by the 1930s he was writing vigorously on religion, as part of his nervous hand-wringing over the fate of that British culture to which he had acclimated himself since the First World War. It is one such work—*The Idea of a Christian Society* (1939)—that I now wish to address.

This must be among the most foolish of Eliot's literary productions. Chief among its many failings is a complete, and at times maddening, imprecision of language and thought, and a lack of a proper definition of the central terms utilized in his argument. The essay was written in 1938–39, after the Munich conference but just prior to the outbreak of World War II, and it is clearly dominated by Eliot's perceived need to combat two obnoxiously anti-Christian tendencies, Russian communism and German and Italian fascism. For Eliot, the society at large must again become vigorously Christian, especially in its morality, in order to achieve the uniformity of culture that he appears to consider desirable. How this uniformity of culture is itself to avoid becoming totalitarian, and how the religious revival is to come about without the use of force are issues that never occur to Eliot; indeed, he seems disturbingly unaware of the numerous fascistic elements in the very proposals he himself is outlining.

What is astounding is how ignorant Eliot remains, from the beginning to the end of his screed, of the degree to which the intellectual foundations of Christianity have been demolished by the advance of knowledge. He appears to regard widening disbelief—the development of non-Christian or anti-Christian attitudes and morals—as somehow self-generated, or perhaps caused by industrialism. Not once does he bother to demonstrate that any point of Christian doctrine is actually *true*; he merely assumes that it *is* self-evidently true. He begins his treatise by noting that Christianity must be treated "with a great deal more *intellectual* respect than is our wont" (I 6). This is not encouraging, since it is exactly that intellectual respect that it has inexorably lost. Eliot in fact maintains that it is very bad to "advocate Christianity, not because it is true, but because it might be beneficial" (I 46) — but he himself makes no attempt to prove that it is true! Does he really fancy that no such proof is now required?

Eliot repeatedly contrasts a "Christian" with a "pagan" society, without once making even a token effort to define either term. He may perhaps have some minimal justification for failing to define the former, although the plain fact that Christianity has broken into numerous competing sects, and also has altered or discarded many of its fundamental tenets (or, at least, its emphasis upon them) over the centuries, makes his stance a bit more problematical. But neglecting to define "pagan" is inexcusable. Does Eliot mean the term literally — the worship of the Greco-Roman pantheon? It does not seem so. Is he using the term more generally to refer to a sort of innocent pleasure in a life close to nature — especially one without a concern for that stern judge in the sky who will consign a majority of the human race to everlasting perdition? This is also doubtful, not only because it would seem difficult for anyone — even Eliot — to object to such an attitude to life but because Eliot actually states dogmatically (without, predictably, supplying any evidence) that "religion, as distinguished from modern paganism, implies a life in conformity with nature" (I 48). There are times when "paganism" seems to serve as a kind of overarching religion or philosophy behind fascism: "The fundamental objection to fascist doctrine . . . is that it is pagan" (I 15); and much later: "If you will not have God (and He is a jealous God) you should pay your respects to Hitler or Stalin" (I 50). Perhaps Eliot is referring (as he does in one of the notes to his essay) to the Nazis' pretense of founding their ideology on a pre-Christian religion. But in reality, paganism for Eliot appears to mean an unthinking acceptance of the inevitability of a mechanized industrial society: "If your real ideals are those of materialistic efficiency, then the sooner you know your own mind, and face the consequences, the better" (I 16). The effect of industrialism, for Eliot, is to produce a mob "detached from tradition, alienated from religion and susceptible to mass suggestion" (I 17).

One wonders why Eliot refuses to believe that political liberalism will be sufficient to ward off the dangers of totalitarianism and regimentation. He finds liberalism merely "negative" (I 13), presumably because it allows individuals to decide matters of thought and belief for themselves, and thereby fails to enforce the "traditional way of life of the community" (I 28) that he frantically yearns for. But how can we return to traditional ways of life when new inventions, and new knowledge, have irrevocably and fundamentally changed the very bases of our social, political, religious, and economic life? Can we uninvent the automobile or the washing machine? More pertinently, can we forget that the doctrine of evolution has destroyed the Christian argument from design, or that physics, biology, and chemistry have rendered monstrously implausible the account of human origins found in Genesis? Eliot is in danger of lapsing not merely into a crudely sentimental nostalgia but into actual anti-intellectualism.

Because Eliot fails to account for growing unbelief in society, he is totally at a loss to determine how his previously Christian sociey can have become "pagan." In an essay, "Church, Community, and State" (1937) appended to *The Idea of a Christian Society,* he writes: "To the unreasoning mind the Church can often be made to appear to be the enemy of progress and enlightenment" (I 74). Note the craftiness of the language: it is only "unreasoning" people who think that the Church can be "made to appear" hostile to enlightenment. By implication, no reasonable person can find that the church actually *is* (as history plainly shows that it is) hostile to enlightenment. Would Eliot lump Bertrand Russell or H. L. Mencken—to name only two of the most significant anticlericalists among Eliot's own contemporaries—in with this "unreasoning" crowd? (Probably he would, given his monotonously snide and disparaging comments on these and many other secular thinkers, including Anatole France and Sigmund Freud.)

In this same essay Eliot equates "what is [morally] wrong" with "what is inconsistent with Christian doctrine" (I 76), as if the two are logically identical. It is staggering to imagine that Eliot cannot conceive of the viability of a secular ethic, but let that pass for the moment. Does he really believe that every feature of Christian doctrine is still morally viable? Since Eliot—here as elsewhere—rarely supplies examples of such doctrines, it is difficult to say, but it seems fair to take him at his word. Let us consider a single moral issue: contraception, an issue on which Eliot explicitly supports the church's position (SE 331). And yet, even in his day the church's repeated and increasingly furious condemnations of it were routinely ignored. Does this mean that all the people who ignored it—whether nominally Christian or not—were evil and corrupt? Or can it mean that the "evil" of contraception was no longer perceived by a society that regarded sensible methods of birth control more relevant to social welfare than adherence to the dictates of a horde of priests (in this case lacking even the security of scriptural support)? Eliot, oddly enough, actually seems to be aware that many moral precepts recommended by the church are merely precepts common to any reasonable society, religious or secular: "the specifically religious emotions must be a kind of extension and sanctification of the domestic and social emotions" (I 24), but he fails to demonstrate the need for this "extension and sanctification"; why are the "domestic and social emotions" not sufficient on their own to engender the kind of morality he wants? Elsewhere Eliot states: "It is not enthusiasm, but dogma, that differentiates a Christian from a pagan society" (I 47). Once again Eliot fails to specify which dogmas he means. Does he believe in the dogma of the divine right of kings (sanctioned by the Bible)? the condoning of slavery (sanctioned by the Bible)? witchcraft (sanctioned by the Bible)? the subordination of women (sanctioned by the Bible)? Given these absurdities, it is remarkable that Eliot can still whine for "a *respect* for the religious life" (I 48).

But how is such a Christian society to come about, given that so many people have lapsed into "paganism"? Again, Eliot is vague and imprecise, but it is in this matter that he begins to sound increasingly fascistic. "[T]he idea of a Christian society implies, for me, the existence of one Church which shall *aim at* comprehending the whole nation" (I 43). Eliot is of course aware of England's numerous Christian and non-Christian sects, and he disavows the notion of any kind of forced uniformity or conversion, but it is difficult to see how else such a church could come into being. In "Church, Community and State" Eliot vigorously rejects the notion that the "Church has no right to interfere with the organisation of society, or with the conduct of those who deny its beliefs" (I 72). He fails to elaborate on this ominous utterance. Elsewhere, in his most disturbing statement, he writes: "A positive culture must have a positive set of values, and the dissentients must remain marginal, tending to make only marginal contributions" (I 36). This, really, is the core of Eliot's cultural totalitarianism. How, exactly, is one to make sure that the "dissentients" (presumably atheists, agnostics, secularists, and even non-Anglicans) remain "marginal"? Does one not allow them to be published in leading magazines and newspapers? Does one suppress their own books, magazines, and newspapers? Eliot does not mention any such thing, but again it is difficult to understand how else he could achieve his aim.

Given that, for Eliot, the idea of a Christian society can only "be realised, in England, through the Church of England" (I 37), it is hardly surprising that he vehemently rejects any thought of the disestablishment of the Anglican Church. Such an action "separates [the church] more definitely and irrevocably from the life of the nation than if it had never been established" (I 39). But hasn't this happened anyway in England? "The national faith must have an official recognition by the State, as well as an accepted status in the community and a basis of conviction in the heart of the individual" (I 41). The first of these is still extant, even if nominally, but the latter two seem to have fallen by the wayside, and there doesn't seem any way to restore the church to its once lofty position.

How has Eliot reached such a pass? How could he, in 1938, so entirely and deliberately ignore the intellectual arguments against the truth of his religion, and therefore against its moral precepts? In 1935 John Beevers, in a discussion of Eliot's own work in *World without Faith*, had written tartly: "I do not believe that Christianity holds anything more of importance for the world. It is finished, played out. The only trouble lies in how to get rid of the body before it begins to smell too much."[9] No doubt Eliot would have been outraged at this remark, if he ever read it, but the mere fact that it and numerous other statements of the same kind could be plausibly written and published should have made Eliot wonder whether the foundations of his faith were quite as firm as they had been two or three or ten centuries ago.

How did this son of St. Louis Unitarians, who read Baudelaire and Laforgue at Harvard and flirted with Buddhism there (and perhaps later as well), suddenly announce his allegiance to Anglo-Catholicism in 1929? It is not as difficult to account for as it appears on the surface. Throughout his life Eliot was terrified of chaos and disorder, and in the end he found no alternative to them but dogmatic religion. Influenced by the idealist philosopher F. H. Bradley, Eliot was haunted by the thought of an irreconcilable subjectivism wherein every person's perception of the world remained unique and incommunicable (he quotes Bradley's "The whole world for each is peculiar and private to that soul" in the notes to *The Waste Land*), and he was also disturbed by the cultural heterogeneity of the West in the aftermath of World War I; accordingly, he desperately sought some haven of safety. As early as 1913 he came upon the French thinker Charles Maurras, who declared himself "classique, catholioque, monarchique"—a phrase Eliot would copy almost verbatim a decade and a half later. In 1916 he wrote: "The present day movement is partly a return to the ideals of the seventeenth century. A classicist in art and literature will therefore be likely to adhere to a monarchical form of government, and to the Catholic Church."[10] However grotesque this may be as analysis, it points clearly to Eliot's eventual conversion. He was first baptized and received into the Church of England in a secret ceremony on June 29, 1927, and then later declared, in the preface to *For Lancelot Andrewes* (1929): "The general point of view [of the essays in the book] may be described as classicist in literature, royalist in politics, and anglo-catholic in religion."[11] The pomposity of this declaration quickly elicited from the intelligentsia the ridicule it deserved and, ironically, alienated Eliot from exactly those individuals—particularly such long-standing colleagues as Virginia Woolf and his erstwhile mentor Ezra Pound, both of whom condemned Eliot's religiosity as an intellectual cop-out—he hoped would lead a moral and religious regeneration of English culture.

I do not wish to treat Eliot's literary views here, although it is quite apparent that they are exactly in accord with his religiopolitical views regarding order and stability. His emphasis on the writer maintaining contact with literary "tradition" (see "Tradition and the Individual Talent" [1919]) led to, and was nurtured by, his adoption of "classicism." But that classicism was of a very peculiar sort. We have already seen that his appeal was to the seventeenth century, but it is difficult to believe that he was unaware that the true age of European classicism was the eighteenth century. It was exactly here that the intellectual control of emotion that Eliot himself regarded as a desideratum reached its pinnacle. But for Eliot, the eighteenth century was a century that did not exist. Through the long course of his life he wrote copiously on the sixteenth, seventeenth, nineteenth, and twentieth centuries, in literature, politics, and religion; but on eighteenth-century literature and thought we find only the solitary late essay "Johnson as Critic and Poet" (1944). No doubt the rampant atheism and secularism of the French Enlightenment and its British and American offshoots were highly offensive to Eliot, even before his conversion (Samuel Johnson, being safely pious, was a happy exception to the rule).

Not once after his conversion (nor, for that matter, before) does Eliot ever address the intellectual foundations of his own belief in Anglo-Catholicism. In the lecture "Catholicism and International Order" (1933) he states, incredibly, that "only the Christian thinker is compelled to examine all his premises, and try to start from the fundamental terms and propositions" (C 117), but there is not one shred of evidence that Eliot himself ever performed this necessary task. He does not realize how perfectly he is describing his own dogmatic mindset when he states in "Religion without Humanism" (1930): "Religious belief, when unquestioned and uncriticised, is liable to degeneration into superstition."[12]

This brings up one of the more repugnant sides of Eliot's religiosity: his persistent denigration of all other views—especially secular ones—merely because they happen to disagree with Christianity. Eliot repeatedly makes seemingly magnanimous claims of giving serious attention to non-Christian (but never to anti-Christian) thinkers in regard to social and political reform, but this attention is always accompanied by a snide condescension. Consider the following:

The Catholic should have high ideals—or rather, I should say *absolute* ideals—and moderate expectations: the heretic, whether he call himself fascist, or communist, or democrat or rationalist, always has low ideals and great expectations. For I say that all ambitions of an earthly paradise are informed by low ideals. I am not condemning all schemes for the betterment of mankind which are not the product of Catholic thinking; but only affirming that all such schemes, as well as our own when we are occupied with immediate temporal emergencies, must be submitted to such examination as only Catholic wisdom can supply. Confronted with any definitely anti-Christian system of society, we are sure that such a system, because founded on falsehood, cannot ever work properly. (C 126–27)

Unthinking dogmatism can go no further.

Only once does Eliot even approach the issue of the intellectual foundations of religious belief. In the context of a discussion of communism, he writes in 1933:

The only end to the battle, if we live to the end, is holiness; the only escape is stupidity, and stupidity, for the majority of people, is no doubt the best solution of the difficulty of thinking; it is far better to be stupid in a faith, even in a stupid faith, than to be stupid and believe nothing. For the smaller number, the first step is to find the least incredible belief and live with it for some time; and that in itself is uncomfortable; but in time we come to perceive that everything else is still more uncomfortable.[13]

I am not entirely sure what this is supposed to mean, nor which hypothetical group—the "stupid" who believe in a "stupid faith" or the "smaller number" (presumably more intelligent) who find "the least incredible belief"—he wishes to align himself with. I will assume, given Eliot's repeated condemnations of the ignorance of the populace ("the number of persons in any generation capable of being greatly stirred intellectually is always and everywhere very, very small" [SE 322]), that he places himself in the latter group. But is religious belief really "less incredible" than atheism? (Let it pass that Eliot is in error if he is referring to atheism as "believing nothing." Atheism is far from being merely a negative stance. The belief that God does not exist carries with it a variety of positive metaphysical, political, social, and ethical corollaries.) Is it really less incredible to believe that lightning is sent by God to punish sinners than that it is caused by the collision of negative and positive particles in clouds? Is it less incredible to believe that Jesus rose from the dead than that the writers of the Gospels were fools and liars?

Similarly, only once does Eliot address the issue of why religious belief has since the Middle Ages declined so precipitously among the intellectual classes, but in doing so he reveals such an astounding ignorance of science, philosophy, and history as to throw one into paroxysms of despair or laughter. In the essay "Religion and Science: A Phantom Dilemma" (1932), Eliot maintains that "no scientific discovery influences people either for or against revealed religion, except insofar as there already exists an atmosphere either favourable or unfavourable to religion."[14] But how can this "atmosphere" develop except through the cumulative effect of scientific and other advances in knowledge? Could it have happened for no reason—especially in light of the rigid control of thought (enforced by murder or imprisonment of heretics and infidels) for which the Middle Ages and Renaissance are so well known? Eliot goes on: "It is not science that has destroyed religious belief, but our preference of unbelief that has made illegitimate use of science." But again, how did this "preference" come about except that intelligent people began to believe that a naturalistic conception of the universe was more plausible than the religious—for the very good reason that it accounted for phenomena in a far more satisfactory way? If the belief that the earth revolves around the sun is shown to be true, what does that do to Christian dogma, which maintains the reverse? Eliot concludes with the plainly false assertion that "the movement away from Christianity came before scientific discovery, and merely made use of it." He must have a very poor grasp of history. The first time in Western civilization that secularism and atheism ever held dominant sway among the intelligent (it has never held sway among the ignorant) was in eighteenth-century

France; can it be plausibly maintained that this was anything but a product of the scientific advances of Copernicus, Kepler, Galileo, Newton, and dozens of others?

By failing to present any intellectual defense for religious belief, Eliot is reduced to the expedient of maintaining that religion is somehow unavoidable, that it is inextricably associated with society or "culture." This is the burden of the opening chapter of *Notes towards the Definition of Culture* (1949), virtually Eliot's last word on the subject. Here he is intent on maintaining that "no culture has appeared or developed except together with religion" (N 87). But this historical argument is full of awkward pitfalls. Two hundred years ago it could have been plausibly maintained (and was indeed maintained) that no society or culture could exist without slavery. A hundred years ago it could have been plausibly maintained (and was indeed maintained) that no society could function if women were given the right to vote. Fifty years ago it could have been maintained (and was indeed maintained) that the intermingling of the putatively separate "races" of humanity would produce cultural and social disaster. All this points to the danger of accepting "tradition" in an uncritical and wholesale manner. Eliot elsewhere asserted, as an argument for retaining religion as a central component of culture, that "we must *use* our heredity, instead of denying it" (SE 421). But how does one "use" slavery, misogyny, and racism? Should these long-standing cultural artifacts not be entirely eradicated from any culture that wishes to call itself civilized?

In any case, is it true that, as Eliot, quoting an anonymous contemporary, notes in *The Idea of a Christian Society*, it is "impossible" for a society to live without religion (I 4)? It is most especially at this point that Eliot's deliberate ignorance of eighteenth-century culture most grievously betrays him. Surely it is difficult to deny that the France and England of that century saw a greater proportion of highly developed intellects and artists than almost any other period can boast, but because the majority of this intelligentsia were atheists or, at best, deists, Eliot cannot bring himself to take notice of them. Much the same could be said of the intellects of Periclean Athens or Augustan Rome, for whom observance of the Greco-Roman religion was merely a polite fiction. It is still an open question whether a society *as a whole* can be secular (I do not count the enforced atheism of communist societies, which is as artificial and dogmatic as the enforced religiosity of an earlier stage of Western society), but the growing secularism of European society at all levels seems to suggest a distinct possibility.

Eliot's entire political, social, and religious thought is vitiated by his inability to conceive of the viability of a secular ethical and political system. As noted, he assumes that such an ethic would be merely focused upon material objectives—the objective of a clean bathroom or an automobile or some such thing. In "Religion and Literature" (1935) he actually writes that "the assumptions of what I call Secularism . . . concern themselves only with changes of a temporal, material, and external nature; they concern themselves with morals only of a collective nature" (SE 354). His long-running argument against the humanism of Irving Babbitt and others rests upon exactly this basis: humanism is merely a "substitute" (SE 420) for religion and (from an ethical perspective) largely parasitic of it; elsewhere he remarks that "I cannot understand a system of morals which seems to be founded on nothing but itself" (SE 432). Unfortunately (as I shall demonstrate in chapter 10), ethics *is* and *must be* founded upon itself; in any case, the metaphysical foundations of religious morality have by now crumbled, so some alternative must be found. Eliot's views on this subject were apparently influenced by T. E. Hulme. Eliot quotes with approval Hulme's pronouncement: "I hold the religious conception of ultimate values to be right, the humanist wrong. From the nature of things, these categories are not inevitable, like the categories of time and space, but are *equally objective*. In speaking of religion, it is to this level of abstraction that I wish to refer" (SE 438). Hulme's simile is most unfortunate, since Einstein established that "time and space" are *not* "objective" but relative.

What Eliot only intermittently notices is that even when religious and secular ethics aim toward approximately similar goals the absolute bases of these goals differ widely. Consider the Golden Rule: "Do unto others as you would have them do unto you." At this point it is scarcely necessary to observe that it was by no means an invention of Jesus; in its negative formulation it can be found five hundred years before Jesus' existence, in the writings attributed to Confucius. Secularists could find this rule an entirely satisfactory—if purely ideal and never wholly realizable—basis for the organization of society, but they do so not on the same grounds as those of the religious. The latter follow the rule because they wish to be obedient to the commands of a god, the former because it is conducive to the functioning of a free society. There is surely a great difference in *attitude* between these two motivations, however much the *results* (or intended results) may be approximately similar. And yet, the degree to which Eliot finds a secular system of social, or even domestic, ethics literally inconceivable is encapsulated by the grotesque remark: "Without the love of God there is no love at all."[15]

By the mid-1930s Eliot had become so dependent upon Catholicism for psychological solace that he even began looking at literature from a religious point of view. The most notorious document in this regard is, of course, *After Strange Gods: A Primer of Modern Heresy* (1934), a series of lectures given at the University of Virginia in 1933. It is here that he wages a vicious *ad hominem* attack on a variety of writers whom he accuses of scorning or abandoning religion, including D. H. Lawrence (a "sick man") and even Ezra Pound. It is all rather sad: the iconoclastic modernist degenerating into the dour Puritan. The comment that caused the greatest embarrassment for Eliot was his reference to the number of "free-thinking Jews" who have infiltrated American civilization. Eliot later repudiated the lectures and attempted to excuse himself by saying that he was a "very sick man" when delivering them, but this does not adequately account for why he allowed such remarks to remain when he later prepared the lectures for publication.[16]

But I am happy to dispense with *After Strange Gods* as evidence of Eliot's views on this issue; the essay "Religion and Literature" (1935) will serve adequately for my purposes, although it of course lacks any snide racist references. Eliot states his position bluntly:

> We must remember that the greater part of our current reading matter is written for us by people who have no real belief in a supernatural order, though some of it may be written by people with individual notions of a supernatural order that is not ours. And the greater part of our reading matter is coming to be written by people who not only have no such belief, but are even ignorant of the fact that there are still people in the world so "backward" or so "eccentric" as to continue to believe. (SE 353)

The harried and defensive tone of this utterance is notable: Eliot manifestly sees himself as part of an ever-dwindling minority of the pious waging a furious rearguard battle against the godless. What is not entirely clear, however, is the degree to which religious (or religio-moral) considerations are actually supposed to affect our judgment of literary works. Is, say, an atheistic novel "bad" *because* it is atheistic, even though it may have other, purely literary virtues? Eliot seems to dodge the question, probably because it will brand him as an antiquated Pecksniff ("I do not want to give the impression that I have delivered a mere fretful jeremiad against contemporary literature" [SE 352]); but since he now no longer believes that there is any such thing as a "purely" literary virtue ("The 'greatness' of literature cannot be determined solely by literary standards" [SE 343]), he is reduced to making statements such as the following: "For literary judgement we need to be acutely aware of two things at once: of 'what we like,' and of 'what we *ought* to like'" (SE 353). Evidently we ought not to like atheistic or secularist novels, poems, or other literary works, because we will in some ill-defined way be "harmed" (SE 353) by them—perhaps because they will wear down our Christian morals, or make us doubt the "primacy of the supernatural over the natural life . . . which I assume to be our primary concern" (SE 352) or, in a worst-case scenario, actually make us atheists and secularists ourselves!

Let us turn the tables and see the results. Suppose I were to assert that it is harmful to read any literature written by the pious, or literature that fosters (or is designed to foster) piety. Not merely am I in that case not allowed to read such things as Dante's *Divine Comedy* or Milton's *Paradise Lost* but, presumably, also Homer's *Iliad* and *Odyssey*, even though these latter works make use of a religion that is now defunct. Nevertheless, there are gods in it, and as a dogmatic atheist I don't even want to read anything about gods, even those that are universally assumed to be false! Instead of adopting a rational attitude—reading Homer, Dante, and Milton because they are great poets and have many interesting and profound things to say about human beings, even if their theologies are by turns comical, horrific, and insane—I am to shield myself against their sirens song in order to preserve my fragile atheism intact. It would surely seem that I am impoverishing my aesthetic sensibility by this kind of self-censorship, and yet, elsewhere Eliot maintains that the Christian—who has to make corresponding sacrifices if he is to be suitably pious—"can have the more varied, refined and intense enjoyment of life" (SE 324)!

In the event, Eliot's social, political, and religious screeds have all gone for naught. They are utterly irrelevant to present-day concerns. For all his whining about the need for Christians to stand up to fascism and communism, it was not Christianity that caused the downfall of these political systems but the very liberalism of America and Western Europe that Eliot despised—with a considerable helping hand from the political, economic, and military might that accompanied it. Eliot was actually aware that Catholicism could itself lapse into either a kind of totalitarianism or a kind of communism: "The ideas of authority, of hierarchy, of discipline and order, applied inappropriately in the temporal sphere, may lead us into some error of absolutism or impossible theocracy. Or the ideas of humanity, brotherhood, equality before God, may lead us to affirm that the Christian can only be a socialist" (C 122). But he cannot bring himself to acknowledge that liberalism and religious toleration are the only means to avoid these opposite poles of political chaos. Eliot's views on toleration are, if nothing else, refreshingly honest: "I think that the virtue of tolerance is greatly overestimated, and I have no objection to being called a bigot myself" (C 135). As early as 1927, in a smug, snide, and deeply ignorant review of Bertrand Russell's lecture *Why I Am Not a Christian*, Eliot proclaimed: "[Russell] has a wholly unreasoning prejudice in favour of freedom, kindliness and such things, and the same unreasoning prejudice against tyranny and cruelty."[17] Let it pass that Russell's "prejudice" was not in any way "unreasoning"; even if it was, one suspects that a majority of intelligent people would share it rather than Eliot's implied preference for their opposites.

And as for Anglicanism being the savior of British society—that has proved to be even more of a sham and a mockery than Eliot could have imagined in 1939. In 1990 the number of active members in the Church of England descended, for the first time, to below 2 million people, or about 5 percent of the adult population. (Roman Catholics numbered just over 2 million people, only a few percentage points higher.)[18] No doubt there are many more "passive" Anglicans, but Eliot would probably regard them with scorn and hostility. There is no sign that they are doing anything for the spiritual or cultural regeneration of Great Britain. And yet, Eliot remained resolutely hostile to political liberalism and secularism, although some of his later utterances have the disturbing effect of whistling in the dark. Consider "Thoughts After Lambeth" (1931):

> The World is trying the experiment of attempting to form a civilized but non-Christian mentality. The experiment will fail; but we must be very patient in awaiting its collapse; meanwhile redeeming the time: so that the Faith may be preserved alive through the dark ages before us; to renew and rebuild civilization, and save the World from suicide. (SE 342)

Eliot's shade will, I fear, be waiting a very long time.

NOTES

References to G. K. Chesterton's works occur in the text as follows: B = "The Blatchford Controversies," *The Collected Works of G. K. Chesterton*, vol. 1 (San Francisco: Ignatius Press, 1986); C = *The Catholic Church and Conversion*, in *Collected Works*, vol. 3 (San Francisco: Ignatius Press, 1990); E = *The Everlasting Man*, in *Collected Works*, vol. 2 (San Francisco: Ignatius Press, 1986); H = *Heretics*, in *Collected Works*, vol. 1; O = *Orthodoxy*, *Collected Works*, vol. 1.

References to T. S. Eliot's works occur in the text as follows: C = "Catholicism and International Order," in *Essays Ancient and Modern* (New York: Harcourt, Brace, 1936); I = *The Idea of a Christian Society,* in *Christianity and Culture* (New York: Harcourt, Brace, 1966); N = *Notes towards the Definition of Culture,* in *Christianity and Culture*; SE = *Selected Essays* (New York: Harcourt, Brace, 1950).

1. George Eliot, "Evangelical Teaching: Dr. Cumming" (1855), *The Writings of George Eliot,* vol. 21 (Boston: Houghton Mifflin, 1908), pp. 163–65.

2. H. P. Lovecraft, "The Defence Remains Open!" (1921), in *Miscellaneous Writings,* ed. S. T. Joshi (Sauk City, Wisc.: Arkham House, 1995), p. 164.

3. Percy Bysshe Shelley, "A Refutation of Deism" (1814), *The Complete Works of Percy Bysshe Shelley,* ed. Roger Ingpen and Walter E. Peck (London & New York: Julian Editions, 1929), vol. 6, p. 48.

4. H. L. Mencken, "Homo Neandertalensis," *Baltimore Evening Sun,* June 29, 1925, p. 1.

5. Kurt Aland, *A History of Christianity,* vol. 1 (Philadelphia: Fortress Press, 1985), p. 56. A translation of *Geschichte der Christenheit* (1980).

6. Pennethorne Hughes, *Witchcraft* (1952; reprint Harmondsworth, England: Penguin, 1967), p. 61.

7. Bertrand Russell, "Is There a God?" (1952), in *The Collected Papers of Bertrand Russell,* ed. John G. Slater and Peter Köllner (London: Routledge, 1997), vol. 11, p. 543.

8. H. L. Mencken, "The Literary Olio," *Smart Set* 27, no. 2 (February 1909): 154–55.

9. John Beevers, *World without Faith* (London: Hamish Hamilton, 1935), p. 64.

10. Quoted in Peter Ackroyd, *T. S. Eliot: A Life* (New York: Simon & Schuster, 1984), p. 75.

11. Preface to *For Lancelot Andrewes* (Garden City, N.Y.: Doubleday, Doran, 1929), p. vii.

12. "Religion without Humanism," in *Humanism in America,* ed. Norman Foerster (New York: Farrar & Rinehart, 1930), p. 105.

13. "A Commentary," *Criterion,* no. 48 (April 1933): 472.

14. "Religion and Science: A Phantom Dilemma," *Listener,* no. 167 (March 23, 1932): 428–29.

15. "The Search for a Moral Sanction," *Listener,* no. 168 (March 30, 1932): 446, 480.

16. Ackroyd, *T. S. Eliot: A Life*, p. 201.

17. Review of Russell's *Why I Am Not a Christian, Criterion* 6, no. 2 (August 1927): 178–79.

18. Grace Davie, *Religion in Britain Since 1945* (Oxford: Basil Blackwell, 1994), p. 46.

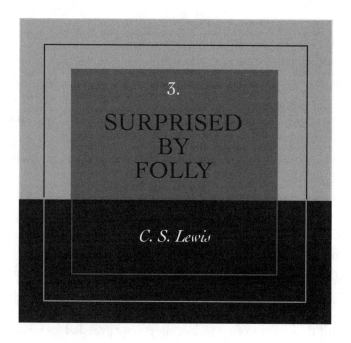

3.

SURPRISED BY FOLLY

C. S. Lewis

A certain air of sanctity hovers around British novelist and theologian C. S. Lewis (1898–1963). A decade ago his most objective biographer, A. N. Wilson, wrote that Lewis "has become in the quarter-century since he died something very like a saint in the minds of conservative-minded believers."[1] Although professional theologians appear not to be much impressed with the cogency of Lewis's many defenses of Christianity, less sophisticated readers regard him with a kind of personal fondness and reverence usually reserved for some doe-eyed neighborhood cleric. Lewis's books have sold in excess of seventy million copies; a large majority of them remain in print half a century or more after their writing; no fewer than seven journals, at a minimum, are or have been devoted exclusively to him; he has been the subject of television plays and films (most notably *Shadowlands*, telling of his love affair with the American divorcée Joy Davidman Gresham). One could say—if one wished to risk inciting the outrage of his devotees—that Lewis has become a kind of cult. Books about him—biographies, critical studies, defenses of his theology—continue to pour off the press in an unending stream, from major publishers, academic publishers, and small presses alike.

Of course, much of this adulation stems not directly from his theological writings but from the works of fiction that have captivated both children and adults, most notably the seven-volume Chronicles of Narnia (1950–56) and his science fiction trilogy *Out of the Silent Planet* (1938), *Perelandra* (1943), and *That Hideous Strength* (1945). To be sure, these works are saturated with Christian special pleading as well, to the point that they become unreadable to anyone not in sympathy with their point of view, but they are nevertheless written with a verve and panache that can sustain them in spite of their heavy burden of moralizing. And, if one is entirely ignorant of Christianity—as I was when I read the Chronicles of Narnia at the age of ten—they can be read with unaffected pleasure as merely entertaining stories. Lewis has also won many readers by his touching autobiographies, *Surprised by Joy* (1955) and *A Grief Observed* (1961).

In all honesty, Lewis deserves to survive not as a defender of Christianity but as a literary critic. A student and later a professor at Oxford (he moved to Cambridge in 1954), he produced several unquestionably distinguished works of literary criticism, chiefly *English Literature in the Sixteenth Century Excluding Drama* (1954), a volume in the prestigious Oxford History of English Literature. One can also mention such things as *The Allegory of Love* (1936), *A Preface to Paradise Lost* (1942), *The Four Loves* (1960), *Studies in Words* (1960), *An Experiment in Criticism* (1961), and *The Discarded Image: An Introduction to Medieval and Renaissance Literature* (1964). These books show Lewis at his best, and his literary standing would be far more secure if he had restricted himself to works of this kind.

The scope of Lewis's Christian apologetics is somewhat difficult to ascertain, since a number of them are "allegories" or half-fictional works—*The Pilgrim's Regress* (1933), *The Great Divorce* (1945), and abve all *The Screwtape Letters* (1942), one of his most frequently reprinted books—that contain little logical reasoning. I shall, accordingly, deal with them only tangentially here. Lewis's main work as a theologian stems from a number of (mercifully short) volumes, including *The Problem of Pain* (1940), *Broadcast Talks* (1942, reprinted in the United States as *The Case for Christianity*), *Christian Behaviour* (1943), *Beyond Personality* (1944), and *Miracles: A Preliminary Study* (1947). The three small booklets of 1942–44—originating as broadcasts to Royal Air Force soldiers during the war—were gathered, with slight revisions, as *Mere Christianity* (1952). *The Abolition of Man* (1943), chiefly a treatise on education, is not explicitly theological but is of importance in ascertaining the thrust of Lewis's moral stance. Lewis wrote a great many short essays on Christian subjects for a wide array of middlebrow British and American periodicals, but gathered only a few of them himself, chiefly in the small book *The World's Last Night and Other Essays* (1960). Since his death, his indefatigable editor Walter Hooper has assembled several more volumes of theological essays, including *Christian Reflections* (1967), *God in the Dock* (1970, published in the United Kingdom as *Undeceptions*), *First and Second Things* (1984), and *The Business of Heaven* (1985), but they add little to the substance of the books prepared by Lewis himself, and in many cases merely contain early versions of sections of his principal treatises.

It would not seem necessary to conduct any detailed dissection of Lewis's theology, for the job has already been done by John Beversluis, who in *C. S. Lewis and the Search for Rational Religion* (1985) has keenly, pungently, but entirely without malice and rancor knocked down every pillar of Lewis's defenses of God, Jesus, and Christianity. (Richard H. Purtill's sorry attempt at rebutting Beversluis only proves that Lewis's advocates are, on the whole, even less worthy of consideration than he was himself.)[2] Beversluis exposes the manifold fallacies of Lewis's mode of argumentation: question-begging, false dichotomies, sheer ignorance of philosophical complexities, rhetorical sleight of hand, and much more. Perhaps his most frequent error is the enunciation of his opponents' views in a highly superficial and even misleading manner, to the point that they become caricatures of the positions he is attempting to refute. As Beversluis notes: "His tendency is to rush into battle, misrepresent the opposition, and then demolish it. The demolition is often swift and the victory decisive, but the view refuted is seldom a position anyone actually holds."[3] One gains the strong impression that Lewis was simply unwilling, or perhaps even afraid, to deal forthrightly with views he disagreed with. It would be surprising to find someone of his general (but not philosophical) intelligence making such crude and grotesque errors in reasoning, were it not that he manifestly considered his opponents not merely factually wrong but morally repugnant and even dangerous, so that he set about attacking them with every weapon available, legitimate or otherwise.

The evolution of Lewis's religious position is of some interest, although *Surprised by Joy*—which purports to trace that evolution—is a highly unreliable document in suppressing key incidents in his life that manifestly affected his piety and in making his conversion from disbelief to belief seem a more purely intellectual matter than it was. Born in Belfast, Lewis was the product of a family both sides of which boasted dogmatic, bigoted Christians. He lost his mother prior to the age of ten—an overwhelming emotional blow from which, apparently, he never recovered. And yet, Lewis maintains that, like G. K. Chesterton (a significant influence on his thought), he lost his faith as a teenager and actually became for a time an atheist—initially from reading pre-Christian literature (the Greco-Roman classics) and then under the influence of a freethinking tutor. This secularism lasted throughout his years as an Oxford undergraduate—a time, incidentally, when he began an affair with a married woman twenty-five years his senior, Janie Moore, whose estranged husband was away in Ireland. This affair, a bizarre psychosexual union with a woman Lewis himself referred to as his "adopted mother," continued unbroken until Moore's death in 1951. Lewis's reconversion, first to nondoctrinal theism in 1929 and then to full-blown Christianity in 1931, occurred, suggestively, not primarily through logical reasoning but through literature—Donne, Herbert, George Macdonald—and through discussions with such devout friends as J. R. R. Tolkien and Owen Barfield. The death of Lewis's father—with whom he had a tortured love-hate relationship—in 1929 is mentioned in only the briefest of sentences in *Surprised by Joy*, for, as A. N. Wilson states:

> He was frightened that hostile readers of his theological work would be able to say that his religion could be "explained" in terms of the Oedipus complex . . . ; and that he was only able to find peace for his heart by coming to terms with a Heavenly Father of his own projection when he had seen the last of his earthly father in Belfast. So much did he dread that his own was a case of "redemption by parricide" that he emphasized the unwillingness with which he accepted the divine call with language which is exaggerated and almost coarse. He was a "prodigal who is brought kicking, struggling, resentful and darting his eyes in every direction for a chance of escape."[4]

After this, he settled into a comfortable Anglican faith, always remaining a bit suspicious of Roman Catholicism (an attitude that eventually soured his relations with the Catholic Tolkien) but saving his greatest wrath for the watering-down of Christian doctrine by other theologians, especially the modernists. He first came into correspondence with Joy Gresham in 1950, while she was still married and, in spite of his strong objections to divorce, he not only married her in 1957 but was outraged that several Church of England clerics refused to perform a church service for them. Already ill with cancer, she died in 1960, and his *A Grief Observed* was published the next year. He was one of three notable individuals who died on November 22, 1963; the others being John F. Kennedy and Aldous Huxley.

Lewis strikes one as a man full of seething emotions over which he had little control—emotions that affected the course of his intellectual development far more than he himself was willing to recognize. And yet, I have no intention of discounting Lewis's theological arguments merely by an appeal to biography; their sources would be of no great importance if they were logically sound. It is precisely because they are not sound—and because the great majority of his readers, manifestly naive and untutored in philosophy, do not perceive their unsoundness—that an analysis of them becomes necessary.

Lewis attempts to establish the existence of God in several ways that strike me as extremely roundabout. His chief argument, oddly enough, stems from the existence of human reason, which he regards as an actually "supernatural" (M 36) phenomenon. His arguments are convoluted and full of ambiguities, but their basic outline—as expounded in chapter 3 of *Miracles*—is something like this:

There are two types of people, the Naturalist and the Supernaturalist. The Naturalist believes that "Nature"—everything that visibly exists in the universe—is "the whole show" (M 17) and that there is nothing external to it. The Supernaturalist, of course, maintains that there is at least one thing, i.e., God, that is outside Nature, and indeed that caused Nature to come into being. It is, however, Lewis's claim that the very existence of reasoning power in human beings cannot be explicated by Naturalist means: "Rational thought or Reason is not interlocked with the great interlocking system of irrational events which we call Nature" (M 33). This is because *"no thought is valid if it can be fully explained as the result of irrational causes"* (M 28). And yet, the Naturalist holds exactly this position:

> But Naturalism, as commonly held, is precisely a theory of this sort. The mind, like every other particular thing or event, is supposed to be simply the product of the Total System. It is supposed to be that and nothing more, to have no power whatever of "going on of its own accord". And the Total System is not supposed to be rational. All thoughts whatever are therefore the results of irrational causes, and nothing more than that. (M 28)

Therefore, the Naturalist lapses into self-contradiction: "The Naturalist cannot condemn other people's thoughts because they have irrational causes and continue to believe his own which have (if Naturalism is true) equally irrational causes" (M 28). Our only recourse is to believe that reason came to us from outside, i.e., from God.

The fallacies in this line of reasoning are so numerous that it is difficult to enumerate them. In the first place, the argument (like so many of Chesterton's) is an argument of *words*, not of *facts*. It is painfully evident that Lewis was simply ignorant of the facts of science. Learned as he was in the realms of literature, his knowledge of the hard sciences appears to have ranged from feeble to nonexistent. He is cataclysmically ignorant of the immense amount of research conducted even in his day by paleontologists, anthropologists, psychologists, biologists, and historians that established unequivocally that primitive man had indeed slowly and gradually developed reasoning power over the course of the past two million years of evolution. Or perhaps we are to imagine our caveman ancestors dwelling for thousands of years in a state of "irrationality" and then waking up one day suddenly endowed by their Creator with the divine gift of reason!

Incredibly, in *The Problem of Pain* Lewis actually puts forth a theory of human development of exactly this sort. In a weird mingling of theology and Darwinism, he avers that "For long centuries God perfected the animal form which was to become the vehicle of humanity and the image of Himself"; then, "in the fullness of time [whenever that might be], God caused to descend upon this new organism, both on its psychology and physiology, a new kind of consciousness which could say 'I' and 'me,' which could look upon itself as an object, which knew God, which could make judgements of truth, beauty, and goodness, and which was so far above time that it could perceive time flowing past" (PP 68). It is difficult to credit any sane person adhering to such a doctrine, which is not only completely at odds with the creation story in Genesis (where, among other things, there is no suggestion that God created such irrational proto-human beings and only later endowed them with reason) but completely in defiance of the facts of human development as known to anthropology. It is no help that Lewis refers to this merely as a "myth," since, in a footnote, he defines the word as "an account of what *may have been* the historical fact" (PP 68). All this makes one doubt whether Lewis had even the faintest comprehension of Darwin's theory of evolution. Although he pays lip service to evolution here and there (see, e.g., MC 169), it is clear that he was mightily uncomfortable with it, for a full acceptance of the theory would present insuperable difficulties to numerous facets of his theological reasoning. In a discussion he had in the late 1940s with the critic Helen Gardner, he had stated that the first person he would wish to meet in Heaven was Adam. When Gardner asserted that "Adam" was likely to be some scarcely articulate Neanderthaloid ape-man, Lewis snapped back: "I see we have a Darwinian in our midst."[5]

But the real fallacy in Lewis's argument is a deceitful and tendentious exploitation of the ambiguities inherent in the words *rational*, *irrational*, and *cause*. (The philosopher G. E. M. Anscombe took exactly this line of reasoning when she wrote her devastating rebuttal to Lewis's account of Naturalism.)[6] By an "irrational cause" Lewis evidently means the physiological account of brain-function, but such an account neither validates nor invalidates any particular thought or thought in general, because that is not its purpose: the determination of whether a given thought is "valid" (i.e., is a true account of the facts of the universe) is an independent process. In any event, it is highly bizarre to maintain that "irrational causes" have somehow led to the formation of the human brain. Lewis quotes J. B. S. Haldane's utterance that "If my mental processes are determined wholly by the motions of atoms in my brain, I have no reason to suppose that my beliefs are true . . . and hence I have no reason for supposing my brain to be composed of atoms" (M 28–29). Lewis seems to fancy that since a given atom is "irrational" (M 29) then no conglomeration of atoms could ever produce rationality. But by this argument no conglomeration of atoms could produce anything. A given atom of a rabbit is not itself a rabbit, so, on Lewis's reasoning, no conglomeration of such atoms could ever produce a rabbit. Lewis also entirely ignores the plain evidences of substantial rationality in animals. His theology cannot encompass the extension of rationality to any species beyond the human, because in his view only human beings have free will and are therefore "fallen" (i.e., are the victims of original sin). Elsewhere Lewis broadens the definition of "rational souls" as follows: "By this I include not merely the faculty to abstract and calculate, but the apprehension of values, the power to mean by 'good' something more than 'good for me' or even 'good for my species'" (WLN 85).

This emphasis on values is critical for Lewis, for he is convinced that the mere existence of a moral sense in human beings is another testimonial to the existence of God. I do not wish to discuss in detail here the vexed question of religion and ethics (see chapter 10), but it can be noted that Lewis's argument on this point is even more careless and easily demolished than his argument in regard to reason. The first part of *The Case for Christianity* is actually titled "Right and Wrong as a Clue to the Meaning of the Universe." Here Lewis asserts that human beings all appear to have a fairly fixed standard of right and wrong. In past ages, he claims, there was much more agreement on such issues than there is now: "they [prior generations] thought that the human idea of Decent Behaviour was obvious to every one. And I believe they were right" (CC 4). When confronted with assertions that different cultures have differed widely in their ethical presuppositions—which would lead one to suspect that morals are largely, or exclusively, the product of social conditioning—Lewis simply utters a flat denial: different cultures have "only had *slightly* different moralities" (CC 5)—a statement would make any anthropologist laugh his head off. Lewis himself, with his deep readings in Greco-Roman literature, should have known better, and probably did. One of the central features of ancient Greek morality—embodied in Medea's memorable line "[I am] hard on my enemies but well-disposed to friends" (Euripides, *Medea* 809)—is not merely "slightly" different from but antipodal to the Christian doctrine enunciated by Jesus: "But I say unto you, Love your enemies, bless them that curse you, do good to them that hate you" (Matt. 5:44). It makes no difference that almost no Christian has ever practiced this moral axiom (Lewis, especially in his debates with opponents, certainly did not); it nonetheless remains, and must remain, the avowed doctrine of every Christian by virtue of its presumed utterance by Jesus. Instances of fundamental moral differences—between one culture and another, between a single culture at different stages in its development, and of course between individuals within a culture or in different cultures—could be multiplied *ad infinitum.*

And yet, even if everyone agreed absolutely in their moral views, this would still not establish that morals are *objective,* which is what

Lewis wishes to establish and believes that he has in fact established ("It seems, then, we are forced to believe in a real Right and Wrong" [CC 6]): this uniformity could simply be a result of universal error. If everyone believed that the earth was flat, the world would not therefore be flat. (In chapter 10 I will argue that moral statements are not subject to truth or falsity at all.)

Lewis puts forward another claim to support the objectivity of morals by declaring that there are many instances when we wish to pursue some course of action that we ourselves know is wrong. Why he thinks this conflict cannot be accounted for by recourse to social conditioning rather than by the assumption that a god has infused a sense of morality in us from outside is beyond my understanding. In any case, this account runs into immediate trouble when we face the plain fact that different individuals have antipodally different ideas of what is right and what is wrong. A man raised in a monogamous society who comes to believe in polygamy will inevitably face an internal conflict as to what he wants to do (practice polygamy) and what he has been conditioned to believe he ought to do (practice monogamy). But a man in a polygamous society who comes to believe in monogamy will face an exactly analogous situation, except that what he wants to do and what he thinks he ought to do will be exactly reversed. In such a scenario, which belief accords with the "real" Right and Wrong that Lewis thinks has been implanted by a god? Lewis would merely be begging the question if he asserted that the belief he himself felt more comfortable with (presumably monogamy) is "real" or "true" while the other is "false" or "not true."

In *Miracles* Lewis maintains that those who assert that morals are not objective are inconsistent in recommending some particular moral or social practice over others:

> The Naturalist can, if he chooses, brazen it out. He can say, "Yes. I quite agree that there is no such thing as wrong and right. I admit that no moral judgment can be 'true' or 'correct' and, consequently, that no one system of morality can be better or worse than another. All ideas of good and evil are hallucinations—shadows cast on the outer world by the impulses which we have been conditioned to feel." Indeed many Naturalists are delighted to say this.

But then they must stick to it; and fortunately (though inconsistently) most real Naturalists do not. A moment after they have admitted that good and evil are illusions, you will find them exhorting us to work for posterity, to educate, revolutionise, liquidate, live and die for the good of the human race. (M 45–46)

Among the numerous errors here, the chief one rests in putting into the Naturalist's mouth both the assertion that "no moral judgment can be 'true' or 'correct'" and that "no one system of morality can be better or worse than another." The latter does not follow from the former, for the very notion of "better or worse" slyly reintroduces an objective standard of morality which it is the express purpose of the Naturalist to deny. Morals may be nothing more than preferences, but those preferences, even if not "true" (i.e., not derived from some objective standard), are still "real" in the sense that they are real preferences. As I noted in the introduction, my liking of chocolate ice cream is not "truer" than your liking for vanilla ice cream, but it is a real liking, and there is no reason why I, as a moral subjectivist, should not wish my own preferences in regard to more substantive matters, i.e., social or moral organization, to become more widespread, and why I should not try to convince others to adopt them.

The Abolition of Man is Lewis's most sustained polemic against the notion of the subjectivity of values, but it adds little to the discussion. Once again he asserts that some moral axioms are "so obviously reasonable that they neither demand nor admit proof" (AM 53), and that these axioms must be accepted unquestioningly, otherwise "you will destroy all values, and so destroy the bases of your own criticism as well as the thing criticized" (AM 59–60). Lewis even goes on to declare that those who undertake this kind of criticism of what he calls the *Tao* (the basic moral values that, in his view, all cultures and civilizations have shared) are not even, or are no longer, fully human: "It is not that they are bad men. They are not men at all. Stepping outside the *Tao*, they have stepped into the void. Nor are their subjects necessarily unhappy men. They are not men at all: they are artefacts. Man's final conquest has proved to be the abolition of Man" (AM 74). Lewis goes on to paint a lurid portrait of some future society in which the moral subjectivists (which he deems the "Conditioners" because they seek to brainwash all members of society into their outlook) have produced a society in which everyone acts merely on the impulse of the moment. He concludes ominously: "A dogmatic belief in objective value is necessary to the very idea of a rule which is not tyranny or an obedience which is not slavery" (AM 81). But this is merely hyperventilated bluster; Lewis is simply writing science fiction.

The emphasis on reason and morality as infusions from God leads Lewis directly to several of the central tenets of Christianity, which in his view suddenly become more plausible. Specifically, the miraculous incarnation of God into a human being in the figure of Jesus is rendered less bizarre: "If we did not know by experience what it feels like to be a rational animal—how all these natural facts, all this bio-chemistry and instinctive affection or repulsion and sensuous perception, can become the medium of rational thought and moral will which understand necessary relations and acknowledge modes of behaviour as universally binding, we could not conceive, much less imagine, the thing happening" (M 134). The entire burden of *Miracles* is to make the various supernatural events associated with Christianity seem not merely not impossible but actually "probable" (M 160). It would not seem that a focus on miracles would be the best way to justify Christian doctrine, since it is exactly these miracles—the Incarnation, the Resurrection, and the death of Christ for our "sins"—that are now subject to such skepticism, even on the part of believing Christians. But Lewis is aware of the centrality of the issue: "The accounts of the 'miracles' in first-century Palestine are either lies, or legends, or history. And if all, or the most important, of them are lies or legends then the claim which Christianity has been making for the last two thousand years is simply false" (M 97).

Lewis's focus is on the figure of Christ. In one of the most notorious of his utterances (first propounded in rudimentary form in *The Problem of Pain* [PP 21] and expressed definitively in *The Case for Christianity*), he maintains that given Jesus' own assertions that he was the son of God and that he would one day return and pass judgment on our sins we have only two alternatives in our attitude toward him:

I'm trying here to prevent anyone from saying the really silly thing that people often say about Him: "I'm ready to accept Jesus as a great moral teacher, but I don't accept His claim to be a God." That's the one thing we mustn't say. A man who was merely a man and said the sort of things Jesus said wouldn't be a great moral teacher. He'd either be a lunatic—on a level with the man who says he's a poached egg—or else he'd be the Devil of Hell. You must make your choice. Either this man was, and is, the Son of God: or else a madman or something worse. You can shut Him up for a fool, you can spit at Him and kill Him as a demon; or you can fall at his feet and call Him Lord and God. But don't let us come with any patronising nonsense about His being a great human teacher. He hasn't left that open to us. He didn't intend to. (CC 45)

This is, prototypically, an instance of a false dichotomy: it might be called the fallacious either-or argument. As several other commentators have pointed out, it does not leave room for a third or fourth possibility—specifically, that Jesus was not mad but merely mistaken.[7] I confess that I myself have no particular difficulty in regarding Jesus as insane, but perhaps that is merely a personal bias. Lewis, in any event, is making an appeal not to reason but to raw emotion: he is counting on the high probability that even the most brazen-faced atheist will not care to offend many millions of people by bluntly declaring that Jesus was a ripe candidate for the booby hatch. Lewis himself seems to fancy that the possibility of Jesus' insanity is not even worth the bother of discussing (all he says on the matter is "Now it seems to me obvious that he wasn't either a lunatic or a fiend" [CC 45]). But the likelihood that Jesus, though sincerely convinced that he was the son of God, was merely mistaken seems highly plausible after even a superficial examination of the historical circumstances of his emergence in "first-century Palestine." As Beversluis notes:

Theologians have long insisted that Jesus' messianic claims must be viewed against the background of Jewish eschatology and the immanent expectation of the One who would deliver the Jewish nation. All devout Jews shared this hope. They believed that sooner or later someone would answer to the description of the promised

Messiah—if not Jesus, then someone else. Consequently, the credentials of each claimant had to be investigated one by one. For those who proved deficient, the proper assessment was not "Another lunatic," but rather "This is not he for whom we look." Lewis's discussion suggests that all individuals of all times and places who say the kinds of things Jesus said must be dismissed as lunatics if their claims are rejected. But this overlooks the theological and historical background that alone makes the idea of a messianic claim intelligible in the first place.[8]

It may be worth noting that for all Lewis's insistence on studying the historical context of literary texts and the language in which they are composed he was singularly uninterested in understanding the historical circumstances out of which his own religion emerged. He also expressed quick disdain and extreme ignorance of the biblical criticism that in the century preceding had produced such luminous insights into the composition of the Bible and its social, political, and theological background. In the essay "Religion without Dogma?" (1946) he delivers this incredible aside:

> The Biblical criticism which began in the nineteenth century has already shot its bolt and most of its conclusions have been successfully disputed, though it will, like nineteenth-century materialism, long continue to dominate popular thought. What I can say with more certainty is that that *kind* of criticism—the kind which discovers that every old book was made by six anonymous authors well provided with scissors and paste and that every anecdote of the slightest interest is unhistorical, has already begun to die out in the studies I know best. (U 104)

It may also be worth noting that Lewis's discomfiture with regarding Jesus as *only* a "great moral teacher" rests precisely in his awareness that in this scenario there is no compelling reason to follow his teachings as opposed to the teachings of any other moralist, such as Confucius or Socrates or even Bertrand Russell (assuming, for the moment, that Lewis could regard him as a "great moral teacher"). For

Lewis, Jesus' moral utterances had to have the force of a commandment, otherwise they were useless to his purpose. (Whether Jesus
actually was a "great moral teacher" may itself be subject to doubt.
Anyone who presumably asserted that those who are not baptized are
going straight to hell [Mark 16:16], that the majority of the world's
people will end up in hell anyway [Luke 13:24], and that non-Christians should be forced to convert to Christianity [Luke 14:23] should,
at the very least, expect to find his moral eminence open to question.)

Once Lewis has established Jesus' divine credentials to his satisfaction, he is compelled to assume that all his utterances are true and
correct; for surely the son of God—in fact, one who is actually God
himself—could not possibly be in error. He does leave himself a little
wiggle room by claiming that "I certainly think that Christ, in the
flesh, was not omniscient—if only because a human brain could not,
presumably, be the vehicle of omniscient consciousness" (PP 120).
But to say that Christ didn't know *everything* is very different from
saying that he was actually *wrong* about something. In a later essay,
"The World's Last Night" (1952), Lewis confronts head-on what he
candidly calls "the most embarrassing verse in the Bible" (WLN 98):
*the obvious fact that Jesus' prediction of his second coming as destined to occur
within the lifetime of those who heard him was erroneous.* This prediction is
repeated in all three of the synoptic gospels (Matt. 16:28; Mark 9:1;
Luke 9:27), with minimal changes of language. If Jesus was wrong on
so central an aspect of his eschatology, how can it be plausibly maintained that he was the son of God? With this error he descends to the
level of one more false prophet carrying a sandwich board predicting
the end of the world, while the world passes calmly by without giving
him a moment's notice. On the basis of this one error alone, the entire
edifice of Christianity comes tumbling down.

Lewis tries to dodge this issue by first quoting another verse that
is not quite so explicit on the matter ("Verily I say unto you, this generation shall not pass, till all these things be fulfilled" [Matt. 24:34]),
then by quoting Jesus' subsequent comment: "But of that day and
hour knoweth no man, no, not the angels of heaven, but my Father
only" (Matt. 24:36). Lewis believes that this latter utterance allows

him to conclude that "Jesus professed himself (in some sense) ignorant, and within a moment showed that he really was so. To believe in
the Incarnation, to believe that he is God, makes it hard to understand
how he could be ignorant; but also makes it certain that, if he said he
could be ignorant, then ignorant he really could be" (WLN 99).

I have no idea what that is supposed to mean. In any case, even if
we assume that Jesus was uncertain of the "day and hour" of his
second coming, that uncertainty seems to apply, in context, within the
"this generation" remark two verses earlier; Jesus is still maintaining
here that he will return within the lifetime of those who hear him, but
that the exact date of that return is unclear. So it is not the case that
Jesus is merely "ignorant"; he is still mistaken, in that he clearly did
not return within "this generation." And the other passages I have
cited, which Lewis does not discuss, make no such confessions of
"ignorance" on the matter.

As an historical aside, it is interesting to note that as early as 1
Thessalonians (purportedly written by Paul in the early 50s C.E.), we
find that Jesus' second coming will occur, in that memorable phrase,
"as a thief in the night" (5:2)—in other words, he may come back so
well disguised that no one will know that the second coming is happening! If you can believe that, then there is a bridge nearby that I'd
like to sell you. Still later, in 2 Peter (written around 150 C.E.), there
is an attempt to quell early Christians' pitiable worries on this point
("Where is the promise of his coming?" [3:4]) with the manifest
sophism "one day is with the Lord as a thousand years, and a thousand years is one day" (3:8)—an apparent allusion to the "day and
hour" ambiguity cited by Lewis. The only problem is that elsewhere
Jesus himself did not mention days or months or years in regard to
his coming, but stated plainly: "But I tell you of a truth, there be some
standing here, which shall not taste of death, till they see the kingdom
of God" (Luke 9:27).

Every Christian theologian is obliged to face up to what is
unquestionably the most difficult crux in the entire doctrine: how a
god who is conceived to be both omnipotent and benevolent can allow
"evil" (i.e., suffering) to exist. It is the old dilemma of "why bad things

happen to good people." Lewis addresses the issue at length in his first work of apologetics, *The Problem of Pain* (1940). He does so not by repudiating either God's omnipotence (as many liberal theologians have done) or his benevolence (as relatively few, understandably, have done) but by thrusting the blame fully upon human beings. In effect, "bad" things do not happen to "good" people because there *are* no "good" people. Everyone is "fallen," i.e., the victims of Adam's original sin. That sin is precisely defined by Lewis as "the abuse of . . . free will" (PP 61). In other words, God allowed us to have free will, but an essential part of that free will is the freedom to do bad things, which every one of us does repeatedly and with relish; therefore, no one is guiltless.

This is, in fact, an entirely satisfactory "solution" of the problem of suffering, although Lewis is in error in thinking that it thereby does not entail the notion of a vengeful and retributive God.[9] But of course it paints a rather glum view of the moral status of the human race—a view that Lewis was, indeed, not hesitant to embrace: "A recovery of the old sense of sin is essential to Christianity. Christ takes it for granted that men are bad. Until we really feel this assumption of His to be true, though we are part of the world He came to save, we are not part of the audience to whom His words are addressed" (PP 51). Later Lewis asserts that "the whole human race . . . is, in fact, . . . a pocket of evil" (PP 56); "we actually are, at present, creatures whose character must be, in some respects, a horror to God" (PP 60). Lewis is so insistent on this point that he suddenly has to draw back a bit, declaring nervously that he is not putting forth "a restatement of the doctrine of Total Depravity" (PP 59): we are not *totally* depraved, it would appear (otherwise we could not be "redeemed"), but we're in pretty bad shape, nonetheless.

Even with this dark view of humanity, however, Lewis is forced to confront the plain fact that people who are not obviously "depraved" nonetheless suffer pain on occasion: "We are perplexed to see misfortune falling upon decent, inoffensive, worthy people—on capable, hard-working mothers of families or diligent, thrifty little tradespeople, on those who have worked so hard, and so honestly, for their modest stock of happiness and now seem to be entering on the enjoyment of it with the fullest right" (PP 86). How to deal with this "perplexity"? Lewis's answer is that too much happiness is not good for us: we become so immersed in pleasure that we forget how (morally) wretched we are and also forget that we are totally dependent on God's favor! Suffering, therefore, is God's "warning" (PP 86) that we must constantly abase ourselves before him: "Suffering is not good in itself. What is good in any painful experience is, for the sufferer, his submission to the will of God, and, for the spectators, the compassion aroused and the acts of mercy to which it leads" (PP 98).

There is, however, a point Lewis never mentions—the awkward question of whether such suffering actually leads people back to God. There are surely a great many who, under the pressure of intense pain or misfortune, have come to believe in the absence of a divine spirit in the world. Indeed, if John Beversluis is correct, Lewis himself might have been one of them. There are strong indications in *A Grief Observed* that the death of Lewis's wife caused him momentarily to conceive of God as a kind of "Cosmic Sadist" who enjoyed toying with people's emotions. Even if Lewis ultimately came to reject this conception and somehow managed to preserve his notion of the goodness of God, he seems to have done so in a manner that is neither emotionally satisfying nor logically convincing. As Beversluis writes:

> We are emphatically assured by one expositor after another that the agonizing experience recounted in *A Grief Observed* does not constitute a falsification of the assertion that God is good. But then what would? Lewis's final answer appears to be: Nothing. But that is a fatal admission. It reveals that his belief in God's goodness has become wholly vacuous, that there is no way to deal with the problem of contrary evidence. Lewis claims that his faith somehow survived. I am sure that it did. But it no longer invites the assent of the rational man.[10]

Lewis's notion of devils apparently works into his entire conception of pain and suffering, although in a manner that frankly baffles me. This notion runs through the entirety of his work and is of course at the heart of *The Screwtape Letters*. In a later preface to that volume, Lewis flatly asserts his belief in the existence of devils ("I believe in angels, and I believe that some of these, by the abuse of their free will, have become enemies to God and, as a corollary, to us" [SL vii]), although he demurs at picturing them in the conventional way—bats' wings, tridents, etc. Note that devils here are themselves accused of an "abuse of . . . free will," exactly the same moral flaw that led to humanity's fall from grace. But the problem becomes how, if at all, does the existence of devils help to account for humanity's own "abuse of free will"? In *The Problem of Pain* Lewis dances around the whole issue, stating only that "when man fell, someone had, indeed, tempted him" (PP 120), that someone being, presumably, the Devil (the head honcho in this case, not some subordinate devil like Wormwood in *The Screwtape Letters*). But does this not cause a problem with the whole notion of human free will? If the Devil tempted Adam, isn't *he* (the Devil) to blame for our woes, rather than Adam? Perhaps Lewis imagines that Adam exercised free will by allowing himself to be tempted. But if so, what then are we to make of a strange passage in *Christian Behaviour* that provides a kind of analysis of the human soul? "There are two things inside me, competing with the human self which I must try to become. They are the Animal self, and the Diabolical self" (MC 80). Does this mean that there was a diabolical self built into the human soul at its creation, or that we have somehow internalized the Devil's blandishments and made them our own? And what of a passage in *Miracles* that states that God, in allowing both human beings and angels to exercise free will by sinning, "thus surrender[ed] a portion of His omnipotence" (M 147), even though in *The Problem of Pain* he claimed that God's omnipotence is unlimited except "the intrinsically impossible" (PP 25)? This whole notion of devils is simply an incoherent mess in Lewis's theology. He states cocksurely that "My religion would not be in ruins if this opinion [on devils] were shown to be false" (SL vii), but Lewis would have been better off if he had omitted it entirely.

So humanity is "fallen," and a number of us are going to be consigned to hell (there is an entire chapter on hell in *The Problem of Pain*).

What then becomes of Christ's power to "redeem" us? In *The Case for Christianity* Lewis maintained that "The central Christian belief is that Christ's death has somehow put us right with God and given us a fresh start" (CC 46). A fresh start to do more sinning? If so, what exactly was the point of Christ's death in the first place? It doesn't seem to have accomplished anything. Surely it cannot be asserted that the human race is, morally speaking, much better after Jesus' death than before. Lewis almost lets the cat out of the bag when he pictures "a God so full of mercy that He becomes man and dies by torture to avert that final ruin [i.e., hell] from His creatures, and who yet, where that heroic remedy fails, seems unwilling, or even unable [!], to arrest the ruin by an act of mere power" (PP 106). Adam and all his descendants sinned; Christ came along and died to give us a "fresh start"; we sin some more and are going to hell. Not a very effective system of moral improvement, it seems to me.

And yet, the most remarkable chapter of *The Problem of Pain* is the one dealing with animal pain. Since Lewis denies rationality or free will to animals, he must confront the obvious dilemma of why God allows animals to suffer as much pain as they do: what good does it do them, since they are not "fallen" and therefore cannot be redeemed? In a series of logical somersaults difficult to follow, Lewis first asserts that "a great deal of what appears to be animal suffering need not be suffering in any real sense" (PP 119), since it is not evident that animals, though "sentient," are "conscious" and therefore are sufficiently aware of themselves as self-standing entities to understand that it is they who are suffering the pain. I think Lewis would have benefited by seeing some programs on the Discovery Channel, which show fairly conclusively that animals suffer pretty excruciating pain when being devoured by other animals. He then suggests that animals might have been corrupted by Satan (PP 120) and therefore, presumably, deserve to suffer, and, as a final coup de grâce, he conjectures that perhaps animals have immortal souls after all (PP 122)! But not all of them: unlike those horrible atheists who maintain that only "wild" animals are "natural" and tame ones are "artificial" (PP 123), the reverse may well be the case. Tame animals, you see, might have

absorbed a certain trace of our own humanity by osmosis, and therefore they gain a kind of self-awareness denied to those ignorant beasts
in the forest, and so "it seems to me possible that certain animals may
have an immortality, not in themselves, but in the immortality of their
masters" (PP 125). How comforting to think that Fido will join me in
heaven! But why stop here? Perhaps even a few wild animals are also
immortal, although, of course, "their immortality would . . . be related
to man" (PP 126). How so? Lewis expounds: "If Christian cosmology
is in *any* sense (I do not say, in a literal sense) true, then all that exists
on our planet is related to man, and even the creatures that were
extinct before men existed are then only seen in their true light when
they are seen as the unconscious harbingers of man" (PP 127). So the
dinosaurs were, unbeknownst to themselves, lumbering for millions
of years to prepare the way for glorious *Homo sapiens!* To which the
only legitimate riposte is Bertrand Russell's wry description of theologians' arguments for the existence of God from evolution:

> The world was once lifeless, and when life began it was a poor sort
> of life consisting of green slime and other uninteresting things.
> Gradually by the course of evolution, it developed into animals and
> plants and at last into MAN. Man, so the theologians assure us, is
> so splendid a Being that he may well be regarded as the culmination
> to which the long ages of nebula and slime were a prelude. I think
> the theologians must have been fortunate in their human contacts.
> They do not seem to me to have given due weight to Hitler or the
> Beast of Belsen. If Omnipotence, with all the time at its disposal,
> thought it worth while to lead up to these men through the many
> millions of years of evolution, I can only say that the moral and aes-
> thetic taste involved is peculiar.[11]

It would be vastly to the benefit of Lewis's reputation as a theologian if this chapter on animal pain could be expunged from existence.
It is not only the nadir of Lewis's work in terms of logical thought, it
reveals an appalling callousness to suffering that brings only Calvin or
Luther to mind. Its mere existence is a standing refutation of all the
arguments Lewis puts forth for Christianity as a religion that can be

justified rationally. If one is forced to undergo the kind of mental and emotional gymnastics as are undertaken in this chapter merely for the sake of preserving a belief in God, then it would certainly appear that that belief is not intellectually justifiable.

As it is, John Beversluis has delivered a laconic epitaph on Lewis's entire venture into Christian apologetics, and beyond this very little need be said:

> Taken as a whole, then, Lewis's apologetic writings do not embody a religion that satisfied his own definition of rationality. His arguments for the existence of God fail. His answer to the Problem of Evil is unacceptable. His characteristic way of misrepresenting the views of the opposition stands as a permanent warning to future apologists. He is even guilty of trying to harmonize incompatible philosophical traditions. And so the failures accumulate, the inconsistencies remain, and the case for Christianity has not been made.[12]

NOTES

References to C. S. Lewis's works occur in the text as follows: AM = *The Abolition of Man* (1943; reprint New York: Simon & Schuster, 1996); CC = *The Case for Christianity* (New York: Macmillan, 1943); M = *Miracles: A Preliminary Study* (New York: Macmillan, 1947); MC = *Mere Christianity* (New York: Simon & Schuster, 1952); PP = *The Problem of Pain* (1940; reprint New York: Simon & Schuster, 1996); SL = *The Screwtape Letters* (1942; reprint New York: Macmillan, 1962); U = *Undeceptions*, ed. Walter Hooper (London: Geoffrey Bles, 1971); WLN = *The World's Last Night and Other Essays* (New York: Harcourt, Brace & Co., 1960).

1. A. N. Wilson, *C. S. Lewis: A Biography* (London: Collins, 1990), p. x.
2. See Richard H. Purtill, "Did C. S. Lewis Lose His Faith?" in *A Christian for All Christians: Essays in Honor of C. S. Lewis*, ed. Andrew Walker and James Patrick (London: Hodder & Stoughton, 1990), pp. 27–62. Like Lewis himself, Purtill knocks down a straw man: he contends that in *A Grief Observed*, Lewis, according to Beversluis, "lost" his faith in the rationality of Christianity, when in fact Beversluis maintains that that faith survived, after a

fashion, but had become philosophically untenable. Purtill also summons as an ally a hostile review of Beversluis's book by Thomas V. Norris of Notre Dame, declaring that he is "not a partisan of Lewis"—as if such a pious gent is not likely to be far more sympathetic to Lewis's enterprise than Beversluis's.

3. John Beversluis, *C. S. Lewis and the Search for Rational Religion* (Grand Rapids, Mich.: William B. Eerdmans Co., 1985), p. 41.

4. Wilson, *C. S. Lewis: A Biography*, p. 111.

5. Ibid., p. 210.

6. G. E. M. Anscombe, "A Reply to Mr. C. S. Lewis's Argument that 'Naturalism' Is Self-Defeating" (1948). See Beversluis's discussion (pp. 65–68).

7. The point was first made by W. Norman Pittenger, "Apologist Versus Apologist," *Christian Century* 75 (1 October 1958): 1104–1107. See also Beversluis (pp. 54–57) and Robert M. Price, *Beyond Born Again: Toward Evangelical Maturity* (Upper Montcair, N.J.: Apocryphal Books, 1992), ch. 7.

8. Beversluis, *C. S. Lewis and the Search for Rational Religion*, pp. 55–56.

9. On this issue see Walter Kaufmann, *The Faith of a Heretic* (Garden City, N.Y.: Doubleday, 1961), ch. 6.

10. Beversluis, *C. S. Lewis and the Search for Rational Religion*, p. 161.

11. Bertrand Russell, "Is There a God?" (1952), in *The Collected Papers of Bertrand Russell*, ed. John G. Slater and Peter Köllner (London: Routledge, 1997), vol. 11, pp. 544–45.

12. Beversluis, *C. S. Lewis and the Search for Rational Religion*, pp. 166–67.

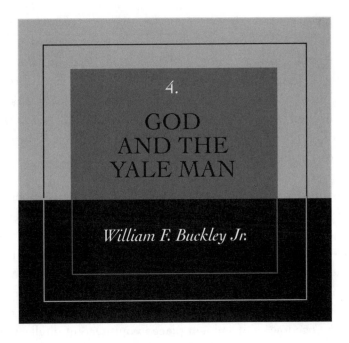

4.

GOD
AND THE
YALE MAN

William F. Buckley Jr.

William F. Buckley Jr. (b. 1925) is the founder of the modern conservative movement. It is not entirely clear what role he has had in the origin of modern religious conservatism, especially given the fact that what we call the religious right is largely a Protestant phenomenon, and its leaders have on occasion suggested that Buckley's form of dogmatic Roman Catholicism is unwelcome within its camp. But Buckley's first book, *God and Man at Yale* (1951), with its complaints about the increasing godlessness of the American university, could well have laid a seed that grew to fruition more than two decades later. Buckley's prodigally copious writing is by no means dominated by religious concerns, and it required more than forty years for him to produce another treatise on the subject, *Nearer, My*

God: An Autobiography of Faith (1997). His editorials in the *National Review*, the conservative paper he founded in 1955, discuss religious issues of the day from time to time, but his two major books are all that are needed to gain a sense of his faith and his doctrine. Another early book, *McCarthy and His Enemies* (1954), will prove to be of some relevance in a slightly different context.

I suppose it is unreasonable to expect Buckley to be an adept philosopher. After all, he is only a political journalist—which on the order of intellectual accomplishment is roughly on the same level as a hack fiction writer and a magazine editor (both of which Buckley also happens to have been). In *Nearer, My God* he makes the scarcely necessary admission that "I am not remotely qualified as a theologian or historian of Christianity" (N xvii), and we will find his discussions superficial and confused to the point of grotesquerie. And yet, because he occupies a prominent place in our current intellectual culture (not, to be sure, specifically for his religious views), his work demands some scrutiny.

God and Man at Yale is a priceless buffoonery. In it, Buckley announces that "during the years 1946 to 1950, I was an undergraduate at Yale University. I arrived in New Haven fresh from a two-year stint in the Army, and I brought with me a firm belief in Christianity and a profound respect for American institutions and traditions." Accordingly, he looked to Yale "for allies against secularism and collectivism" (G ix). He was, of course, bitterly disappointed, and the rest of his treatise—condemning the prevalence of godless secularism and lack of respect for religion—alternates between a whine and a rant. To someone of Buckley's way of thinking, it would certainly not do to have one's religious, moral, and political presuppositions disturbed by a college education. Why, at that rate, one might actually be exposed to new ideas and, accordingly, come to believe that one's earlier views were wrong! No, it was hardly to be countenanced. It is beyond Buckley's capacity, then or now, to imagine that he could be mistaken about anything—either his religion or his politics. And so, when he finds professors at Yale whose views do not chime with his, he can only assume that they are not merely wrong, but evil.

And yet, in the preface to his book Buckley makes the following remarkable statement:

> I should also like to state that I am not here concerned with writing an *apologia* either for Christianity or for individualism. That is to say, this essay will not attempt to prove either the divinity of Christ or to defend the advantages of conducting our lives with reference to divine sanctions. Nor shall I attempt to demonstrate the contemporary applicability of the principal theses of Adam Smith.
>
> Rather, I will proceed on the assumption that Christianity and freedom are "good," without ever worrying that by so doing, I am being presumptuous. (G xiii)

This is a fatal admission. To be sure, Buckley is not being presumptuous in his assumptions; he is merely being a fool. With no attempt to establish the *truth* of his religion (he axiomatically assumes that "we are right and they [his intellectual opponents] are wrong" [G xii]), his entire treatise becomes nothing but a sniffing out of all those professors, and others affiliated with his university, with whom he happens to disagree.

Buckley's use of "good" in this passage is more than a little curious, especially as he himself includes it within quotation marks. He never defines in what sense he thinks Christianity to be "good"; can he mean that it is "good" for people to believe it whether it is true or not (the evident position of William James)? This seems unlikely, given his later contempt of "relativism, pragmatism, and utilitarianism" (G 25). In a footnote to the second paragraph quoted above, he writes: "In point of fact, the argument I shall advance does not even require that free enterprise and Christianity be 'good,' but merely that the educational overseers of a private university should *consider* them to be 'good'" (G xiii). This goes from bad to worse, for it manifestly implies exactly the kind of relativistic and utilitarian approach that Buckley claims to scorn. Bertrand Russell, summarizing William James's moralistic argument for belief in God ("we ought to believe in God because, if we do not, we shall not behave well"), notes:

The first and greatest objection to this argument is that, at its best, it cannot prove that there is a God but only that politicians and educators ought to try to make people think there is one. Whether this ought to be done or not is not a theological question but a political one. The arguments are of the same sort as those which urge that children should be taught respect for the flag. A man with any genuine religious feeling will not be content with the view that the belief in God is useful, because he will wish to know whether, in fact, there is a God. It is absurd to contend that the two questions are the same. In the nursery, belief in Father Christmas is useful, but grown-up people do not think that this proves Father Christmas to be real.[1]

To complete his excursion into imbecility, Buckley announces at the start: "I think of Yale . . . as a nondenominational educational institution not exclusively interested in the propagation of Christianity" (G 4). This is entirely disingenuous, for the remainder of Buckley's book makes it abundantly clear that the propagation of Christianity is exactly what he thinks Yale *should* be interested in. How Buckley can reconcile this remarkable statement with the equally remarkable assertion that the Yale faculty should, in his opinion, be "committed to the desirability of fostering . . . a belief in God" (G x) is something only he can explain.

Buckley devotes a long chapter, "Religion at Yale," to an examination of specific professors in the departments of religion, sociology, philosophy, and psychology, and unleashes a barrage of disapproval for all those pedagogues whom he believes to be insufficiently devout. He is forced repeatedly to state that he has no criticism of the academic credentials of any of these individuals, but he bridles whenever they either lampoon religion, express atheistic, agnostic, or secular remarks, or merely *ignore* religion in the course of their work. There is no question that he would like to impose a Christian litmus test upon the Yale faculty. In remarking that one professor, Ralph E. Turner of the history department, has "little respect for the values that most undergraduates have been brought up to respect" (G 13), it does not occur to Buckley to wonder whether those values are worthy of respect. In noting that "many instructors [of sociology] believe that [religion] is distinctly harmful benightedness" (G 14), it never occurs to him to wonder whether it might be. In claiming that another professor, Raymond Kennedy of the sociology department, "subverted the faith of numbers of students who, guilelessly, entered the course hoping to learn sociology and left with the impression that faith in God and the scientific approach to human problems are mutually exclusive" (G 17), Buckley never pauses to consider whether the faith of these students wasn't very strong or well-founded to begin with, and whether religion and science are indeed mutually exclusive. This same professor, Buckley complains, "reveals his biases freely and frankly" (G 18)—it was his misfortune, evidently, not to have the same biases as Buckley himself.

Buckley winds up with a grand peroration following his scorn of "relativism, pragmatism, and utilitarianism":

> And there is surely not a department at Yale that is uncontaminated with the absolute that there are no absolutes, no intrinsic rights, no ultimate truths. The acceptance of these notions, which emerge in courses in history and economics, in sociology and political science, in psychology and literature, makes impossible any intelligible conception of an omnipotent, purposeful, and benign Supreme Being who has laid down immutable laws, endowed his creatures with inalienable rights, and posited unchangeable rules of human conduct. (G 25–26)

It is difficult to believe that even Buckley, fresh out of school and a callow lad of twenty-six, could utter such gibberish. It is amusing to see him criticizing the demise of "absolute" truths, since it is exactly this that allowed so many religionists in the twentieth century to maintain that religion *might* be true given that science was no longer *definitively* true. In any case, what are the "immutable laws" and "unchangeable rules of human conduct" laid down by the Supreme Being? That the sun revolves around the earth, that slavery is acceptable, that wives are the property of their husbands? All these views are found in the Bible, a document that Buckley presumably accepts unconditionally. Buckley no doubt thinks that his mention of "inalienable rights" is a clever rhetorical stroke, but it only augments the folly of his remark. It is of course derived from the beginning of the Declaration of Independence ("We hold these truths to be self-evident, that all men are created equal, that they are endowed by their Creator [!] with certain unalienable [*sic*] Rights . . ."). Perhaps Buckley regards this text as some kind of secondary Bible, for no "inalienable rights" can be found in the Bible itself. Indeed, since the Bible repeatedly endorses the divine right of kings (to choose one passage among many: "Let every soul be subject unto the higher powers. For there is no power but of God: the powers that be are ordained of God": Rom. 3:1), one could be justified in regarding democracy and "inalienable rights" to be contrary to Christian teaching.

Buckley's intolerance extends well beyond mere atheists, agnostics, and secularists. By vaunting Christianity so exclusively, he condemns all other religions to perdition. He notes bluntly that "Christianity is the true religion" and that "all genuine Christian leaders proclaim it to be, thus committing themselves logically to the proposition that all other religions are untrue" (G 28) — exactly what the proponents of Judaism and Islam are obliged to do as well, but rarely do nowadays. In 1951 Yale sponsored a Religious Emphasis Week, its principal speaker being Reinhold Niebuhr. A *Yale Daily News* editorial noted: "'In these tragic times we are all faced with re-evaluating our beliefs.' So reads the Christian Mission's brochure on the Niebuhr talks. But now that they're all over, we fail to see how they have helped in this search. The next time a Religious Emphasis Week rolls around, we would propose the following: let's have a forum in which we'd hear, as well as the Christian, the Taoist point of view, the Buddhist, the Mohammedan, the Jewish, the Hindu, and so on. Here would be some real meat for thought: here would be a real basis for re-evaluation of beliefs." Buckley remarks in high dudgeon: "This was too much for even the Yale student carefully nurtured in tolerance and relativism. Sample reply: 'Today's editorial is a bogus and a phony, pretending to the merit of honest criticism but really possessing only the false splendor of irrelevance and condescension. . . .'" (G 32n).

So what does Buckley think should be done about this lamentable situation? Since Yale is a private university it can, presumably, hire anyone it likes, for any reason it likes, and Buckley emphatically declares that that is exactly what should be done. If faculty members do not toe the line on religion and individualism, they should not be hired to begin with, and, if already hired, they should be promptly dismissed. Buckley is therefore obliged to dismiss as a "hoax" (G 182) the entire notion of academic freedom. He does it in a most curious way. First, he asserts that Yale does not actually practice academic freedom. He advances some instances of professors who would not be acceptable to the faculty of a given department because they do not themselves espouse the party line on some issues, e.g., a professor of English who champions Joyce Kilmer as a great poet, a sociologist who advocates Aryan supremacy, a political scientist who deprecates democracy. Let it pass that these are *purely hypothetical* cases, and Buckley does not present a single instance of any actual professor being rejected on such grounds. All he has proven is that people do not always practice what they preach; he has made no case against the principle of academic freedom itself.

It is in the course of this section that Buckley, at long last, feebly and hesitantly broaches the central issue involved—the actual truth or falsity of Christianity (and individualism)—but he does so only to drop it forthwith. Acknowledging that truth may be difficult to arrive at in these cases, and conceding magnanimously that "Christianity— or even the existence of God—in the opinion of some people, is not demonstrable" (G 154), Buckley then states: "Let us say that Christianity *may not be truth,* but that in the eyes of Christians it is at least the *nearest thing to unrevealed* and *perhaps inapprehensible ultimate truth*" (G 154). If there is a greater instance of a tautology, I have yet to hear of it. Of course Christians regard Christianity as the "nearest thing" to the truth; if they didn't, they wouldn't be Christians. But Jews, Muslims, Hindus, Buddhists, and the followers of every other religion similarly regard *their* religion as the nearest thing to the truth. Atheists regard their nonreligious views as the closest thing to the truth. What then? How has there been any advance in the argument? One begins to develop the suspicion that Buckley is simply incapable of demonstrating the "truth" of Christianity; he himself throws in the towel by remarking: "Let us not pursue the point" (G 154).

In a later passage Buckley proclaims, "In the absence of demonstrable truth, the best we can do is to exercise the greatest diligence, humility, insight, intelligence, and industry in trying to arrive at the nearest values to truth" (G 156). I leave it to readers to determine whether Buckley himself has followed this sane course, either in his religious or in his economic views. It certainly seems as if youthful brainwashing has led Buckley to grasp fervently, and perhaps desperately, at a religion that he cannot now bring himself to question. A little later we find that religion and individualism are "noble doctrines whose ascendancy is the best guaranty of man's freedom and man's selfless dedication to the good" (G 173). (Do I hear "God Bless America" playing somewhere in the background?)

Toward the end Buckley becomes both a trifle paranoid and contradictory. He is so worried that the collectivist policies recommended by the faculty will be widely embraced that they will end up bankrupting the wealthy alumni of the college, resulting in "the impoverishment of every imaginable financial supporter of Yale, except the government" (G 171). The last time I checked—fifty years after Buckley's screed, and when many of the abhorred "collectivist" policies had been embraced as a matter of routine economic policy by the American government—Yale was still financially well endowed.

Then there is the matter of the actual influence of the teachers upon the students. Throughout his book Buckley worries himself into a tizzy about the baleful effect of all those atheists and collectivists upon the "impressionable" minds of the wide-eyed neophytes under their charge. After all, the faculty "addresses itself to the task of persuading the sons of these supporters [i.e., the Yale alumni, who are all presumably Christian individualists] to be atheistic socialists" (G xi–xii). And yet, in his discussion of academic freedom, he says the very reverse. Buckley believes that his own religious and economic values—which he maintains, on no compelling evidence, are the values of the majority of the alumni and of the overseers of the college—should be taught, but when university president Charles Seymour objected to the idea that the faculty should teach a single, monolithic set of values, Buckley protests: "A value orthodoxy in an educational institution need not *in any circumstances* [my italics] induce credulity in the student, nor deny the value of skepticism as a first step to conviction" (G 194). Which is it to be? It appears that the atheistic socialists are successful in brainwashing their hapless students, but that the Christian individualists are not. Certainly a lamentable state of affairs!

What Buckley is really whining about is that *his own* prejudices and biases, religious and economic, are not being taught. He is resentful that the views he grew up with—and that he regards as sacrosanct and self-evidently correct—are not shared by leading scholars of his day. Since he is unwilling or unable to defend his own views intellectually—since, indeed, he cannot conceive how he could be mistaken—he can only assume that there is some evil conspiracy to propagate the views he despises, and so his only recourse is to demand the dismissal of his opponents. It is difficult to imagine that Buckley could, even in 1950, believe the intellectual foundations of Christianity to be as well-founded as they were a century or two earlier; he was, after all, born in the very year of the Scopes trial. He grudgingly admits that there is a distinction between *"refining* a given set of values, and *displacing* them altogether in favor of others" (G 174), but can he truly be unaware that the advances in human knowledge and civilization over the past four centuries have profoundly shaken the "truth" of his religion? How can there be talk of "refining" certain biblical views that have been shown to be demonstrably false?

I have no interest in Buckley's political or economic views except insofar as he himself, in *God and Man at Yale,* sees the fields of religion and economics as inextricably linked. It will be a surprise to those who have followed Buckley's subsequent journalistic career to hear him stating ponderously at the outset: "I myself believe that the duel between Christianity and atheism is the most important in the world. I further believe that the struggle between individualism and collectivism is the same struggle reproduced on another level" (G xii–xiii).

Buckley has, of course, devoted a greater proportion of his energies to the second point rather than the first. In any event, his long chapter on "Individualism at Yale" is a reprise of his religion chapter, made doubly absurd by his frank admission that "my remarks in this chapter in no way attempt to rebut the arguments of the collectivist" (G 47). The result is still more finger-pointing at collectivists, socialists, and other folk who earn Buckley's disapproval.

I am not concerned with the actual accuracy of Buckley's comments, either on the religiosity or the economic orthodoxy of the Yale faculty. This point was sufficiently taken care of by McGeorge Bundy's pungent review in the *Atlantic Monthly* (November 1951), when he charged Buckley with being "dishonest" and concluded: "I can imagine no more certain way of discrediting both religion and individualism than the acceptance of Mr. Buckley's guidance."[2] For my part, I have two other issues to raise with Buckley's entire approach.

The first is that, for all his linking of secularism and collectivism as twin evils of modern society and education, he fails utterly to note a connection very hurtful to his cause: the religion of Jesus Christ (I hesitate to call it Christianity, since it does not seem to have been practiced by anyone in the last two thousand years) advocated as complete a collectivist society as any ever proposed. Can Buckley really be unaware that Jesus himself was a pure communist? The assertion is, indeed, a commonplace, perhaps most pungently expressed in George Bernard Shaw's preface to *Androcles and the Lion*. At this stage it seems hardly necessary to cite Jesus' well-known condemnations of wealth and property ("Lay not up for yourselves treasures upon earth" [Matt. 6:19]) and his recommendations to give up all the property one has ("If thou wilt be perfect, go and sell that thou hast, and give to the poor, and thou shalt have treasure in heaven" [Matt. 19:21]), so that the description in Acts of the early Christian community ("And all that believed were together, and had all things common; and sold their possessions and goods, and parted them to all men, as every man had need" [2:44–45]) is only a logical extension of Jesus' own teaching.

The other problem is with Buckley's whole approach of identifying by name the individuals he dislikes, without the least attempt to show that they are actually mistaken in their beliefs. Buckley assumes at the outset that they are mistaken ("we are right and they are wrong"), so he hardly need trouble himself on the matter. Buckley has a great nose for atheists and collectivists. Ralph E. Turner of the history department is "emphatically and vigorously atheistic" (G 13); Brand Blanchard of the philosophy department is "an earnest and expansive atheist" (G 18); Buckley even becomes outraged that a student magazine devoted to Christianity, *Et Veritas*, is insufficiently pious and proselytizing. As for the economists, Alexander Brooks "was an outspoken socialist" (G 87); other instructors are "doctrinaire Keynesians" (G 87); Professor Lindblom's "philosophy . . . is, manifestly, collectivist in the extreme" (G 92), and he "strongly supports the socialist government of Great Britain" (G 95). Even nonprofessors come under the lash, such as Garrison Ellis, editor of the *Yale Daily News*, who is "a pronounced, emphatic, undeviating left-winger" (G 105), as opposed to Buckley himself, who is a pronounced, emphatic, undeviating right-winger.

What does all this remind us of? What else but McCarthyism?

Buckley's long-winded and sycophantic defense of McCarthy, *McCarthy and His Enemies*, speaks in exactly the same tone. And yet, for all its painfully detailed and frequently sophistical dismissal of the "Liberal" attacks on McCarthy, it is surprisingly silent on the overriding issue of that bleak period: the plain fact that the House Un-American Activities Committee did not merely pursue supposed communists in government, but expanded its scope to persecute a wide variety of intellectuals—writers, film actors, and artists in general—solely on the basis of their opinions or of their support of liberal, humanitarian (even if, in some cases, nominally communist) causes, and who could not possibly be regarded as "threats" to the government. This is the true threat of McCarthyism, and it is what made him far more dangerous to American institutions than any of the communists he sniffed out. Buckley blithely asserts that "McCarthyism . . . has little in common with pogroms and concentration camps" (M

317), but that is only because McCarthy was not able to do more than harass and destroy the careers of his opponents. The true parallels to McCarthy (and to Buckley in his attitude toward Yale) is not to the pogroms, but to the witchcraft persecutors of the Middle Ages and Renaissance—and, in a still greater irony of which Buckley himself remains to this day oblivious, to the very Soviet communists he professes to despise. If McCarthy and Buckley did not carry out the purges that Lenin and Stalin effected, it was only because they lacked the political and military power to do so. They all went in with the same attitude: they were definitively right and everyone else was conclusively wrong; their opponents' errors were pernicious and must be rooted out—by force, innuendo, smear campaigns, guilt by association, and any other tactics that came to hand. Extremism on both the right and left has an uncanny habit of meeting—and it meets on the ground we call fascism.

Buckley claims to be a libertarian, but his libertarianism, like that of so many others, extends only in certain limited directions. He is all for "maximum freedom" (G 51n), but only in the sphere of economic exploitation by capitalists without tedious and bothersome government interference; in matters of opinion and expression he sings a very different tune. In *McCarthy and His Enemies* he hoped wistfully for a constitutional amendment to outlaw the expression of communist views (M 6), and he also saw no problem with the Atlanta city government's banning of a pro-African American film, even though no one was being forced to see the film (M 322–23). No, Mr. Buckley does not seem inclined to bestow "freedom" upon opinions he doesn't like. Let us heed the words of a true libertarian, H. L. Mencken: "I am, in brief, a libertarian of the most extreme variety, and know of no human right that is one-tenth as valuable as the simple right to utter what seems (at the moment) to be the truth. Take away this right, and none other is worth a hoot; nor, indeed, can any other long exist."[3]

Buckley casually denies that any "reign of terror" existed during the McCarthy period. But that is only because his own views were never in danger of being persecuted; he might have thought differently if he were on the other side. And yet, in denying that McCarthy was trying to silence all opposition, especially from liberal sources, Buckley makes an ominous prediction:

> Some day, the patience of America may at last be exhausted, and we will strike out against Liberals. Not because they are treacherous like Communists, but because, with James Burnham, we will conclude "that they are mistaken in their predictions, false in their analyses, wrong in their advice, and through the results of their actions injurious to the interests of the nation. That is reason enough to strive to free the conduct of the country's affairs from the influence of them and their works." (M 333)

This is, as I say, ominous, but not in an obvious way, nor in a way that Buckley himself has even now realized. Buckley and Burnham are of course entitled to this belief, just as I am entitled to believe the exact opposite. The real question is: What is to be done about such undesirables? Shall we institute an Inquisition to get them out of government and other influential areas of society and culture? Certainly, this is conceivable; what happened once may happen again. But what Buckey fails to grasp is that at some future date the government could decide that his own reactionary conservatism is "mistaken in its predictions," etc., etc., and so seek to eliminate him and his cohorts from political and cultural power. The only reprieve for Buckley is that liberals are not in the habit of persecuting others solely for their opinions. If atheism and religion, liberalism and conservatism are not allowed the freest possible airing in the intellectual arena—without the threat of crackdowns on unpopular opinions or of firings from teaching positions—then no advance in knowledge and civilization can occur. The only alternative is fascism, where one side is right and the other is wrong. Buckley may find it difficult to credit, but many intelligent people do not regard his views as self-evidently correct. He needs to make a case for them, not merely assert them by fiat and condemn his opponents simply because they hold alternative opinions.

It took Buckley more than forty years to present an actual defense of Christian doctrine; the result is *Nearer, My God: An Autobiography of Faith*

(1997). This book, too, provides much merriment at Buckley's expense. Because it is presented somewhat loosely as an "autobiography of faith," it lacks coherent structure, and, oddly enough, the autobiographical framework is dropped after the opening chapters. But we now learn definitively what we suspected all along—that Buckley had been thoroughly indoctrinated into Catholicism from infancy onward, in part by his father but mostly by his mother; it is a fact Buckley openly admits: "I grew up . . . in a large family of Catholics without even a decent ration of tentativeness among the lot of us about our religious faith" (N 241).

But the book suffers from more serious flaws than mere rambling or padding, although there is plenty of both in it. Buckley maintains that his mode of reasoning in his book "tends to be argumentative" (N xvii), but because (as I noted at the outset) he does not regard himself as an "expert" either on Catholic theology or history, he frequently hides behind the views of others, and it is not always clear what views he himself espouses. On occasion it almost seems as if he does not have the courage of his convictions. He appears to advocate the principle of papal infallibility, but presents only John Henry Newman's arguments in support of it. Elsewhere he notes in passing the opinion of Irving Kristol and Michael Kinsley on the matter of prayer in public schools: such a prayer, in the minds of opponents, would compel students of a different faith to accept a prayer in which they do not believe, but "Kristol and Kinsley simply deny the force of this objection" (N 28). That is all that is said, and neither the reasoning of Kristol and Kinsley supporting this remarkable assertion nor Buckley's own thoughts on the matter (aside from a predictably Falwellian sneer at the "Supreme Court's war against religion in the public schools" [N 37]) are ever recorded. Elsewhere, Buckley gathers an informal panel of experts— some of them actual theologians, others well-informed laypeople, but all of them Catholics and conservative friends of long standing—to expound their views on various theological conundrums, but he rarely adds his own views, acting in large part only as a reporter. This seems to me a strange kind of autobiography. Nevertheless, I shall attempt as far as possible to discuss Buckley's own opinions, although on occasion I will address those of others with which Buckley appears to agree.

It is amusing to see how desperately Buckley and his pals assert the distinctiveness, and even the divinity, of the Catholic Church. Much is made of the antiquity of their faith (see, e.g., N 247). The argument is not a good one. If the truth of a religion is based upon its antiquity or longevity, then Catholicism—and Christianity as a whole—will have to bring up the rear in comparison to many Eastern religions, several of which have outlasted it by a millennium or more, to say nothing of Judaism itself, of which Christianity is a bastard off-spring. So far as I can tell, the world record in this regard goes to the Egyptians: their religion existed for close to four thousand years, from no later than 3110 B.C.E. (the beginning of the 1st Dynasty) to at least 642 C.E. (the Arab conquest of Egypt, when Islam became the state religion). Isis beats Jesus, and even Moses, hands down! Even Greco-Roman paganism lasted for nearly two millennia (from at least 1200 B.C.E. to about 600 C.E.), and would no doubt have lasted longer if Christianity had not suppressed it. Buckley himself is impressed by the single-minded determination of the Apostles to spread their belief: "It is unimaginable to me that such a thing could happen except under such extraordinary auspices as moved Peter and his fellow Apostles" (N 279). Hardly. This kind of fanaticism has been seen in religion time and time again: it is no more remarkable that the early Christians martyred themselves for their faith than that Jim Jones's followers drank poisoned Kool-Aid™ at his command. One fellow, George Rutler (an Anglican priest who converted to Catholicism in 1981), actually sees something "evidently supernatural" in the appearance of Pope John Paul II "at this tumultuous period in world affairs" (N 243–44)! No doubt there was also something blessedly supernatural in the sudden death of the liberalizing John Paul I under suspicious circumstances after only a month in office.

Buckley begins his treatise with the impressive assertion that "the [Catholic] Church is unique in that it is governed by a vision that has not changed in two thousand years" (N xix). This is a singularly unfortunate formulation: there is nothing "unique" about the Catholic Church in this regard. Virtually every religion—Hinduism, Buddhism, Confucianism, to name only three of many that predate Christianity by centuries—has remained true to its first principles: if you think you have the word of God on your side, you don't have much incentive to change. And no doubt the various Protestant denominations all believe that they have preserved this "vision"—"that we are not accidental biological accretions, we are creatures of a divine plan; that the God who made us undertook to demonstrate his devotion to us as individual human beings by submitting to the pain and humiliation of the Cross" (N xix)—better than the Catholic Church has. It is a view Buckley would have difficulty refuting, and in fact he makes no attempt to do so, although he utters various passing comments of a blandly snide nature on the hapless fate of Protestants who have "no magisterium to pronounce conclusions by which the faithful are bound" (N 84). In other words, whereas Protestants are plagued by having to figure out points of doctrine for themselves, Catholics are relieved of the burden of thinking by recourse to an infallible pope! A comforting thought, indeed.

But how does Buckley justify his continuing faith in an era of widespread skepticism (among the intelligentsia, at any rate)? He has surprisingly little difficulty in the matter. "Science has not discredited religious faith. Christianity is as viable in the post-Einstein world as when it caught fire in the West" (N 39). Buckley does not do much to justify this astounding utterance; he seems to regard it as obvious. In two sentences, therefore, Buckley dispenses to his satisfaction with half a millennium of scientific inquiry. I wish I could gain this kind of self-confidence. But the idea that relativity, quantum theory, or any other advance of modern science makes it any more likely than before that the resurrection of the dead, birth by immaculate conception, or any other such rubbish is possible or even probable is one that has polluted much loose thinking in both religious and scientific circles for half a century or more.

Buckley goes on to declare: "What keeps Christians afloat is the buoyant knowledge that no devastating damage has in fact been done to Christian doctrine" (N 55). Ah, blessed Bill!—how strong a shield your ignorance must be! I suppose one should not be surprised at Buckley's staggering ignorance of science, ancient and modern, but one might expect him to have a slightly better notion of the scientific and philosophical implications of many of the Christian doctrines in which he professes to believe. And although he claims to have read much in the area of Catholic apologetics, he seems wondrously unaware of the multitude of skeptical tracts that have, for many intellectuals, shattered the foundations of religious belief, whether it be Robert G. Ingersoll's *Some Mistakes of Moses* (1879) or Joseph Wheless's *Is It God's Word?* (1926) or Bertrand Russell's *Religion and Science* (1935), all the way down to Antony Flew's *Atheistic Humanism* (1993), Carl Sagan's *The Demon-Haunted World* (1995), and beyond.

Buckley is aware of the importance of shielding the Bible from critical scrutiny, and specifically of denying that anyone has found any "errors" in it: "If any part of the Bible is subject to 'error,' as distinguished from misinterpretation, then the whole of it must be so regarded" (N 83). I need not rehearse my discussion, in the previous chapter, of Jesus' clearly erroneous prediction of the date of his second coming — one of many errors in the Bible that could be cited. Buckley, however, is protected from any cataclysmic consequences of this and any other biblical error by his contention that only the (Catholic) Church is allowed to interpret scripture! It almost appears as if, for Buckley, the Catholic Church is superior to the Bible. No doubt a legion of clever theologians over the past two millennia have managed to explain away all manner of "errors" as being something other than what they are, so that no one's faith need be jeopardized. Buckley presents a final dodge by remarking: "We cannot . . . confidently assume that we have heard correctly the word of God as given to us in the Bible" (N 85). I have no idea what this is supposed to mean. Is he now saying that there *are* errors in the Bible — even if only errors of "transmission"? Did the numerous and heterogeneous authors of the Bible have wax in their ears as they listened to the Divine Message?

After this, it would seem that any other of Buckley's follies would be an anticlimax. Still, it is amusing to consider some of them. In two chapters he asks his posse of pious friends to assess the evidence regarding Jesus' "miracles" and, in particular, his resurrection from the dead. It would be tiresome to examine the succession of sophistries, evasions, question-beggings, circular reasonings, and wish-fulfillment fantasies in which his various authorities indulge (as when Jeffrey Hart thinks he has validated the miracles on the basis of the resurrection— as if one incredible event provides evidence for another), so let us focus only on the resurrection idea. All the devotees believe in it, of course, but Russell Kirk makes a rather plangent comment:

> The Resurrection lacking, what we call Christianity would be a mere congeries of moral exhortations, at best; and exhortations founded upon no more authority than the occasional utterances of an obscure man whose hints of divinity and half-veiled claims of power to judge the quick and the dead might be regarded as manifestations of delusions of grandeur. . . . Without that Resurrection, which prefigures our own resurrection and life everlasting, one might as well turn again to the gods of the Greeks, or to Epictetus, Marcus Aurelius, and Seneca. (N 124)

Just so! Well then, how do Buckley's authorities "prove"—or even make plausible—the notion of Jesus' resurrection from the dead? Basically it is a matter of the supposed fact that as early as 1 Corinthians (traditionally dated to around 56 C.E.—twenty-three years after the crucifixion) Paul mentions its occurrence. But what our distinguished theologians fail to point out is (as Robert M. Price, one of the most learned of New Testament scholars, has observed) that the mention (1 Cor. 15) is *not* of a bodily resurrection at all, but of a *spiritual* one (in other words, some kind of ghost)—a resurrection exactly contrary to the physical resurrection asserted in the Gospels (written at least two to four decades later).[4] What has clearly happened is that the myth has grown in the telling—a myth quite analogous (as Price suggests) to the "miraculous" disppearance of Apollonius of Tyana (born a few years after Jesus but living far after him, almost to the end of the first century C.E.) as recorded by Philostratus. Indeed, numerous features in the life and death of Apollonius—the "miracles" attending his birth, his scorn of wealth and property, his wonder-working (including healing by touch), and the supposed fact that at the end of his life, "he entered the temple of Athene [at Lindus] and disappeared within it"[5]—sound suspiciously similar to celebrated events in some other person's life. . . . On the basis of this "evidence" it would seem entirely plausible to found a religion based upon the life and death of Apollonius of Tyana (Apollonianity?).

Buckley also places much value on the supposed existence of eyewitness accounts of Jesus' resurrection, as found in the Gospels. Even if these accounts could be trusted, the argument is not a good one. People see what they want to see. That the grief-stricken followers of Jesus—obviously a charismatic and appealing fellow—saw him in their mind's eye days after his crucifixion is a phenomenon entirely accountable on psychological grounds. Given the fact (assuming it is a fact) that, according to the Gospels, Jesus himself predicted his own death and resurrection (see, e.g., Mark 8:31), it is understandable that his followers would, even if subconsciously, make sure that that prophecy was seen to be fulfilled. My own mother saw my father (her husband of more than forty years) come to her in a dream a few days after his death. It is a short step from this to believing that she saw him in the flesh while awake. Indeed, in antiquity, when it was a common belief that dreams came from the gods, the dream itself would have been sufficient proof of some kind of resurrection. This is, after all, how the notions of "soul" and "life after death" probably originated in primitive cultures: visions of dead people in dreams.

Only a few years after the disappearance of Ambrose Bierce in Mexico in late 1913 (he was almost certainly killed in the Mexican Civil War in early 1914), numerous individuals of reasonable credibility attested to seeing Bierce in a variety of locations in North America, South America, and Europe; one of them even maintained that he saw Bierce serving alongside Lord Kitchener during World War I! On the basis of this "evidence" it would seem entirely plausible to found a religion based upon the death and resurrection of Ambrose Bierce (Biercianity?).

And let's not forget Elvis. . . . (Presleyanity? No, we must draw the line somewhere.)

What Buckley and his devout cohorts don't seem to grasp is that "supernatural" or "miraculous" events must cross an exceptionally high threshold of proof in order to be accepted. Because such events defy known laws of entity that have been established by innumerable scientific tests and by the common experience of humankind, and because the possibility of error, bias, chicanery, and (in Tom Paine's memorable phrase) "pious fraud" is so high, we are right in requiring an overwhelming amount of clear and well-documented evidence. That the dead cannot return to life is so well-established a principle, contradicted by no recorded case (except that of Lazarus, which of course suffers from the same evidentiary problems), that the likelihood of Jesus' having risen is very, very small. Question-begging responses like "God could have effected it," or "Jesus was both human and divine," or "The Bible says so" won't do the trick, for the existence of God, the divinity of Jesus, and the inerrancy of the Bible are the very points at issue.

In one chapter Buckley hesitantly and nervously treats the problem of evil. How could a God, postulated as being both omnipotent and benevolent, cause or allow bad things to happen? The focal point of Buckley's reflections is an earthquake in Turkey "a few years ago" (N 163), which resulted in the death of some four hundred men, women, and children. (One assumes that his hand-wringing and nail-biting were radically increased by an earthquake in the same region in 1999, when more than 10,000 souls received an express ticket to heaven.) Buckley acknowledges that few of the victims were morally deserving of this horrible death, hence his quandary. He initially lapses into the age-old evasion conveniently encapsulated by William Cowper's "God works in mysterious ways" ("we don't know all of the purposes of God" [N 163]), then he makes the curious statement, "Earthquakes do not contradict reason. They just happen" (N 163). But Buckley's own theology does not allow him to believe this. Earthquakes *do* contradict reason and *don't* "just happen" if one assumes, as a Christian is obliged to do, that God directly causes all events and yet is also totally benevolent. In this matter there really is no getting around David Hume's compact formulation: "Is he [God] willing to prevent evil, but not able? then is he impotent. Is he able, but not willing? then is he malevolent. Is he both able and willing? whence then is evil?"[6] In other words, either the postulate of God's omnipotence or of his benevolence must be abandoned. But of course Buckley does neither; instead he asserts lamely that we really ought to be very grateful to God "for being alive and a candidate for perpetual life" (N 164)—a thought that will no doubt be comforting to those Turks who gained their eternal rest after only a few years in this vale of tears—and then, after some further inconclusive reflections, ends his disquisition abruptly, as if this excursion into casuistry has given him a headache.

The "God works in mysterious ways" idea may be worth a little examination. The notion is that our "limited" intellects are incapable of comprehending what appear to us as God's inscrutable decrees and actions. This may well be the case, but it becomes equally plausible to hypothesize that a devil or an extraterrestrial entity caused that earthquake in Turkey as that God did: we have no more evidence for the one than for the other. If we are unable to fathom God's purposes, then we have no more reason to postulate the existence of God than of a devil or an extraterrestrial. In other words, we have—as Leslie Stephen cleverly asserted well over a century ago—lapsed into agnosticism:

> Is not the denunciation of reason a commonplace with theologians? What could be easier than to form a catena of the most philosophical defenders of Christianity who have exhausted language in declaring the impotence of the unassisted intellect? . . . Trust your reason, we have been told till we are tired of the phrase, and you will become Atheists or Agnostics. We take you at your word: we become Agnostics. What right have you to turn round and rate us for being a degree more logical than yourselves? . . . You say, as we say, that the natural man can know nothing of the Divine nature. That is Agnosticism. Our fundamental principle is not only granted, but asserted.[7]

In reality, however, what all this futile discussion about God's "purpose" in causing earthquakes and other such things really points to is, curiously enough, a lack of sympathy on the part of Christians. We have already seen this in C. S. Lewis's unconscionably vicious and cruel discussion of animal pain. Christians are so determined to preserve their God's attributes (omnipotence and benevolence combined), in spite of their inherent paradoxes, that they willingly glide over the human cost of suffering. Buckley himself unwittingly acknowledges this when he remarks at the very outset of his discussion that he was accustomed, when faced with news of such disasters, to dismiss them without much thought: "Years of experience had warned me to resist the impulse; even so, I gave in to it. *Why does He permit such suffering* — self-evidently unrelated to human misbehavior?" (N 163). That phrase "resist the impulse" is the key; as Walter Kaufmann remarked in *The Faith of a Heretic* (1961), "Those who believe in God because their experience of life and the facts of nature prove his existence must have led sheltered lives and closed their hearts to the voice of their brothers' blood."[8] On a purely logical level, even a *single case* of unjustified suffering shatters the belief in either God's omnipotence or his benevolence; but there is, and has been, *so much* unjustified suffering that it becomes rather appalling and even evil to say that God must have had some purpose in it all. It is only the inveterate will to believe in a cheerful deity that prevents most people from lapsing into Manicheism, or the belief in two equal and opposed entities, a god of good and a god of evil. A character in Joris-Karl Huysmans' novel of Satanism, *Là-Bas* (1891), observes: "[Manicheism] is one of the oldest and it is *the* simplest of religions, and it best explains the abominable mess everything is in at the present time."[9]

Buckley is, to be sure, not entirely blind to the demerits of the Catholic Church. He laments the fact that the church did not do much, for the better part of two millennia, to end the institution of slavery. But, one might ask, how could it, given that slavery is condoned and, at times, emphatically approved in both the Old and the New Testaments? Buckley then proceeds to the following fatuity:

> Imagine the fate of slavery and of the Inquisition in a moral vacuum in which the magnetic reach of Christianity was unfelt. Mightn't it be said that, but for Christianity, there is reason to wonder whether slavery would even *now* be extinct in the Christian world? And that whatever the historical slowness of its reflexes, the stability of

Catholic-dominated Christianity continues to be central to the moral health and prospects of the human race? (N 67)

A more grotesque instance of special pleading would be difficult to find. In the first place, the conjecture is idle: it is impossible to say what would have happened to Western civilization if Christianity had not come along. In the second place, there never was any "moral vacuum" that Christianity came in the nick of time to fill; indeed, at the time of Christianity's very origins there were several vibrant and thriving moral systems that could well have produced a far more rational and viable social and cultural ethic than Christianity has ever provided. It is eminently plausible to believe that the continuance of the Greco-Roman tradition of secular philosophy (for it was the Stoics and Epicureans who first broached the unity of the human race, regardless of class or station) would have ended ancient slavery long before the early nineteenth century. But all this is useless speculation.

The moral black marks against the Catholic Church are many and various; I choose here only one—the persecution of witches. Let us be clear on the truly appalling ferocity and barbarism of this enterprise—an enterprise that lasted fully *fifteen hundred years,* off and on (mostly on) from as early as 373 C.E. to the end of the eighteenth century, and, moreover, that had *complete and unequivocal scriptural support.* This is not a case of individual "bad eggs" in the Catholic Church running amok (as in the recent cases of pedophilia among priests and subsequent cover-ups by bishops and archbishops); this is something that had the full approval of the church at the highest levels. Witchcraft was, after all, not merely an ordinary crime but a heresy—a defiance of the biblical injunction "Thou shalt not suffer a witch to live" (Exod. 22:18). No one needs to recount the horrors of this long and dismal chapter of human folly, but for the benefit of the historyless I present some fragments of evidence, culled chiefly from the witchcraft scholar Pennethorne Hughes.

Let us first examine the farcical procedures of the witchcraft trials. The standard medieval handbook on the subject, Sprenger and Kramer's *Malleus Maleficarum* (1490), is described by Hughes as follows:

It defied all that we mean by the laws of evidence. It presumed guilt and it advocated torture. It allowed virtually no defence, yet it made suggestions for ways to confuse and betray the prisoner. It advocated as punishment cruel and protracted death. It used devilish ingenuity to trap a devil who can rarely have been present. It provided a weapon to send to a writhing death thousands of misguided, superstitious, and ignorant souls, of whom only a few were perhaps actuated consciously by the motives and beliefs it sought to destroy.[10]

Our modern totalitarians seem not to have held a candle to the sober churchmen of the fifteenth and sixteenth centuries.

Would you like some torture? The witchcraft persecutors were particularly good at that: "The whip, the fires, the rack, the thumbscrew, a horrible studded chair slowly heated from below, or whatever inhuman ingenuity could contrive."[11] And let's not forget the water torture (although this was favored not by the Catholics but by the Scots Presbyterians), based upon the idea that "water, being a sacred substance, would reject suspects if they were guilty, and they would only sink if innocent":

It appears to have involved the suspect being hustled to the waterside, naked or in a shirt, and thrown in with the hands and feet bound crosswise, the left foot to the right hand and vice versa. A rope round the waist was supposed to secure rescue if she sank, but it very often did not do so. If the witch floated—and many people would do so, in spite of the ministrations of sympathetic bystanders with poles to push them in—she was guilty. If she did not float, the experiment could be, and often was, repeated. Ultimately the original symbolism was forgotten, and ducking merely became a cruel form of punishment, rather than a test.[12]

At a conservative estimate, ten million witches were killed throughout Europe. To be sure, a tiny proportion of these might actually have been "witches" in the sense that they practiced herbal magic or actually participated in Black Masses, but were even these people deserving of death for these derelictions? In any event, I trust that most of us today are convinced that these wretches were not endowed with supernatural powers. (Buckley, I fear, is in an awkward position on this point: given that he implicitly accepts the principle of papal infallibility, he is obliged to believe—following countless papal bulls, including Pope Innocent VIII's bull of 1484—that witches with supernatural powers actually exist and must be extirpated.) The persecution of witches must surely rank as one of the great crimes against humanity, no better or worse than the pogroms of Hitler, Stalin, or Pol Pot. Hughes himself comes to a similar conclusion: "The Papacy fought against [witchcraft] . . . with an abandon comparable to the last anti-Jewish furies of the retracting Reich in 1945."[13]

It is not a good defense of the witchcraft persecutors that they lived in an age when torture and other barbarities were tolerated (the shallow "historical relativism" argument—an argument that could be used to excuse the atrocities of almost any historical figure, including Hitler). In point of fact, torture was *not* habitually used in ordinary criminal cases in the Middle Ages and Renaissance, but witchcraft was thought to be such a dangerous heresy that any and all means were acceptable. It is an even worse defense that the persecutors were, by and large, quite sincere in their beliefs rather than sadists or adventurers: the world has much more to fear from the earnest zealot than from the mere opportunist. In reality, the true failing of the persecutors is exactly Buckley's own failing: *the inability to believe that they were wrong.* But they *were* wrong: wrong in maintaining that witches were supernatural creatures, and wrong in believing the Bible to be inerrant, at least on this particular point.

Let us also be very clear that the decline of witch-belief was entirely—I cannot emphasize this strongly enough—*entirely* the product of religious skepticism, first with the members of the Royal Society in England in the seventeenth century, then with those horrible deist, agnostic, and atheist philosophers of Enlightenment France—including such British and American analogues as David Hume, Edward Gibbon, Thomas Jefferson, and Thomas Paine. The Catholic Church did not reform itself on this matter; it was forced by outside pressure to reform. To be sure, the Protestant churches were no better in this regard; it is simply that they had less time—only two or three centuries—to engage in the torching of witches. After all, John Wesley, the founder of Methodism, stated quite correctly that disbelief in witches meant a disbelief in the Bible. Far from Christianity civilizing the West, it was manifestly the West that (partially and belatedly) civilized Christianity.

One need not go on. Torture and execution of heretics and infidels; opposition to every sort of intellectual advance, from cosmogony (don't forget Galileo) to biology (dare we mention Darwin?) to geology (but the world, after all, is only 6,000 years old!) to medicine (the church "attributed epidemics to sin or to the Jews; . . . [and] most individual illness to the intervention of devils"[14]); the pestiferousness of missionaries meddling with other people's religions; the "divine right of kings"; fear and hatred of sex, resulting in all kinds of irrational taboos and reticences; systematic misogyny and the degradation of women; anti-Semitism—the list of the Christian (and specifically the Catholic) Church's moral, intellectual, social, and political derelictions could be infinitely multiplied. And it bears repeating that every one of these things has full and unequivocal scriptural authority.

And this is the church that Buckley wishes us to see as a moral exemplar!

I want to return to Buckley's phrase "moral vacuum." The idea, evidently, is that if Christianity did not occupy its position of political and social dominance in the West beginning around 300, Western civilization would have developed without any morals at all. One only has to express the notion to perceive its absurdity. The philosophy of Stoicism, thriving as late as the age of the Antonines, could easily have filled the bill as a workable moral system. The greatest intellectual contribution of classical philosophy was the development of a secular ethic—the first in Western history—and there can be no doubt that we would have seen far less of the intellectual stagnation of the Dark Ages had Christianity not triumphed. Buckley's idea is, in any case, historically inept: if Christianity had not supplied the ethics of late antiquity and the medieval period, then *some* system would have filled the void: a society without morals is an impossibility, given the plain fact that morals are themselves a product of society.

And yet, it becomes eminently clear that Buckley cannot conceive of the possibility—or, at any rate, the viability—of a secular ethic. In a later chapter he looks at the twentieth century and whines, "What became of sin?" (N 231); and elsewhere (in speaking of Catholics' widespread disregard of the Vatican's ban on birth control): "A sense of the sinfulness of an act is hugely important to the moral order. In its absence, there is a terrible void" (N 200). It does not occur to Buckley that a particular act may no longer be regarded as a sin, not because of the moral turpitude of society but because the act in question has come to be perceived as merely an irrational taboo not based upon any social or moral reality but instead only upon a hoary and irrelevant dogma.

I will probe the relation of religion to ethics and politics elsewhere; right now I need only state that even the most cursory examination of history shows that religion has been of no help whatever in restraining immoral (i.e., antisocial) behavior. There was just as much adultery, chicanery, torture, hypocrisy, duplicity, uncharitableness, and sundry other forms of barbarism in pious times as in our secular age. More, the church engendered specific moral evils of its own, as I have indicated above, and it pursued these evils so vigorously for centuries that it finally produced an overwhelming sense of outrage in both religious and secular minds, so that its moral authority was severely compromised. And when the scientific advances of the nineteenth and twentieth centuries dismantled intellectual support for the existence of God, it became preposterous to assert that any action was a "sin" against an entity who probably did not exist. Buckley remarks that when people, in subverting the concept of sin, are "indirectly subverting transcendant authority" (N 231), he begs the question by assuming the existence of a transcendant authority.

A related issue is the relation of religious belief upon our political sensibilities. Buckley appears to find secular assertions of the legal and political equality of all human beings inadequate; he states that the only type of equality between peoples that he can envision is "equal[ity] in the eyes of God" (N 234)—as if the plain fact of our common humanity isn't enough! There is, however, a further problem with Buckley's view: it has no scriptural support, although Buckley seems to think it does. Nowhere in the Bible is it stated that *all* human beings are the "children of God"; instead, what we find is this (to choose one example among many): "For ye are all the children of God by faith in Christ Jesus" (Gal. 3:26).[15] This statement (by Paul) is clearly exclusionary: not only does it leave out atheists and agnostics (a numerically insignificant and contemptible group, of course) but also everyone who is not a Christian; in other words, a majority of human beings in the world. Jesus himself is relentless in practicing this kind of exclusion: "Whosoever shall deny me before men, him will I also deny before my Father which is in heaven" (Matt. 10:33). It was, in fact, several pagan philosophers in antiquity who asserted a genuine common humanity that transcended boundaries of country, class, and belief; compare the Stoic Seneca: "We are all akin by Nature, who has formed us of the same elements and placed us here together for the same end" (*Epistulae* 95.52).

Buckley is, however, quite right in declaring that democratic liberalism, interpreted in its broadest sense, may not be an entirely satisfactory substitute for the religious certainty we have lost, and that certain totalitarian regimes are actually more efficient at enforcing both political and moral uniformity. Citing Richard Weaver, Buckley remarks that "Marxism and Communism are redemptive creeds, while liberalism has no eschatology, no ultimate sense of consummation" (N 234). It should, as a result, be obvious (although Buckley shows no awareness of it) that the appeal of Marxism and communism (not to mention Nazism) to certain minds *is exactly identical* to the appeal offered by religion: moral certainty decreed from above. All these creeds, nominally atheistic, in fact assert their own doctrines with the fervency of an evangelical religion, and in this sense become indistinguishable from a religion. Liberalism, which urges individual citizens to make up their own minds about how to lead their lives, is inevitably messier; it is also unfeasible for those who are intellectually, morally, and socially incapable of having any coherent ideas on how to lead their lives. Buckley, violently hostile to political totalitarianism, nevertheless seems quite happy to submit his own moral vision to the doctrinal totalitarianism of Roman Catholicism.

To those who, having seen me give Buckley the business, think I am engaging in "Catholic-bashing," I have only two things to say:

1) I do not consider Roman Catholicism any more preposterous and absurd than any other religion devised by human folly or madness. No doubt its poetic and mystical aspects can act as a powerful stimulant—somewhat similar, perhaps, to the belladonna that the medieval witches rubbed over themselves to induce hallucinations prior to participating in the Black Mass—although, for my taste, the aesthetic beauty of the Greco-Roman religion is much more appealing, to say nothing of the fact that it offers fewer logical difficulties to the trained intellect.

2) Buckley leaves himself open to this kind of treatment because of the manifest deficiencies found abundantly in his two books on religion. He remarks blithely in *Nearer, My God* that "probably no believing Christian is likely to lose his faith after reading" (N xvii) his book, but I am not so sanguine. Surely any intelligent person who witnesses Buckley swallowing so many absurdities, leaving so many paradoxes unresolved, and uttering so many non sequiturs and logical fallacies would be justified in thinking that only an idiot could accept such a farrago of nonsense.

In truth, Buckley is more to be pitied than scorned. It is transparently evident that he has been brainwashed—and, at a somewhat later stage, brainwashed himself—into Catholicism, to the point that he is incapable of looking at the world except as a Catholic. A large segment of his mind has thereby been crippled, and it is beyond his intellectual powers to consider any sane alternative to his fantastic religion. His religious views are not based upon reason but upon emotion, nostalgia, and wishful thinking. Catholicism is, for him as for so many others, a security blanket. Buckley is now a doddering old man and has largely put himself out to pasture; it would therefore seem as unkind to tear his religion away from him as it would be to take a succulent lollipop from a helpless infant. But this is not likely to happen: he will probably not change his views one iota no matter how much contrary evidence is put forth. But he nonetheless stands as a shining example of how religious indoctrination can lead even an intelligent person into absurdity.

NOTES

References to William F. Buckley's works occur in the text as follows: G = *God and Man at Yale* (Chicago: Regnery, 1951); M = *McCarthy and His Enemies: The Record and Its Meaning* (with L. Brent Bozell) (1954; reprint Washington, D.C.: Regnery, 1995); N = *Nearer, My God: An Autobiography of Faith* (New York: Doubleday, 1997).

1. Bertrand Russell, "Is There a God?" (1952), in *The Collected Papers of Bertrand Russell*, ed. John G. Slater and Peter Köllner (London: Routledge, 1997), vol. 11, pp. 545–46.

2. McGeorge Bundy, "The Attack on Yale," *Atlantic Monthly* 188, no. 5 (November 1951): 50, 52.

3. H. L. Mencken, "The Monthly Feuilleton," *Smart Set* 69, no. 4 (December 1922): 140.

4. Robert M. Price, *Beyond Born Again: Toward Evangelical Maturity* (Upper Montclair, N.J.: Apocryphal Books, 1993), pp. 76–78.

5. Philostratus, *Life of Apollonius of Tyana*, 8.30.

6. David Hume, *Dialogues Concerning Natural Religion* (1779), ed. Henry D. Aiken (New York: Hafner, 1948), p. 66.

7. Leslie Stephen, "An Agnostic's Apology" (1876), in *An Agnostic's Apology and Other Essays* (New York: G. P. Putnam's Sons; London: Smith, Elder & Co., 1903), pp. 7–8.

8. Walter Kaufmann, *The Faith of a Heretic* (Garden City, N.Y.: Doubleday, 1961), p. 180.

9. Joris-Karl Huysmans, *Là-Bas*, trans. Keene Wallace (Paris: privately printed, 1928), p. 59.

10. Pennethorne Hughes, *Witchcraft* (1952; reprint, Harmondsworth, England: Penguin, 1967), p. 180.

11. Ibid., p. 181.

12. Ibid., p. 190.

13. Ibid., p. 173.

14. Ibid., p. 203.

15. Cf. Edward Westermarck's comment that Jesus taught neither "the belief in a common divine fatherhood nor the idea of a common human brotherhood." *Christianity and Morals* (New York: Macmillan, 1939), p. 76.

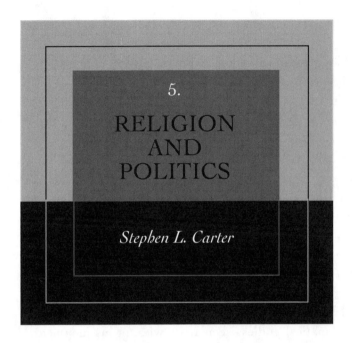

5.

RELIGION
AND
POLITICS

Stephen L. Carter

L aw professor Stephen L. Carter (b. 1954) began his career with a meditation on growing up as an African American, *Reflections of an Affirmative Action Baby* (1991). This book attracted much attention, but his next work, *The Culture of Disbelief: How American Law and Politics Trivialize Religious Devotion* (1993), was even more provocative. Here Carter maintained that the intellectual elite—including the media and most branches of the government, not excepting the Supreme Court—compelled religiously devout individuals to shed their piety when entering into public discourse, since the elite only took cognizance of arguments made in consonance with secular ideals. Carter then wrote two books on the conduct of political discourse—*Integrity* (1996) and *Civility* (1998)—the basic thrust of which is that there should be greater politeness in the discussion of social, political, and moral issues in the public arena. Carter then returned to the subject dealt with in *The Culture of Disbelief* in *The Dissent of the Governed: A Meditation on Law, Religion, and Loyalty* (1998), a revision of the William E. Massey Sr. Lectures in the History of Civilization, delivered at Harvard in 1995. Carter seems intent on writing the same book over and over again, as his most recent effort, *God's Name in Vain* (2000) —yet another reprise of *The Culture of Disbelief*—attests. Nevertheless, he has come to be regarded as an intellectual worth taking seriously on issues of politics, morality, and religion. He has even achieved that ultimate token of intellectual respectability—the op-ed page of the *New York Times*.

Carter proclaims himself as occupying a reasonable middle ground between two extremes—the fanatical religious right and the equally fanatical godless secularists who, in his judgment, dominate politics and the media. But we will find that Carter's inclinations are considerably closer to the first group than the second. He is himself a safe, reasonable, nonfanatical Episcopalian, and in *The Culture of Disbelief* he supplies an affecting portrait of his own faith:

> Prayer is a crucial part of our family life. We pray before important events: meals, trips, sleep. We give thanks for our good fortune, pray for those less fortunate, beg forgiveness for our sins, and ask forgiveness for the sins of others. For us, prayer is an affirmation of our connectedness to God. We have no way of knowing whether God approves of us, and that is not what our prayers are for—we are only mortal, after all, and we have no right to presume. Yet the activity of prayer is our tradition as well as our comfort, and we cannot, as a family, imagine life without it. (C 185)

Carter's arguments on religion are sufficiently displayed in *The Culture of Disbelief*, so that there is little need to examine his other works. And yet, it must be stated at the outset that this treatise is one long excursion into question-begging. He whines that we should abandon the "rhetoric that implies that there is something wrong with religious devotion" (C 6), but never demonstrates that there is anything right about it. He pleads for "restoring religion to the place of honor that it deserves in the pantheon of American cultural institutions" (C 68), without presenting any argument that it deserves any place of honor. He questions whether, in our society, "citizens to whom [religious] rhetoric is precious are accorded the respect that they deserve" (C 45), but fails to prove that it is worthy of respect. Finally, he proclaims as one of the major agendas of his book that "we should stop the steady drumbeat, especially in our popular culture, for the proposition that the religiously devout are less rational than more 'normal' folks" (C 16), assuming as a given that such people are *not* less rational than normal folks when all the evidence points to the contrary.

In other words, Carter snivels indignantly that believers in God are not accorded much respect in our society, especially in the public sphere, but neglects to establish that a belief in God is intellectually justified. Evidently he feels that the mere fact that many millions of people profess such a belief is sufficient to grant it both "respect" and "honor" in the public arena. This is, as I have repeatedly stated, simply a version of the democratic fallacy—the fallacy that truth can be determined by a vote of the majority. Carter actually comes quite close to enunciating this fallacy flawlessly, but without any realization that he is doing so: "Most Americans believe [that] there is a God external to the human mind, and if that God has tried to communicate with us, whether through revelation or some other path, then the human task is surely to discover the contents of that communication" (C 73). Is it sufficient to note the beliefs of "most Americans" as proof that their beliefs are true? Consider a parallel case. Throughout most of human history the majority of people in the world believed that the earth was flat; does that mean that such a view—especially if it continues to be maintained after it has been shown to be false—is to be accorded "respect" and "honor" even if large numbers of people affirm it?

Not once does Carter ever entertain the notion that religious views are not much respected by the intelligentsia because the latter have strongly come to doubt their truth. To be sure, few intellectuals—especially those who write for magazines and newspapers of wide circulation and who therefore cannot afford to alienate any large segment of the population—are quite so tactless as to utter these doubts bluntly, but there can scarcely be any denying that this is the real reason why religiously oriented views on politics and society have come under such suspicion. That any of the world's numerous sacred texts are divinely inspired, or that any sect or individual can legitimately ascertain the "will" of a God who probably does not exist, are now regarded by any intelligent person as so grotesquely unlikely that anyone espousing these views is automatically—and rightly—deemed an escapee from Dayton, Tennessee.

This notion of the will of God produces some incidental amusement at Carter's expense. Although, as he magnanimously declares, we cannot always be sure that we have ascertained the will of God on any moral, social, or political question, he nonetheless seems fairly certain that either he himself or others can in theory arrive at fair certainty in this regard, and have done so in the past. He discusses the furor in the Episcopal Church over the ordination of women priests and bishops and asserts that the issue is not one of politics at all: "The question, for the believing Christian, is not what motivates some self-righteous advocates on either side of the question but what God would want us to do" (C 75). He quickly concludes—without supplying any argument, either from scripture or from natural theology—"I think the ordination of women is closer to God's word" (C 79). Unregenerate Catholics, take note! Still more remarkable is his discussion of the 1992 Republican National Convention. Although mildly deprecating the divisive "God-talk" of such right-wingers as Pat Robertson (especially in regard to their condemnation of homosexuals—a stance that, as Carter fails to point out, has clear scriptural support), he nonetheless believes it possible that "one party might in fact stand for values that are closer than the other's to the will of God" (C 50). So maybe God is a Republican after all! Regrettably, Carter does not offer any guidance as to how that will is to be clearly determined.

And yet, Carter seems dimly aware that religious dogma no longer has the validity it once had. He quotes a character from a Tom Stoppard play as stating that there came "a calendar date—*a moment*—when the onus of proof passed from the atheist to the believer, when, quite suddenly, the noes had it"; he adds without comment the remark of the "philosopher" Jeffrey Stout (a perfect encapsulation of the democratic fallacy): "If so, it was not a matter of majority rule" (C 7). It is interesting to see Carter elsewhere assert, as part of his plea for civility in dialogue: "I do not mean that nobody speaks—*everybody* speaks—but rather that nobody listens" (D x). Certainly, Carter himself has not "listened" to atheist or even agnostic arguments against the existence of God; indeed, one begins to suspect that he is scarcely even aware of their existence.

Only much later does Carter even approach the subject of the truth or falsity of his (or any other) religion, but in doing so he falls into paradox and contradiction. In the course of a tedious and long-winded discussion of creationists, he declares flatly that they are "wrong," but censures us nasty liberals for declaring that they are also "irrational or fanatical" (C 176). It is not entirely clear to me why Carter—who accepts the Bible overall as some kind of authoritative text—does not believe literally in the Genesis story; he himself never provides any reason why he does not. If it is because he thinks that account is somehow meant symbolically, he is on a very dangerous slippery slope: if that is the case, why is the very notion of God not meant symbolically? But that is neither here nor there. Carter is quite correct in maintaining that creationists actually claim that their belief is a true belief and that evolution is a "pack of lies" (C 176) which they are outraged that their children are being taught. But if Carter believes creationism to be wrong, how can he avoid the corollary that the first eleven chapters of the sacred text he himself professes to believe are also, in some sense, wrong? Carter, however, can never bring himself to say this. Instead, he beats around the bush by saying that evolution and creationism are really only epistemologically different—that they start with different criteria for what passes for truth. This allows Carter to proclaim: "To the extent that creationism is the result of the application of the hermeneutic of inerrancy to the opening chapters of Genesis, it is certainly rational" (C 174); and still more boldly, "Given its starting point and its methodology, creationism is as rational an explanation as any other" (C 175). Oh, yeah? I'm sure I could found an entirely "rational" (i.e., logically consistent) system of metaphysics, and even of ethics and politics, based upon the initial premise that the earth is flat, but would this entire procedure be any less irrational? Carter also observes soberly: "There is no way to disprove, for example, the old creationist claim that physical evidence that appears to run against the biblical account is only a trap set by the devil for the unwary" (C 175). The old fossil trick! Carter is correct, of course, but because he fails to bring in the principles of *probability* and *verifiability* (the real bases of scientific truth), he is blissfully unaware of the absurdity of the claim. One could respond that it is equally impossible to ascertain whether a god or a devil created the universe. Given the course of human history, one becomes strongly inclined to favor the latter.

Carter actually admits that the differences between religious truth and scientific truth are differences of fact and not belief; in regard to the issue of whether there is life after death, he notes: "The question is whether something exists or not; it is a question designed to discover a fact. Calling a fact a belief cannot quite get around that central point. After all, whatever else might be said about life after death, one thing seems sure: either there is one or there is not" (C 222). But Carter then returns to his perceived epistemological difficulty, maintaining that these religious "questions generate no hypotheses testable against observation of the natural world. The hypotheses the questions generate are testable only against God's word" (C 222). But this obviously begs the question, for the actual existence of "God's word" (i.e., the divine inspiration of the Bible or any other sacred text) is the very point at issue. In any case, if the creationist claim is to be judged by "God's word," then it is difficult to see how Carter can declare it to be wrong, since it obviously *accords* with God's word as purportedly revealed in Genesis.

The lengths to which Carter will go to accord "respect" to even the most foolish religious beliefs becomes evident in his discussion of the beliefs of Jehovah's Witnesses that a blood transfusion is tantamount to drinking blood, which will presumably jeopardize their chances of salvation. I personally am perfectly happy to see the gradual departure of Jehovah's Witnesses from this vale of tears as a result of their refusal to receive transfusions, but the state has evidently decided that it has an interest in preserving the lives of its citizens, even if they are buffoons. Carter pleads against assuming that "anyone who believes that God can heal diseases is stupid or fanatical" (C 21), but how else can one possibly view such a preposterous belief? It is interesting to note that Carter, in this context (or, for that matter, anywhere else in his book), fails to mention Christian Science—specifically, the numerous instances where Christian Scientists have been convicted for causing the deaths of their children by refusing them medical attention. Even Carter, one supposes, would find it difficult to defend such appalling instances of religious fanaticism.

Carter's main argument is that in our liberal secular society religious persons must shed their beliefs—or, at any rate, the religious motivations of their beliefs—in order to get a hearing on political or social issues. In this he reveals a fundamental, indeed crippling, misconstrual of the very nature of the American political experiment. The United States was the first secular government in the world—the first to refuse to set up an established church and the first to create a wall of separation of some kind (the exact parameters of which have always been in debate and in flux) between church and state. The one and only unifying force in this country is each citizen's presumed allegiance to the U.S. Constitution. Certain political commentators are fond of stressing the rhetorical citation of "the Laws of Nature and of Nature's God" in the first sentence of the Declaration of Independence (a "Creator" gets mentioned in the second sentence), which proves to their minds that religion of some kind is at the heart of American politics. But our nation's government is not founded upon the Declaration of Independence, but rather the Constitution—and there is no God or Creator mentioned there. This obvious fact, taken in conjunction with the Establishment Clause and the plain reality of religious diversity throughout the United States, must mean that secular arguments for political and social policy are the *only* ones that can attain *universal* validity. This is not to say that everyone will agree on any given secular policy decision but that the secular *basis* of that decision is the only one to which *all* American citizens can, in theory, agree. If *any* religious basis is asserted, then the adherents of all other religions—not to mention the not insignificant number of atheists, agnostics, and secularists—will question the *basis* of that decision even if they may happen to agree with the decision itself. If, for example, someone asserted that murder is wrong because it is contrary to the will of God, a variety of awkward questions would ensue even among those (the majority of us, one hopes) who agree about the wrongness of murder: "How do you know there is a God? How do you know he has a will? How have you ascertained that will?" And so on. But if one asserted that murder is wrong because it would be impossible to conduct a civilized society if murder were permitted, then that is surely something that everyone can agree upon. If someone then wishes to assert that murder is *also* contrary to the will of God, he is free to do so, although it will not add anything to the discussion.

More than a century ago, Robert G. Ingersoll made this very point in arguing against the "recognition" of God in the Constitution:

> In 1776 our fathers endeavored to retire the gods from politics. They declared that "all governments derive their just powers from the consent of the governed." This was a contradiction of the then political ideas of the world; it was, as many believed, an act of pure blasphemy—a renunciation of the Deity. It was in fact a declaration of the independence of the earth. It was a notice to all churches and priests that thereafter mankind would govern and protect themselves. Politically it tore down every altar and denied the authority of every "sacred book," and appealed from the Providence of God to the Providence of Man. . . .
>
> The Government of the United States is secular. It derives its power from the consent of man. It is a Government with which God has nothing whatever to do—and all forms and customs, inconsistent with the fundamental fact that the people are the source of authority, should be abandoned. . . .
>
> A nation can neither be Christian nor Infidel—a nation is incapable of having opinions upon these subjects. . . . Of course it is admitted that the majority of citizens composing a nation may believe or disbelieve, and they may call the nation what they please.

A nation is a corporation. To repeat a familiar saying, "it has no soul." There can be no such thing as a Christian corporation. Several Christians may form a corporation, but it can hardly be said that the corporation thus formed was included in the atonement. For instance: Seven Christians form a corporation—that is to say, there are seven natural persons and one artificial—can it be said that there are eight souls to be saved?[1]

Carter makes still further blunders on this issue when he asserts (in a discussion of religious and secular morality):

For vast numbers of Americans, another agency of settlement for moral dilemmas—another authority—*is* available: divine command. Liberal theory might scoff at the idea that God's will is relevant to moral decisions in the liberal state, but the citizen whose public self is guided by religious faith might reasonably ask why the will of any of the brilliant philosophers of the liberal tradition, or, for that matter, the will of the Supreme Court of the United States is more relevant to moral decisions than the will of God. So far, liberal theory has not presented an adequate answer. (C 226)

In the first place, the Supreme Court is *not* the arbiter of "moral decisions." It is only the arbiter of legal decisions, and if these decisions have moral implications, that is an entirely secondary and coincidental matter; in any case, such implications are subject to widely differing interpretations by different individuals. In the second place, the Supreme Court has this power in making decisions regarding constitutional law because the U.S. Constitution says so, and we, as citizens of the United States, have granted the Supreme Court that power because we at least implicitly accept the Constitution (and no other document or set of beliefs) as the bedrock legal and political foundation for this country. It is the *only* foundation that *all* citizens can accept; "God's will" will not do.

What is amusing in all this is that Carter all but admits that religion is irrational, but goes on to maintain that this very irrationality should nevertheless not be discounted in matters of public policy.

"Today's political philosophers see public dialogue as essentially secular, bounded by requirements of rationality and reason," says Carter. "It is not easy to fit religion into that universe" (C 42). Why? Because "religion is really an alien way of knowing the world—alien, at least, in a political and legal culture in which reason supposedly rules" (C 43). But exactly how does one incorporate irrationality into a discussion of political, social, and moral issues? How to adjudicate between the claims of competing irrationalities? Is there not, indeed, already enough irrationality in politics and society as it is?

Carter may, indeed, be correct in believing that many secularists today look with insouciance when religion is used to bolster causes they support but become suspicious and alarmed when religion becomes the bulwark of causes (mostly right-wing) they dislike. The formulation is, I believe, a bit too simple—the right-wing causes not infrequently aim at coercion of all citizens into practices dictated by religious dogma, whereas the left-wing causes are chiefly in the interests of liberation and political equality—but let that pass for a moment. Carter is particularly exercised by the fact that no one complained when Martin Luther King Jr. drew upon his Christian heritage to advance the cause of civil rights. But what Carter fails to realize is that if King did indeed think that the Bible advocated the racial equality that he (and, presumably, most of the rest of us) wanted, he was clearly in error. I have already noted, in regard to William F. Buckley's notion that "equality before God" is the only kind of equality between persons that he can envisage, that no such unequivocal "equality" can be found in the Bible. Let me quote in full the scriptural passage I cited there, when Paul states: "For ye are all the children of God by faith in Christ Jesus. For as many of you as have been baptized into Christ have put on Christ. There is neither Jew nor Greek, there is neither bond nor free, there is neither male nor female: for ye are all one in Christ Jesus" (Gal. 3:26–28). Here again, certain types of exclusion— exclusion by race or ethnic origin, social status, and gender—are replaced by another type: faith in Christian dogma, specifically the rite of baptism. Anyone who is not baptized cannot possibly be included in the formulation "children of God."

What is more, Carter is no doubt aware that slave owners both before and after the Civil War made repeated attempts to justify slavery by appeals to the Bible, but he is probably unwilling to acknowledge the plain fact that these slave owners had far better scriptural authority, both in the Old and the New Testaments, for their views than the abolitionists did. Charles Bradlaugh made this point many years ago:

> I am unaware of any religion in the world which in the past forbade slavery. The professors of Christianity for ages supported it; the Old Testament repeatedly sanctioned it by special laws; the New Testament has no repealing declaration. Though we are at the close of the nineteenth century of the Christian era, it is only during the past three-quarters of a century that the battle for freedom has been gradually won. It is scarcely a quarter of a century since the famous emancipation amendment was carried to the United States Constitution; and it is impossible for any well-informed Christian to deny that the abolition movement in North America was most steadily and bitterly opposed by the religious bodies in the various States. Henry Wilson, in his *Rise and Fall of the Slave-Power in America;* Samuel J. May, in his *Recollections of the Anti-Slavery Conflict,* and J. Greenleaf Whittier, in his poems, alike are witnesses that the Bible and pulpit, the church and its great influence, were used against abolition and in favor of the slaveowner. I know that Christians in the present day often declare that Christianity had a large share in bringing about the abolition of slavery, and this because men professing Christianity were Abolitionists. I plead that those so-called Christian Abolitionists were men and women whose humanity— recognizing freedom for all—was, in this, in direct conflict with Christianity. It is not yet fifty years since the European Christian Powers jointly agreed to abolish the slave trade. What of the effect of Christianity on these Powers in the centuries which had preceded? The heretic Condorcet pleaded powerfully for freedom, whilst Christian France was still slave-holding. For many centuries Christian Spain and Christian Portugal held slaves. Porto Rico freedom is not of long date, and Cuban emancipation is even yet newer. It was a Christian king, Charles V., and a Christian friar, who

founded in Spanish America the slave-trade between the Old World and the New. For some 1,800 years almost all Christians kept slaves, bought slaves, sold slaves, bred slaves, stole slaves.[2]

Carter asserts that religions can serve as some kind of bulwark against state tyranny. This idea would provoke mirth in anyone who has any awareness of the long tradition of religions siding with government for domination of the populace. A. J. Ayer has noted, with delicate understatement, "The tendency of religious hierarchies to side with the oppressors rather than the oppressed."[3] But Carter goes further and declares that "the religions, to be truly free, must be able to engage in practices that the larger society condemns" (C 24). I am not certain that Carter realizes the implications of this astounding utterance. Exactly how far is one to engage in such practices? What if someone (I do not necessarily mean a Southerner) were to declare that he will reinstitute slavery on his property? What could Carter possibly say to such a person? All that the latter would have to do is to appeal to Ephesians 6:5 ("Servants, be obedient to them that are your masters according to the flesh, with fear and trembling, in singleness of your heart, as unto Christ"), among many other texts, and declare that slavery is scripturally sanctioned. Carter might, I suppose, say that slavery is now outlawed by the Thirteenth Amendment to the U.S. Constitution, but this line of argument would not be open to him because he has already declared (in a paraphrase of Martin Luther King) that the "authority of God [is] *superior to* the authority of the state" (C 38), so that merely human laws could not possibly abrogate God's law condoning slavery.

Carter is remarkably—and, it seems to me, unconscionably—callous and cavalier in regard to the "horrors" committed in the name of religion. In an early passage he notes parenthetically: "No comments, please, about how people's willingness to kill and die for their religious traditions shows why those traditions must be kept out of the public sphere—after all, people are also willing to kill and die for freedom and equality" (C 56). The parallel is wholly specious. The motivations for religious killing—and it has gone on for thousands of years with little surcease except in the last two centuries—are manifestly connected with the perceived need to maintain a ruthless religious orthodoxy; in other words, the killing is assocated with oppression, coercion, and fascistic control of the populace—not very analogous to the "freedom and equality" for which others have killed and died. It is as if Carter were saying: "People have killed for freedom and people have killed for tyranny; therefore, freedom and tyranny are morally equivalent."

Elsewhere Carter bravely claims to have read accounts of religious "horrors"—chiefly James A. Haight's *Holy Horrors: An Illustrated History of Religious Murders and Madness* (1990)—but dismisses the subject by blandly maintaining that "it is rarely accurate to attribute the parade of horrors to religion as such. Generally, it is the alliance of religion and government that makes these evils possible" (C 85). But is this not a perfect counterargument to Carter's own claim that religion should be more closely associated with government? What Carter also fails to grasp is that all religions that claim *exclusive* knowledge of the truth—and that includes the "big three" of the West: Christianity, Judaism, and Islam—are *inherently totalitarian.* If you believe you are right and everyone else is wrong (as all Christians, Jews, and Muslims are commanded by their respective scriptures to believe), then you have no option but to force your beliefs upon others. Indeed, such coercion will, on this hypothesis, be for *their* benefit: one does not, after all, wish more people to go to hell than is absolutely necessary. Punishment of heretics is sanctioned by nearly every sacred text in existence. It is, in fact, precisely because the believers of the Middle Ages and Renaissance were adhering rigidly and faithfully to their scriptures that they produced the "horrors" we now decry. The only reason these horrors have ceased is because the decline of religious belief caused more and more people to question whether the scriptures *were* in truth the words of a god, and therefore whether the appalling acts of cruelty and viciousness committed for centuries on end could be theologically or morally justified. The real reason most Christians, Jews, and Muslims do not kill heretics is not because of some fancied movement toward "toleration" (an issue I shall discuss elsewhere), but because they lack the courage of their convictions. Christians and Jews no longer really believe it when the Psalmist pleads: "Thou therefore, O Lord God of hosts, the God of Israel, awake to visit all the heathen: be not merciful to any wicked transgressors" (Ps. 59:5), or when Paul commands Christians to have nothing to do with unbelievers (2 Cor. 6:14)—a command echoed in the Koran (5:56), which instructs Muslims not to have Jews or Christians as friends.

Then there is Carter's treatment of the Ayatollah Khomeini's fatwa against Salman Rushdie for his supposed blasphemy against Islam in *The Satanic Verses*. Although mildly deprecating it, Carter cannot bring himself to condemn even this most flagrant case of religious bigotry, claiming that "one should properly fight against official censorship and intimidation, not against religion" (C 10). Can Carter seriously maintain that Rushdie's "crime" was not religious in nature, or at least perceived as such by the Ayatollah? Does he think that if Rushdie had written satirically about, say, Omar Khayyam, the Ayatollah would have been quite as hostile? The punishing of "infidels" is repeatedly, almost monotonously, endorsed in the Koran ("When ye encounter the infidels, strike off their heads till ye have made a great slaughter among them, and of the rest make fast the fetters" [47:4]), so to anyone who believes in the Koran, Rushdie is clearly guilty of a heinous offense. Of course, the matter of whether Rushdie is in fact an "infidel" (a matter not much affected by Rushdie's shabby and hypocritical "conversion" to Islam shortly after the fatwa was issued) and did in fact "insult" Islam are the very points at issue; but if the Ayatollah—the pope of Islam—cannot decide these points, who can? (Lest we in the West pride ourselves that we are above this kind of savagery, it should be noted that trials for blasphemy against the Christian religion were a regular occurrence far into the nineteenth century.)[4]

Incredibly, Carter actually makes the argument that religions are *not* exclusive in their claims to truth:

> A claim of exclusivity is not a moral evil. If one genuinely believes
> that he or she has found the only route to salvation through the one

true faith, one obviously has no choice but to proclaim that other religions are wrong. However, the one doing the proclaiming should make clear what is going on: it is the nature of *that individual's faith,* not the nature of *religion itself,* that dictates the exclusivity. (C 92)

Carter must have a very poor familiarity with sacred texts, including his own. How is it possible to deny that the scriptures of Judaism, Christianity, and Islam each make clear claims to exclusive truth? All we need do is to point to Isaiah 43:11 ("I, even I, am the Lord; and beside me there is no saviour") for the Judaic claim (or, if we wish, we could even appeal to one of the Ten Commandments: "Thou shalt have no other gods before me" [Exod. 20:2]); Mark 16:16 ("He that believeth and is baptized shall be saved; but he that believeth not shall be damned") for the Christian claim; and the Koran 3:17 ("The true religion with God is Islam") for the Muslim claim. To be sure, other religions (such as Greco-Roman paganism and some of the Eastern religions, especially Hinduism) are not exclusive, but the "big three" of the West certainly are, and every believer of each of these faiths is obliged to maintain that the believers of all other faiths are perniciously in error.

Much of Carter's book is a disquisition of the interrelations between religion, politics, and public morality, specifically in regard to various church-state decisions made by the Supreme Court. One point that Carter passes over hastily (it is one that has actually not reached the Supreme Court and may never do so) is the mildly irritating issue of the motto "In God We Trust" affixed to our currency. Carter claims that this motto does not violate the Establishment Clause and that the effort to eliminate it, "if successful, . . . would wipe away even the civil religion" (C 109) of America. Carter never bothers to identify what this "civil religion" is: is it merely the grotesque claim that God has a special place in his heart for citizens of the United States? On a related case Carter becomes a bit more heated: "One of the more interesting cases involved a rather bland 'Motorists' Prayer' to God for safety that North Carolina printed on its official state maps. A federal court, missing the significance of

America's civil religion, held the practice to be a violation of the Establishment Clause" (C 111). This is all that Carter has to say on the subject, but perhaps we can do a little better.

A little history in the matter of "In God We Trust" may be useful. The statement is found approximately in the fourth stanza (which nobody sings, and whose existence is probably not suspected by one American in a million) of "The Star-Spangled Banner": "Then conquer we must, when our cause is just, / And this be our motto—'In God is our Trust.'" This motto was first affixed on the so-called copper-nickel (a 3¢ piece) on March 3, 1865—a clear effort to lend some kind of overarching unity to a nation in the final stages of a devastating civil war. But the motto was optional for other forms of currency; it did not become mandatory until July 11, 1955, when Congress decreed that it be placed on all the coins and paper money printed by the United States. Lawmakers were manifestly striving, in those early days of the Cold War, to gain a moral advantage over those horrible atheistic Russians, as an address by longtime Congressman Charles Edward Bennett (a Democrat [!] from Florida) attests:

> In these days when imperialistic and materialistic communism seeks to attack and to destroy freedom, it is proper for us to seek continuously for ways to strengthen the foundations of our freedom. At the base of our freedom is our faith in God and the desire of Americans to live by His will and by His guidance. As long as this country trusts in God, it will prevail. To remind all of us of this self-evident truth, it is proper that our currency should carry these inspiring words, coming down to us, through our history: "In God we trust."[5]

No doubt this is an utterance to warm Carter's heart, but the degree to which it can be accepted by most intelligent Americans is now considerably in doubt.

Two curious arguments are made in defense of the motto. The first is that it does not actually endorse any specific god in whom we are putting our trust. This argument is itself based upon the assumption that the Establishment Clause does not prohibit a *general*, nondoctrinal support of religion, only a support of *some specific* religion. This interpretation, although advocated by Chief Justice Rehnquist among others of the political right wing, seems plainly false; as a leading scholar of the Establishment Clause, Leonard W. Levy, asserts, these so-called nonpreferentialists have "developed a plausible but fundamentally defective interpretation of the establishment clause."[6] But let us suppose Rehnquist's claim is true: can "In God We Trust" still pass constitutional muster? I hardly think so. It would be preposterous to assume that the Congress in 1955—let alone 1865—was doing anything but endorsing the Christian religion when passing this measure. (It should be noted that the prayer that opened the session of Congress during which Bennett made his speech ended with the words: "Hear us in Christ's name. Amen.") Can one possibly believe that the "God" of "In God We Trust" is anything but the Christian God?

The other defense offered up by partisans is even more bizarre. It is an admission that the words "In God We Trust" are actually meaningless! When in April 2000 a federal appeals panel outlawed the statement "With God, all things are possible" as the state motto of Ohio (a decision later reversed by the full appeals court), some wondered why "In God We Trust" was not similarly suspect. The appeals panel stated that the Ohio motto violated the First Amendment because, being an exact copy of a statement attributed to Jesus in the New Testament (see Matt. 19:26), it thereby constituted an endorsement of Christianity. Let it pass for the moment that "In God We Trust" is pretty close to numerous statements in both the Old and the New Testaments, e.g. Isaiah 36:7 ("We trust in the Lord our God") or 1 Timothy 4:10 ("we trust in the living God"). That is not the point at issue. The American Civil Liberties Union lawyer bringing forth the case against Ohio purported to distinguish the two mottoes in question, remarking of the Ohio emblem: "It's not the same as 'In God We Trust.' No one knows what that means."[7] But if the words are void of meaning, then what advantage is it to have them on our currency—and what harm would it do to remove them?

But assuming that the motto does have some intelligible meaning, what meaning does it have? Who, specifically, are the "we" who trust in God? Who else but the American people? But this puts the estimated 10 to 30 million Americans who are atheists or agnostics in an awkward position: either we are not real Americans (even though we all have passports to prove that we are), or we are somehow to be relegated to the status of second-class citizens, in some nebulous way inferior— purely because of our beliefs—to those more pious than ourselves.

To be sure, this may not be the most burning issue in the matter of church-state relations in this country. I personally have not lost any sleep over "In God We Trust," nor have I been tempted to risk felony prosecution by scraping off the motto from my coins with a file or blotting it off the pitifully few bills in my wallet with a felt-tip pen. Still, it is difficult to deny that this is one of the most flagrant and obvious violations of the "wall of separation" that could be imagined.

Carter works himself into a lather over the apparent fact that "values" are no longer taught in public schools. He feels that they should be so as to make better citizens of us. When the inevitable question—whose values?—is raised, Carter huffily dismisses it as "cynical," adding: "We have moved sharply into a morally relativistic age, and the public schools have certainly felt the sting" (C 201). Carter, poor devil, is lugubriously aware that the foundations of morality are not quite as sound as they used to be; that moral "truths," including those that are derived from some scripture, are no longer regarded as truths, especially given that many of these religious "truths" were plausibly used to support ethical and political positions—racism, slavery, misogyny, theocracy—that few of us are now willing to defend. All that Carter can do in response to this dilemma is to assert the democratic fallacy ("there are some broad values on which vast majorities of Americans tend to agree" [C 203]), even though he is sadly aware that in certain other areas the opinions of "vast majorities of Americans" do not count for much ("Most Americans believe, in the virtual absence of any evidence at all, that Earth has been visited by beings from other planets, and no amount of scientific argument to the contrary seems to shake them" [C 218]). Again the question arises: Which values to teach? That witches and heretics should be killed? That women should not speak in church? That homosexuality is a sin? That slaves are slaves by God's decree and not by the force of circumstance? Each of these doctrines has been taught by several of the great religions of the world, and numerous citations from their scriptures could be adduced to justify them.

In *The Dissent of the Governed* Carter reprises the topic, and in doing so makes a startling assertion:

> A majority of parents say that they would send their children to pri-
> vate religious schools if they could afford to, and the number one
> reason they offer is that they want the schools to reinforce the values
> the parents are trying to teach them. In principle, there is no reason
> that the public schools cannot do the same thing. And if the schools
> refuse to do so, then parents will have a point when they argue that
> the schools are trying—actively trying—to wean their children from
> the religious traditions of the parents. (D 44)

Again, I am not sure Carter is quite aware of the implications of his remark. In the first place, it is impossible for any school, public or private, to teach values that "reinforce" the values of parents: even in a religiously homogeneous group, values are likely to vary considerably (and Carter himself avers repeatedly that religious people do not follow the teachings of their priests or pastors in some kind of robotic lockstep), and this variation will be still wider with the parents of public-school children. No matter how bland and nondoctrinal a set of values are, it could not possibly harmonize with that of every single parent of every child in school; indeed, the more bland and nondoc-trinal it becomes, the less value it will have for raising civically responsible children. Carter never answers the question as to why it is not sufficient for parents to teach their children whatever values they want before and after school hours. And the notion that schools are "actively" engaged in undermining the religious traditions of parents is both preposterous and insulting. If schools provide *facts* that render certain religious tenets unlikely, the problem lies with the tenets and not with the facts. One would otherwise have to imagine a high-school geology teacher stating to his pupils, "The earth is 4.5 billion years old—and by the way, that fact renders the creation story in

Genesis highly problematical." *That* would be an active attempt to undermine religious traditions, but so far as I know, no teacher in the public schools has ever made such an utterance, nor would he or she gain approval if he or she did so. What Carter wants, apparently, is a kind of instruction that would cause no one to question any values or beliefs that he or she grew up with. But is it not one of the essential goals of education to induce the young to give critical scrutiny to ingrained beliefs, so that even if they ultimately embrace those beliefs, they do so intelligently and not in the mechanical manner of programmed robots?

Carter concludes his treatise with a pitiable whine that recalls William James's sheepish persistence in religious belief in spite of all the errors that religion has committed in the past several thousands of years of human history: "Despite all the wrongs that are done in its name, religion at its best will tend to strengthen, not weaken, the values most Americans hold dear" (C 268). I am not so confident of this as Carter is, largely because I so infrequently see "religion at its best." In any case, Carter's worries about the "disrespect" accorded to religious points of view in contemporary American society are misplaced, and for two reasons. Firstly, there is no shortage of religious opinion in this country, even on questions of public policy. Politicians, political philosophers, clerics, scholars, and even ordinary people have unlimited possibilities for the expression of religiously based views, so that Carter's charge that "secular liberals" are somehow muzzling these people is plainly and overwhelmingly false. Secondly, Carter's notion that such views ought by their very nature be accorded "respect" is unreasonable. *Every* view, whether secular or religious, must first *earn* respect. It is precisely because religious views seem to many to be based upon falsehoods—or, at the very least, are based upon a way of looking at the world not shared by those whom decisions of public policy will affect—that they are deemed out of bounds.

The mere fact that someone so theologically and philosophically inept as Stephen L. Carter can be regarded as a leading American intellectual only proves that our society does not have many genuine intellectuals today. His discussions of politics and law are somewhat less incompetent than his various screeds on religion, and he would be well advised to stick to these topics in the future. Otherwise, he will continue to pine vainly for "respect" without having done anything to warrant it.

NOTES

References to Stephen L. Carter's works occur in the text as follows: C = *The Culture of Disbelief* (New York: Basic Books, 1993); D = *The Dissent of the Governed* (Cambridge: Harvard University Press, 1998).

1. Robert G. Ingersoll, "God in the Constitution" (1890), in *The Works of Robert G. Ingersoll,* vol. 11 (New York: Dresden Publishing Co., 1906), pp. 123, 127, 131.

2. Charles Bradlaugh, "Humanity's Gain from Unbelief," *North American Review* 148, no. 3 (March 1889): 297–98.

3. A. J. Ayer, *The Central Questions of Philosophy* (1973; reprint New York: William Morrow, 1975), p. 225.

4. See Leonard W. Levy, *Blasphemy: Verbal Offense against the Sacred, from Moses to Salman Rushdie* (New York: Knopf, 1993).

5. *Congressional Record,* House of Representatives, April 13, 1955, p. 4384.

6. Leonard W. Levy, *The Establishment Clause: Religion and the First Amendment* (New York: Macmillan, 1986), p. 91.

7. Jane Fritsch, "Holy Cow! Ohio Has a Motto Problem," *New York Times,* April 30, 2000, sec. 4, p. 2.

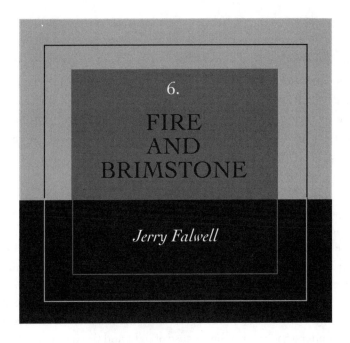

6.

FIRE
AND
BRIMSTONE

Jerry Falwell

The modern Christian fundamentalist movement has customarily been dated to 1978, when Jerry Falwell (b. 1933) established the Moral Majority, contending that as many as fifty to sixty million Americans declared themselves "born again Christians." This movement—simultaneously religious, moral, and political—sought to reverse a tide of secularism that had been growing (among the intelligentsia) over the better part of a century, when evidence had been mounting inexorably that the Bible did not embody "truth" in a literal or even a symbolic sense. To be sure, the great masses of the ignorant had not been much affected by such an intellectual shift, but they never are, and today the overwhelming number of Americans still declare themselves believers in God, although by no means a majority of these are "born again."

Fundamentalism is a recurring phenomenon in the history of religion. The first such movement of which I am aware occurred around the eighth century C.E. in ancient Israel, when the Karaites, led by Anan ben David, sought to read their Bible in its literal simplicity and to practice all the restraints and injunctions found in Exodus, Leviticus, and Deuteronomy, specifically in regard to the Sabbath. The result was not picturesque:

> Karaite literalism forbade anyone on the Sabbath to leave the house, to carry anything from one room into another, to wash the face, to wear a coat, shoes, girdle, or anything except a shirt, to make a bed, to carry food from the kitchen into another apartment, and similar other necessary activities of daily life. Likewise, the Biblical injunction "Ye shall kindle no fires throughout your habitation on the Sabbath day" (Exod. 35.3) was pressed to its literalness, and accordingly understood to prohibit the use of light and fire on the Sabbath. The Karaites consequently were obliged to put out all the lights and fires on the incidence of the day of rest and had to spend Friday night in total darkness, and the Sabbath, even in the most wintry season, in the cold.[1]

The history of the West is replete with similar enterprises. Martin Luther "rejected the authority not only of the Pope and the clergy but even of the Bible itself, except where in his opinion the Bible confirmed his faith."[2] Although evangelicals—such as George Whitefield, John Wesley, even the grotesque Billy Sunday—are not to be confused with fundamentalists, there is at the heart of many such movements a perceived need to return to the basics of biblical teaching in a society that is thought to be discarding or ignoring them.

I maintain, however, that *there is no such thing today as a Christian fundamentalist.* That is to say, there is no one who actually believes in the literal truth of the Bible. I take this to be the primary defining element of fundamentalism, although the movement as a whole is notoriously difficult to summarize in short compass. But I assert, and hope here to show, that not a single individual in today's American society —not even Jerry Falwell—believes every utterance that is made in the Bible. These individuals are either ignorant of the many passages in the Bible that no sane person can now accept, or they deliberately avoid bringing attention to them.

Falwell himself is a mildly amusing phenomenon of modern American civilization. In 1952, while listening to a radio broadcast of Charles Fuller's "Old Fashioned Gospel Hour," he became "born again" and subsequently worked diligently in the Baptist community in Virginia. He himself established a radio show and later a television show, "The Old-Time Gospel Hour," which by the early 1970s was being broadcast on more than 300 stations. He also founded Liberty College to train a phalanx of like-minded theologians. But it was his founding of the Moral Majority that thrust him into the national spotlight; at the same time, however, he became a figure of fun and ridicule as the prototype of the backwoods fundamentalist. He is now likely to be remembered less as a religious leader than as the clownish antagonist of Larry Flynt in the film *The People vs. Larry Flynt,* which portrays his bootless effort to sue Flynt for lampooning him in the chaste pages of *Hustler.*

Falwell has published only a few books; no doubt he is aware that he can reach a far greater number of dupes through television. *Listen, America!* (1980), published only two years after he formed the Moral Majority, is an exhaustive outline of his views, and he does not seem to have modified them significantly in the subsequent two decades. Among Falwell's other works is an autobiography, *Strength for the Journey* (1987), but this was actually ghostwritten by Mel White, a minister who, embarrassingly for Falwell, later admitted to being gay. But we can be confident that *Listen, America!* comes right from the Falwellian pen: it is too illiterate, pompous, evasive, and self-important to be anything but his own creation.

It would be too much to expect Falwell to *justify* his belief in God or in the Bible by any process of philosophical or scientific reasoning. To this simple soul, the Bible is absolutely true, and that is the end of it; anything that contradicts the Bible in any way is ipso facto false. Falwell is, indeed, forthright in his belief in biblical inerrancy: "A thorough study of the Bible will show that it is indeed the inerrant Word of the living God. The Bible is absolutely infallible, without error in all matters pertaining to faith and practice, as well as in areas such as geography, science, history, etc." (L 63). (It should be pointed out that this is the official doctrine of the Catholic Church as well, although a succession of popes have found ways to explain away various awkward or barbaric parts of the Bible, so that not many Catholics can be considered "fundamentalists" in the same sense as Falwell.)

I don't imagine there is much need to refute this utterance through any citation of the numerous inconsistencies, contradictions, errors, and confusions in the Bible; it has been done before by many hands, perhaps most ably in Joseph Wheless's *Is It God's Word?* (1926). The troubles begin at an awkwardly early stage. Is Falwell really ignorant of the fact that Genesis records not *one* account of creation, but *two*, and that these accounts differ significantly? Are we to believe, for example, that God created the animals before he created human beings (Gen. 1:20–26), or that human beings came first (Gen. 2:15–20)? Surely one of these accounts must be in error. How is it possible for Falwell—as well as the Southern Baptists, who assert as part of their essential doctrine that the Bible is "totally true"—to accept both?

One in fact begins to develop the unnerving impression that Falwell himself does not know his own scripture as well as he ought. He actually claims that "if a man is not a student of the Word of God and does not know what the Bible says, I question his ability to be an effective leader" (L 17). The phrasing is singularly unfortunate, for it is difficult to deny that such atheists and secularists as David Hume, Friedrich Nietzsche, H. L. Mencken, and Bertrand Russell knew quite well "what the Bible says," and yet it is unlikely that Falwell would regard these horrible people as "effective leaders." But by his own criterion, he is not one himself. Let us consider a passage early in *Listen, America!* in which Falwell finds the sources of American capitalism in scripture: "The free-enterprise system is clearly outlined in the Book of Proverbs in the Bible. Jesus Christ made it clear that the work ethic was a part of His plan for man. Ownership of property is biblical. Competition in business is biblical. Ambitious and successful business management is clearly oulined as a part of God's plan for His People" (L 13). Well, lordy me! It seems hardly necessary to point out (as I have done in a previous chapter) that Jesus himself seems to have been (or at least is presented in the Gospels as) a pure communist—at any rate, one who scorned wealth and possessions and believed in distributing all his meager belongings among his followers. Or consider again how Falwell urges the use and development of the American military as something biblically sanctioned: "In the verse, 'he beareth not the sword in vain [Romans 13:4],' we find the acknowledgment that those in places of authority, officials in Washington, have the right to bear the sword. The bearing of the sword by the government is correct and proper" (L 98). But what of Jesus' "resist not evil: but whosoever shall smite thee on thy right cheek, turn to him the other also" (Matt. 5:39)? More astute theologians than Falwell have no doubt found ingenious ways to circumvent Jesus' pacifist teachings in order to vaunt Christian warfare, so this particular contradiction need not give us much pause. Somewhat more awkward for Falwell is his assertion that in the garden of Eden it was "Satan, who revealed himself as a serpent" (L 62) and who tempted Eve with the apple. But a quick look at Genesis 3 reveals that the serpent was nothing but a serpent, albeit one endowed with the miraculous power of speech. This notion of the serpent as Satan was a later interpretation, first propounded in the Wisdom of Solomon, a Greek text written no earlier than 30 B.C.E., and, ironically enough, it is found also in the Koran (2:33–34), a text Falwell certainly does not wish to endorse. How Falwell justifies this interpretation in light of his biblical literalism is a question only he can answer. But Falwell's greatest lapse into scriptural absurdity occurs when he asserts (in defense of the value of work as a moral benefit as opposed to welfare) that "we are to earn our bread by the sweat of our brow" (L 74). I beg leave to point out that this injunction (from Gen. 3:19) is God's *punishment* to Adam for disobedience. If Adam hadn't eaten that Granny Smith apple proffered to him by Eve, no one would have to work and we would all be lounging around in Eden, without a care in the world!

But all this is neither here nor there. I am entirely willing, for the sake of the present argument, to regard the Bible as the inerrant Word of God. Let us see if Falwell truly does so as well. He repeatedly states that the Ten Commandments should be the bedrock moral code of the nation; in a prefatory note to *Listen, America!* he actually maintains that "More than eight out of every ten—84 percent of the American people—believe that the Ten Commandments are still valid for today." If this is true, it is only one further indication that most purported Christians—even most fundamentalists—are ignorant of what the Bible actually says.

Two of the commandments clearly endorse the institution of slavery. In the commandment to "Remember the sabbath day, to keep it holy" (Exod. 20:8), there is a further elaboration: "But the seventh day is the sabbath of the Lord thy God; in it thou shalt not do any work, thou, nor thy son, nor thy daughter, thy manservant, nor thy maidservant, nor thy cattle, nor thy stranger that is within thy gates" (Exod. 20:10). No one need be deceived that the terms "manservant" and "maidservant" refer to anything but slaves; we are not dealing with some ancient predecessor of Jeeves. (The Revised English Bible is a bit more forthright on this point, translating the words as "slave" and "slave-girl," respectively.)

(Parenthetically, it may be noted that one significant person is missing from the above enumeration of those who should do no work: the wife. Can this be, as Clarence Darrow pointed out, because she is needed to do the cooking, cleaning, and other work that would allow everyone else to loaf on the Sabbath?)[3]

The tenth commandment is even more interesting from this perspective: "Thou shalt not covet thy neighbour's house, thou shalt not covet thy neighbour's wife, nor his manservant, nor his maidservant, nor his ox, nor his ass, nor any thing that is thy neighbour's" (Exod. 20:17). Let us be clear on what the word *covet* means: to *desire to possess* what belongs to someone else. (The Hebrew and English words are identical in meaning here.) The commandment is enumerating a man's *possessions* in descending order of importance. Accordingly, a man is not only a slave owner but he owns his wife. This commandment is quite distinct from the commandment against adultery ("Thou shalt not commit adultery" [Exod. 10:14])—it means taking a man's wife away from him and making her *your own* possession. Those modern politicians who have recently sought the public display of the Ten Commandments in schools and elsewhere perform a clever ploy by presenting a *Reader's Digest* condensed version of this commandment—"Thou shalt not covet"—leaving it deliberately ambiguous what exactly is being coveted—but this is as legitimate an enterprise as omitting "manservant" and "maidservant" from the Sabbath-day commandment.

My overriding point is this: *All Christian fundamentalists (and Orthodox Jews) are obliged to sanction the institution of slavery and are obliged to regard wives as the property of their husbands. If they do not, they are not fundamentalists.* It is no use to point to the one passage in the Bible where slavery is discounted as insignificant to one's salvation (Gal. 3:26–28), for, as I have shown elsewhere, this statement by Paul is contradicted by Paul and by Jesus himself in which they both sanction slavery as an acceptable feature of any society.

I wish to return to the Sabbath-day commandment for a moment, for it has some interesting ramifications of its own. I am not at the moment concerned with the vexed question of which day of the week actually is the sabbath, or why Jews and Christians differ on this seemingly essential matter. The real point at issue is: What is one to do with anyone who violates the Sabbath?

The matter is elaborated in a later passage: "Six days may work be done, but in the seventh day is the sabbath of rest, holy to the Lord: whosoever doeth any work in the sabbath Day, he shall surely be put to death" (Exod. 31:15).

What was that? Anyone who works on the Sabbath *shall be put to death?* This is no typo. The passage is repeated in Exodus 35:2. In Numbers there is even a convenient narrative exemplifying the point. A hapless fellow was found picking up sticks on the Sabbath. Moses and Aaron, outraged, took him up and asked God what to do with him. "And the Lord said unto Moses, The man shall be surely put to death: all the congregation shall stone him with stones without the camp" (Num. 15:35). Sure enough, the congregation did just that.

Once again I am forced to state: *All Christian fundamentalists (and Orthodox Jews) are obliged to seek the death penalty for violators of the Sabbath. If they do not, they are not fundamentalists.*

So far, I have not heard Falwell or any other fundamentalist urge the death penalty for Sabbath violators, but some of his predecessors were not so shy. In the 1920s a group called the Lord's Day Alliance lobbied numerous state legislatures to outlaw a variety of activities — ranging from playing golf to driving cars to seeing movies — on Sunday. The reasoning was that if people could not engage in these and other activities, some of them might have no recourse but to go to church. Evidently it was acceptable to drive cars in order to attend church. The Lord's Day Alliance also issued a pamphlet called *The Importance of the Death Penalty,* urging that capital punishment be imposed upon violators of the Sabbath.[4]

Let us turn to another moral issue that infuriates the fundamentalists — homosexuality. What does the Bible say on this issue? Garry Wills briefly discusses the matter in *Papal Sin* (2000), although I am saddened to note his sophistical attempt to maintain that the numerous condemnations of homosexuality in the Bible are somehow not applicable to modern Christianity. But let that pass. There are at least four injunctions against homosexuality in the Old Testament and three in the New. The ones that interest me the most are two passages in Leviticus. The first appears straightforward enough: "Thou shalt not lie with mankind, as with womankind: it is abomination" (18:22). Oddly enough, this injunction seems to apply only to men: perhaps God could not even conceive of such a thing as lesbianism. The other Leviticus passage is of considerably greater interest: "If a man also lie with mankind, as he lieth with a woman, both of them have committed an abomination; they shall surely be put to death; their blood shall be upon them" (20:13). Read that one closely: any man who engages in a homosexual act with a man must be put to death.

Therefore, *all Christian fundamentalists (and Orthodox Jews) are obliged to urge the death penalty to active homosexuals. If they do not, they are not fundamentalists.*

There does not seem any way around this. Remember that this is the direct word of God ("And the Lord spake unto Moses." [Lev. 20:1]). Surely Falwell cannot possibly assert that this injunction applies only to Jews, or that the God in question is only the Jewish

God, not the Christian one; in that case, his own support for the Ten Commandments, not to mention the entire creation story (or stories) in Genesis, would be subject to the same reservation. Falwell could similarly not assert that such a measure would violate the U.S. Constitution or other federal or state laws: surely Falwell is the last person on earth to assert that man's laws ought to supersede God's law. In any case, it is by no means clear that the death penalty against homosexuals would be unconstitutional. Since the Supreme Court's 1986 decision (*Bowers v. Hardwick*) upholding a Georgia sodomy law in effect criminalized even consensual homosexual behavior among adults in the privacy of their own homes, there is no reason any state legislature, or the federal government as a whole, could not decree any punishment it wished in regard to this behavior. In that case, opponents would have to undertake further legal action to establish that the death penalty for gays was "cruel and unusual punishment" — and given the current conservative tendencies of the Supreme Court, it is anyone's guess how this issue would be adjudicated. I find it interesting to note that in a town meeting held in Vermont in early 2000 during that state's debate over "civil unions" for gay couples, a pious lady cited the first passage of Leviticus as biblical authority against recognition of homosexuality;[5] but no one seems to have brought up the other passage. And yet, if fundamentalists believe the Bible to be the word of God, they have no choice but to demand the death penalty for homosexuals.

Falwell devotes a small chapter of *Listen, America!* to the subject, in which he actually quotes both passages from Leviticus, but nervously remarks of the latter (the death-penalty injunction): "We are no longer under that law because of Christ's sacrificial death on the cross" (L 181). I have no idea what this could possibly mean, especially as Falwell himself does not elucidate it. Is he attempting to maintain that Jesus himself repudiated the "law" of the Old Testament? Some passages in the Bible appear to point in this direction, but surely not this one: "Think not that I am come to destroy the law, or the prophets: I am not come to destroy, but to fulfil" (Matt. 5:17); even Paul said, "So worship I the God of my fathers, believing all things which are written in the law and in the prophets" (Acts 24:14), suggesting that he, too, believed that all the Old Testament "laws" were still valid, except perhaps those (e.g., on divorce) that Jesus had explicitly overturned. Or perhaps Falwell believes that Jesus' death will redeem everyone, sinner and pious alike. On this vexed point, too, there have been millennia of theological debate. On the one side there are such passages as Acts 24:15 ("And have hope toward God . . . that there shall be a resurrection of the dead, both of the just and unjust"), and on the other side, such passages as John 16:16 ("He that believeth and is baptized shall be saved; but he that believeth not shall be damned"). It seems intrinsically unlikely that Falwell could be of the former camp—the universalists who maintain that no one is in fact going to go to hell, or at any rate that they will remain there for all time—given that he maintains, with a charming redundancy, that "Homosexuality is Satan's diabolical attack upon the family, God's order in Creation" (L 183) and later proclaims: "Those who laugh at a literal hell may someday experience it, for according to the Bible all adulterers, fornicators, homosexuals, and perverts who live and die without a new-birth experience will spend eternity there. (Rev. 21:8)" (L 198). (Well, maybe not. The passage in Revelation 21:8 does not refer explicitly to homosexuals but only to "the fearful, and unbelieving, and the abominable, and murderers, and whoremongers, and sorcerers, and idolaters, and all liars.") In effect, Falwell wants to retain his belief in all the passages in both the Old and the New Testaments on homosexuality except the awkward Leviticus 20:13, which even he apparently finds too barbaric for credence.[6]

Falwell's opposition to legalized abortion is hardly news. He devotes a chapter to this subject in *Listen, America!* beginning: "Life is a miracle. Only God almighty can create life. God said, 'Thou shalt not kill.' Nothing can change the fact that abortion is the murder of life" (L 165). The ineptitude of this utterance almost beggars description. The hauling up of the commandment "Thou shalt not kill" is most unfortunate, in a number of ways. First, it is manifest that the commandment is not to be taken universally: not only does God himself—as well as numerous other worthies in both Testaments—kill with great relish (I am particularly taken by the fact that the prophet Elisha, teased by children for his bald head, "cursed them in the name of the Lord" [2 Kings 2:24], with the result that two she-bears killed forty-two of the little tykes), but a literal reading of the commandment would presumably curtail all forms of killing, whether it be in self-defense, in war, or by the state (i.e., capital punishment). Falwell, of course, does not wish to give up his devotion to capital punishment, which he claims to justify by an appeal to Romans 13:3–4 ("For rulers are not a terror to good works, but to the evil. Wilt thou not be afraid of the power? . . . If thou do that which is evil, be afraid, for he beareth not the sword in vain"), which really has nothing to do with the subject (L 166). But the notion that "abortion is the murder of life" is also clumsily expressed. What kind of life? Animals are alive, and yet we kill them with insouciance for food and other purposes.

It is now a commonplace that there is no scriptural evidence to support opposition to abortion, although one can of course be opposed to it for other reasons. But Falwell thinks he has found three such passages. The first ("Whoso sheddeth man's blood, by man shall his blood be shed, for in the image of God made he man" [Genesis 9:6]) can be easily dispensed with: not only does this beg the question in assuming that a fetus is a "man" (i.e., a human being) — that being the very point at issue — but it would also prohibit all other kinds of killing, as in the commandment "Thou shalt not kill." The next passage is similarly irrelevant:

> For thou hast possessed my reins: thou hast covered me in my mother's womb. I will praise thee; for I am fearfully and wonderfully made: marvellous are thy works; and that my soul knoweth right well. My substance was not hid from thee, when I was made in secret, and curiously wrought in the lowest parts of the earth. Thine eyes did see my substance, yet being unperfect; and in thy book all my members were written, which in continuance were fashioned, when as yet there was none of them. (Ps. 139:13–16)

I still see no injunction against abortion here, even if one assumes that God "saw" the "unperfect" substance of a fetus. Then Falwell cites

Luke 1:39–44, telling of Mary coming to the house of Zacharias, whose pregnant wife Elisabeth greeted her, whereupon "the baby leaped in her womb." How this passage, or any other, is supposed to prove that "the Bible clearly states that life begins at conception" (L 167) is a mystery I shall leave to the learned Dr. Falwell to explicate.

The problems of "biblical inerrancy" for people like Falwell go well beyond moral issues such as those embodied in the Ten Commandments and elsewhere. No one need be reminded of fundamentalists' hostility toward the teaching of Darwinian evolution in schools and their own advocacy of creationism (or, more recently, the minimally reformed notion of "intelligent design"). To be sure, the theory of evolution contradicts the Bible, and anything that contradicts the Bible is, ipso facto, erroneous and evil. Very well; let us adopt this hypothesis and see where it leads.

Consider a famous passage in Joshua, recounting Joshua's battles with the Amorites:

> Then spake Joshua to the Lord in the day when the Lord delivered up the Amorites before the children of Israel, and he said in the sight of Israel, "Sun, stand thou still upon Gibeon; and thou, Moon, in the valley of Ajalon." And the sun stood still, and the moon stayed, until the people had avenged themselves upon their enemies. Is not this written in the book of Jasher? So the sun stood still in the midst of heaven, and hasted not to go down about a whole day. (Josh. 10:12–13)

Whether one believes that such a thing actually happened or not is beside the point; Falwell and his cohorts are obliged to believe that it did. But has it gone unnoticed that this passage makes plain that the writers of at least this section of the Bible believed the sun to revolve around the earth? How else could the day be extended by making the *sun* stand still? The *earth* would have to stand still in order for there to be additional daylight so that Joshua could continue his ethnic cleansing of the Amorites. I do not believe there is any way around this dilemma. It cannot be asserted that the authors of this part of the Bible are merely speaking informally (as we speak of the sun "setting" at day's end): they are clearly writing from a "cosmic" perspective. Certainly, this was the understanding of Martin Luther, who, in arguing against Copernicus, stated: "Sacred scripture tells us that Joshua commanded the sun to stand still, and not the earth."[7] In any case, Falwell cannot allow any kind of "interpretation" in his reading of the Bible; he *must* read the Bible literally if he is to remain true to his faith, because the moment he allows interpretation of any sort, then everything in the Bible becomes subject to interpretation in a variety of symbolic or metaphorical ways, to the point that God himself can be thought of as some kind of symbol or metaphor.

Accordingly, *all Christian fundamentalists (and Orthodox Jews) are obliged to believe that the sun revolves around the earth. If they do not, they are not fundamentalists.* I am therefore puzzled as to why Falwell and his followers do not protest more vigorously at teaching our innocent and malleable children that the earth revolves around the sun, when such a doctrine is clearly heretical. (As I have noted elsewhere, the Catholic Church did not acknowledge the truth of the heliocentric theory until 1822.)

On one point, however, I find Falwell to be admirably forthright: "If a person is not a Christian, he is inherently a failure because he has rejected that one third of his being that must be satisfied—the human spirit. While he is working to please body and soul, he is ignoring the part that yearns for God" (L 62). For once I am inclined to shake hands with Falwell and slap him heartily on the back, even if I myself am manifestly one of the "failures" he deplores. This is because for once in his book, he actually adheres strictly to biblical doctrine, however unpopular and harsh-sounding it may be. *All Christians (not just fundamentalists) are obliged to regard their own faith as the one and only truth about God; if they fail to do so, they cease to be Christians.* The moment you acknowledge that Christianity is simply one religion among many that could conceivably be espoused, you relinquish all claim to truth that Christianity may have, and that the Bible repeatedly declares it to have; the same is true of Judaism, Islam, and all other religions that claim exclusive knowledge of the truth. Once such a concession is made, religion becomes (in Stephen L. Carter's formulation) merely a "hobby": you are tacitly admitting that Christianity is only a preference, no different in kind from a preference of beef over pork. Falwell is aware of this; the only problem is that his religion (like all others) is false.

The whole notion of the "toleration" or "accommodation" of multiple religions is really a sign of religious indifference; indeed, as Charles Bradlaugh long ago noted, it could only be possible in an age in which the "tolerant indifference of scepticism" has become widespread.[8] We may deprecate the vicious persecution of minority religions—Catholics, Quakers, Mormons, and many others—that has cast so ugly a stain on American history (and Falwell does not seem aware that his own religious forbear, the Baptist Roger Williams, was hounded out of the Massachusetts Bay Colony for his own purportedly heretical beliefs and practices), but they at least reveal a devout reading of scripture and a resolute determination to carry out its precepts to the letter. If Jesus said, "He that is not with me is against me" (Matt. 12:30), what choice do you have but to believe that those who do not espouse the Christian religion are doomed to hell? It is, of course, now in rather bad taste for one religion to criticize another, and much worse for one religion to assert that another religion (or, indeed, every other religion) is false, but the end result of this "toleration" is that the believers of all these multitudinous faiths become *unwitting skeptics.*

There is another issue on which I am inclined to pinch Falwell's cheek in delighted approval:

> Why is it wrong to accept the Genesis account of creation? If man is not basically bad; if he is not inherently evil, having received from the fall the very nature of sin and having had death passed upon him and all men; if the depravity of man is not a fact from the very fall in the garden, then the death, the burial, and the resurrection of Jesus Christ were needless and worthless. (L 63)

I am not at the moment concerned with Falwell's insistence on humanity's innate "evil" and "depravity"; in this he is merely following a very long line of sainted theologians, from Augustine to Martin Luther to John Calvin to John Knox and (as we have seen) C. S.

Lewis, who all asserted with a straight face that we are all "born in sin," and that even a helpless infant, from the moment it emerges from its mother's womb, is a "limb of Satan" (in Augustine's words), and that if it happens to die before receiving baptism, it will spend the rest of eternity in hell. This notion of "infant damnation" has been widely ridiculed, but it remains an orthodox tenet of the Catholic Church and of numerous Protestant denominations.

But Falwell is quite correct in declaring that disbelief in Adam's "original sin" is fatal to Christian belief, for in that case there is nothing for Jesus to "redeem." If an actual Adam did not exist, then a fortiori there could have been no one to eat that Golden Delicious apple and thereby condemn the rest of humanity to potential perdition, and therefore Jesus would have no function in coming to our rescue like the U.S. cavalry in old westerns. I maintain, therefore, that *without a literal belief in Adam and Eve, no one can be a Christian.*

I do not wish to trouble myself greatly as to whether this entire doctrine has proper scriptural authority—specifically whether Jesus himself ever had any notion of "saving" humanity from Adam's sin; this is yet another of the extraordinarily complex theological conundrums that have baffled both the pious and the impious for millennia. It can be noted, however, that only once in the synoptic gospels is this salvationism ever attributed to Jesus, and that is when an angel tells Joseph about the future birth of Jesus, who "shall save his people from their sins" (Matt. 1:21). The expression is singularly ambiguous, and it seems hard to interpret "his people" as referring to humanity at large instead of merely the Jews. Indeed, if the synoptic gospels are to be believed, one would be compelled to assume that Jesus was merely an apocalypticist who believed in the imminent end of the world and the need for repentance ("The time is fulfilled, and the kingdom of God is at hand: repent ye, and believe the gospel" [Mark 1:14]). It is abundantly clear that the relation of Jesus to Adam was first made by Paul; the canonical utterance is the well-known passage in Romans: "Wherefore, as by one man [Adam] sin entered into the world, and death by sin; and so death passed upon all men, for that all have sinned" (5:12), therefore "God commendeth his love toward us, in that, while we were yet sinners, Christ died for us" (5:8). For this and many other reasons it would be considerably more accurate to refer to Christianity as Paulianity.

My overriding point is this: those many (nonfundamentalist) Christians—and this appears to include many Catholics—who interpret the creation story in Genesis symbolically place themselves in an inextricable theological bind because they render Jesus' entire life (and, more particularly, his death) pointless; they rob him of the work that the church, for more than a millennium and a half, believed him to have done. To this extent fundamentalists are at least somewhat more logically consistent on this point. The chief problem with fundamentalists is not that they are dogmatic or intolerant or fascistic, although they are all these things and more; it is simply that their religion is false.

The great majority of Falwell's *Listen, America!* is a harried plea for the moral and religious regeneration of the American people, lest they end up in perdition. He is quite certain that America was founded, and remains, under divine guidance: "I believe that God promoted America to a greatness no other nation has ever enjoyed because her heritage is one of a republic governed by laws predicated on the Bible" (L 16); and even more boldly, "God led in the development of that document [the U.S. Constitution], and as a result, we here in America have enjoyed 204 years of unparalleled freedom" (L 22). Well, all of us except Native Americans, African Americans until 1865, women until 1920, immigrants, and sundry other undesirables. But we're in big trouble now: "The disintegration of our social order can be easily explained. Men and women are disobeying the clear instructions God gave in His Word. Because of this, we live in a world of people with confused priorities who are giving maximum time to that which is of minor importance" (L 63–64).

Why Falwell should be so alarmed is a mystery: he wrote *Listen, America!* when an avowed born-again Christian was in the White House, when a great majority of the Congress (who have no doubt read polls stating that half to two-thirds of the American public refuse to vote for an atheist candidate, regardless of his or her views on other subjects) profess some kind of belief in God, and when anywhere from 92 to 97 percent of the American people themselves admit this same belief. Nevertheless, Falwell maintains in his prefatory note that "we, the American people, have allowed a vocal minority of ungodly men and women to bring America to the brink of death." He himself wants to "defend and maintain the freedoms that allow us to live and believe as we choose."

Exactly how Falwell's plans for a moral and religious regeneration of American society will actually enhance our freedoms is a trifle opaque to me. Falwell is charmingly ignorant of the degree to which religions in the past have almost uniformly inhibited the liberties of the populace; indeed, it was only when religion was thrown out of European and American governments in the later eighteenth and early nineteenth centuries that civil liberties began to flourish. Is it necessary, at this late date, to cite the evidence of, say, John Calvin's Geneva in the mid-sixteenth century as a textbook of religious oppression? Here is what a sympathetic historian of Christianity has to say:

> The city was divided into twelve districts, each of which was assigned to one of the elders. The elders were to supervise the families in the districts, even to the extent of having the right to enter any house at any time without invitation in order to examine the moral and other conditions in the house. . . . Every offense, moral as well as religious, and every violation of the civil laws . . . was severely punished. The system of punishments ranged from being reprimanded to doing penance in the church to making a public apology in penitential garb to being excommunicated. . . . Missing worship, playing cards, and even dancing brought severe penalties. Blasphemy and adultery were punished by death; treason and offenses against divine truth were punished by burning at the stake.[9]

Want something a bit closer to home? Consider Paul Johnson's description of the Puritan commonwealth in colonial Massachusetts:

> Puritans saw the individualist as a dangerous loner, meat for the Devil to feed on. As one of them, John Cotton, put it, "Society in all

sorts of humane affairs is better than solitariness." The Puritans believed they had the right to impose their will on this communally organized society.

John Davenport of Connecticut summed up the entire Puritan theory of government thus: "Power of Civil rule, by men orderly chosen, is God's ordinance. It is from the Light and Law of Nature, because the Law of Nature is God's law." They did not accept that an individual had the right to assert himself, in religious or indeed in any matters. When in 1681 a congregation of Anabaptists published an attack on the government of Massachusetts Bay and appealed to what they called the "tolerant spirit" of the first settlers there, Samuel Willard, minister to the Third Church in Boston, wrote a pamphlet in reply, with a preface by Increase Mather, saying: "I perceive they are mistaken in the design of our first Planters, whose business was not toleration but were professed enemies of it, and could leave the world professing they *died no Libertines*. Their business was to settle and (as much as in them lay) to secure Religion to Posterity, according to that way which they believed was of God."[10]

All this sounds remarkably Falwellian, but I do not see anything resembling the augmentation or even the preservation of civil liberties here. And yet, Falwell continues to parrot William Penn's axiom that "Men must be governed by God or they will be ruled by tyrants" (L 95). Possibly his hostility to communism has something to do with it: "Communism is atheistic. When God is taken out of a society, all freedom is lost" (L 90).

Oddly enough, however, Falwell, quoting Romans 13:1 ("Let every soul be subject unto the higher powers"), urges obedience to elected officials, wholly unaware that this passage and several others gave sanction throughout the medieval and Renaissance periods to the doctrine of the "divine right of kings," the greatest inhibitor of civil liberties in European history. Falwell writes: "The authority, 'the higher powers'—the President, the Congress, the judiciary—are ordained of God. This does not imply that all persons in places of authority are godly people. It does, however, mean that they are in their position, whether they are aware of the fact or not, by divine ordination" (L 15). The question, of course, becomes: What exactly is one to do when a particularly ungodly person is in office? In Falwell's mind Bill Clinton (although himself a Baptist) must be such a person, and so Falwell valiantly put aside his reverence for Clinton's God-given office to produce a video suggesting that Clinton was a murderer. Nevertheless, we are to "respect and obey the leaders in authority" (L 15–16)!

What particularly galls Falwell about present-day American society is the proliferation of sex, drugs, rock-and-roll, television, feminism, gays, divorce, and sundry other evils. On the matter of divorce Falwell sounds positively Catholic: "The family is the God-ordained institution of the marriage of one man and one woman together for a lifetime with their biological or adopted children" (L 121). One supposes that Falwell can evade the awkwardness of acknowledging the bountiful instances of incest (the seduction of Lot by his daughters), polygamy (Solomon's thousand wives, three hundred of whom were concubines), and other marital irregularities in the Old Testament by appeal to Jesus' own one-man-for-one-woman decree (Matt. 5:32f.), echoed by Paul (1 Cor. 7:2). Of course, Paul goes on to say that it is best not to marry at all and remain celibate; if you have no other way of getting rid of your horrible sexual urges, you'd better marry ("for it is better to marry than to burn" [1 Cor. 7:9]). Falwell, by some strange oversight, does not cite this passage.

I have already suggested that Falwell cannot bring himself to acknowledge the propriety of husbands' ownership of their wives, even though this is clearly spelled out in the tenth commandment, but on the notion of wives' submission to their husbands he is quite forthright. Citing the standard scripture passages (e.g., Eph. 5:22–23: "Wives, submit yourselves unto your own husbands, as unto the Lord. For the husband is the head of the wife, even as Christ is the head of the church"), Falwell declares:

> Scripture declares that God has called the father to be the spiritual leader in his family. The husband is not to be the dictator of the family, but the spiritual leader. There is a great difference between

> a dictator and a leader. People follow dictators because they are
> forced to do so. They follow leaders because they want to. Good
> husbands are good leaders. Their wives and children want to follow
> them and be under their protection. The husband is to be the deci-
> sionmaker and the one who motivates his family with love. (L 128)

No doubt Falwell took much pleasure in the Southern Baptist Convention's declaration in 1998 that a wife must "submit herself gra-
ciously" to her husband's leadership, even though others were not so
well pleased by the resolution.

But questions are inevitably raised: What if the husband fails to be
this moral exemplar? What if, in fact, he becomes a dictator, or a
drunkard, or a wife-beater, or a child abuser? Falwell has no answers
to these questions, aside from excoriating the women's movement for
taking women out of the home and into self-supporting employment
and lamenting the high divorce rate. Falwell's fulminations against feminism are too absurd even to notice ("Most of the women who are
leaders in the feminist movement promote an immoral life style" [L
124]; "it is shocking how many feminists are lesbians" [L 185]), but the
issue of child abuse deserves some attention. Recent studies have conclusively established that fundamentalists have markedly higher rates
of child abuse than the general population, but Falwell clearly does not
wish to acknowledge the fact.[11] In discussing unruly children, he maintains that "most of the blame must be placed on godless parents who are
rearing children in godless homes and in a godless society" (L 199). I
again ask: How is this possible, with 92 to 97 percent of the American
populace professing belief in God? Or are these people, although purportedly devout, really "ungodly" because they are not born-again
Christians? But Falwell goes on to say, "Parents fail their children
when they do not effectively discipline them" (L 140), and then
addresses the child abuse issue head-on: "In this day and age there is
much talk about child abuse. We are confusing child abuse with discipline, which is necessary if we are to raise healthy children" (L 140).
Falwell will have nothing to do with smart-aleck child psychologists
who have garnered a large body of evidence suggesting that corporal
punishment of children leads directly to violent behavior in later life.

Falwell works himself into a lather in lambasting all the sex and violence (but mostly the sex) on television and the wide availability of pornography. I do not wish to discuss these fulminations extensively, except to note several oddities in his discussion. Firstly, it is unclear why Falwell blames the television and pornography industries for plying their sinful wares so vigorously when the real fault is obviously with the consumers who partake of them. No one, surely, is forcing anyone to watch a given television show; much less is anyone being forced to look at a pornographic magazine or watch an X-rated video. Without a demand, there could be no market for these things. I am aware that actually turning off a television set is regarded by many Americans as something akin to blasphemy, but I assure them that it can be done. Surely the 3 to 8 percent of the populace who claim to be "ungodly" atheists cannot be responsible for the entire consumption of pornography, much less of television; indeed, I have a suspicion that at least a small number of Falwell's sixty million fundamentalists have a video of *The Devil in Miss Jones* hidden away underneath their prayer books.

Falwell knows that he cannot advocate any kind of censorship of these media, although it becomes clear that he is itching to do so. Of television he declares: "I am not advocating doing away with the television set. I believe that television, radio, and the printed page are things we must not destroy but that we must redirect" (L 195). But redirect how? Falwell can come up with nothing more than a boycott (L 195), which has repeatedly proven ineffective. Certainly, he cannot condemn television uniformly, since it has provided him with many millions of tax-free dollars by way of his own television show. Of pornography Falwell states:

> America is a free country. We pride ourselves in freedom of speech and freedom of the press. But freedom ends where someone else's welfare begins. Freedom of the press ends where the welfare of the public and ultimately the welfare of our nation begin. Freedom of speech does not include yelling "Fire!" in a crowded building; it does not include perverting and sickening the moral appetites of men and women. (L 200–201)

This, I fear, is pure sophistry. The analogy of pornography with yelling "Fire!" in a crowded building is so preposterously false as not to require any refutation. This notion of the "welfare of the public" is a dangerous one to use, for it was exactly on these or analogous grounds that Prohibition was advocated (chiefly by the Protestant clergy, notably Methodists), and that such organizations as the New York Society for the Suppression of Vice, founded by the pious Anthony Comstock, sought to ban such standard works of literature as Flaubert's *Madame Bovary,* Gautier's *Mademoiselle de Maupin,* and Joyce's *Ulysses.* On Falwell's own principles, an atheist could maintain that religion itself is harmful to "the welfare of the public" and thereby decree that it be banned. No atheist in America would ever do such a thing because he knows that no one is being forced to listen to any religious speech (except, of course, in the matter of the brainwashing of children into religious dogma by their parents, against which no action can presumably be taken), just as no one is being forced to watch a porno video.

On the matter of prayer in public schools Falwell lapses into further absurdities. Enraged at the 1962 Supreme Court decision that banned enforced prayer in schools, he observes: "Prayer and Bible reading were taken out of the schools because they might 'offend' some child who did not believe in God" (L 210). No, Mr. Falwell, they were removed because these prayers were *coercive* to all non-Christians — Jews, Muslims, Hindus, Buddhists, and the adherents of all other religions, as well as atheists and agnostics. Falwell, dimly recognizing this point, goes on to advocate "the official use of voluntary nonsectarian prayer in the public schools" (L 211). But how can an "official" prayer be "voluntary"? And what is a "nonsectarian" prayer anyway? How is it possible to find a prayer that will somehow harmonize with (or, at any rate, not obviously violate) the tenets of Christianity, Judaism, Islam, Hinduism, Buddhism, and every other religion (leaving aside the atheists and agnostics, who appear not to be of much account in Falwell's scholastic reformation)? It is all too absurd. Those who advocate prayer in schools would do well to consider a situation in which their own religion were a minority faith.

What if, by chance, Buddhism became the most populous religion in the nation, and Buddhists insisted on a school prayer that reflected their own tenets (which, let us recall, do not include belief in an omnipotent deity)? Christians and others compelled to recite this prayer would no doubt feel, at a minimum, "offended," and be among the first to advocate the elimination of enforced public prayer in schools or anywhere else.

Little more need be said. Falwell's own Moral Majority rapidly lost its power and influence, chiefly because Ronald Reagan, whom it helped to elect, did little in matters of public policy aside from paying lip service to the fundamentalists. Falwell's organization was eventually superseded by Pat Robertson's Christian Coalition; but although Robertson has shown considerably greater political and marketing savvy than Falwell, the Christian Coalition itself has remarkably few definite political or theological victories to its credit. No doubt fundamentalists (as commonly understood) will continue to be a force in American political and religious life; but normal people can safely ignore them, especially given that some fundamentalists themselves are now in such despair over the irremediable corruption of American moral and political life that they claim a desire to retreat even further into their own safe, self-contained communities, where they can act and believe as they wish without the irritating presence of the ungodly. As for me, I'll be happy to remain in Sodom.

NOTES

References to Jerry Falwell's *Listen, America!* (Garden City, N.Y.: Doubleday, 1980) occur in the text under the abbreviation L.

1. Isidore Epstein, *Judaism: A Historical Presentation* (Harmondsworth, England: Penguin, 1959), p. 187.

2. Walter Lippmann, *A Preface to Morals* (New York: Macmillan, 1929), p. 13.

3. Clarence Darrow, "The Lord's Day Alliance," *Plain Talk* 2, no. 3 (March 1928): 265.

4. Ibid., p. 260.

5. "Linda Pastelnick ... quoted a verse from Leviticus calling sex between men 'an abomination' and argued, 'God made Adam and Eve, he didn't make Adam and Steve." Carey Goldberg, "Forced Into Action on Gay Marriage, Vermont Finds Itself Deeply Split," *New York Times*, February 3, 2000, p. A16.

6. I do not think much stock need be placed in Falwell's meeting with a group of gay Christians in the fall of 1999, since he explicitly declared at this time that his views on homosexuality were fundamentally unchanged. See "Falwell Speaks to Gay Christians," *New York Times*, October 25, 1999, p. A27.

7. Quoted in Joseph Wheless, *Is It God's Word?* (New York: Knopf, 1926), p. 261.

8. Charles Bradlaugh, "Humanity's Gain from Unbelief," *North American Review* 148, no. 3 (March 1889): 295.

9. Kurt Aland, *A History of Christianity* (Philadelphia: Fortress Press, 1985), vol. 2, p. 186.

10. Paul Johnson, *A History of the American People* (New York: Harper-Collins, 1997), p. 67.

11. See, e.g., H. Danso, B. Hunsberger, and M. Pratt, "The Role of Parental Religious Fundamentalism and Right-Wing Authoritarianism in Child-Rearing Goals and Practice," *Journal for the Scientific Study of Religion* 36 (1997): 496–511.

7.

HAND-WRINGING FROM THE LITERATI

Reynolds Price and Annie Dillard

L iterary folk should not write about religion. It does not require a C. P. Snow to inform us that most of our novelists and poets are seriously, nay appallingly, ignorant of physics, biology, chemistry, geology, anthropology, philosophy, and the many other branches of human knowledge required for even a rudimentarily intelligent opinion on questions of the existence of God, the soul, and the afterlife. But beyond their plain ignorance, there is an added perniciousness in our literati's religious maunderings: their cleverness at word-spinning — even if it is shown to be intellectually vacuous, as it usually is — exercises a fatal attraction upon their equally ill-educated and naive readership. I do not wish to suggest that the ladling out of these honeyed words about God, the immortal soul, and the wonders of heaven is performed by novelists and poets—to whom we may add, in their respective media, painters, sculptors, and composers—in any cynical manner: it is painfully evident that they are themselves taken in by their own ravishing aesthetic products. In other words, although it is plain that such individuals are, in the overwhelming mass, incapable of conducting a course of logical argument outside the narrow field of their own activity (prose, verse, art, or music, as the case may be), they manage to conceal the fact both from their pious readership and from themselves.

Reynolds Price (b. 1933) is a prime example of all these problems. Price is a distinguished novelist, poet, and essayist whose long career has been filled with awards of various kinds. Religion has been at the center of his work from the beginning. Price has also devoted himself to producing translations of various parts of the Bible for contemporary readers, evidently feeling that previous translations are a bit stodgy and inaccessible. *A Palpable God* (1978) is subtitled "Thirty Stories Translated from the Bible with an Essay on the Origins and Life of Narrative." *The Three Gospels* (1996) presents translations of the gospels of Mark and John—plus one of Price's own.

A critical event in Price's life was his bout with spinal cancer, which in 1984 left him paralyzed from the waist down. His struggle with the illness was chronicled in *A Whole New Life* (1994). This event led indirectly to Price's most significant theological treatise, *Letter to a Man in the Fire* (1999), subtitled "Does God Exist and Does He Care?" It is a revised version of a lecture delivered at the Auburn Theological Seminary in New York, and was ultimately inspired by Price's involvement with a young man, Jim Fox, who was himself suffering from cancer and was seeking Price's help and advice on matters of faith. Price naturally felt a bond with Fox, but the poor fellow had the bad luck to die before he could read Price's words of wisdom.

In *A Palpable God* Price ingenuously admits that he had been indoctrinated into the Christian religion as early as the age of three, when his grandmother gave him Josephine Pollard's *Wonderful Stories of the Bible;* the next year his parents fed him Hurlbut's *Story of the Bible* (PG 11). The matter is of some importance because in *Letter to a Man in the Fire,* Price makes it abundantly clear that his chief reason for believing in God is not an abstract study of the universe (he happily acknowledges that his knowledge of physics and other sciences does not amount to much [LM 102]) but a series of visions or hallucinations that he has experienced at random points in his life. We have already seen, in our study of William James, how dubious such a line of argument is, especially when it is abundantly clear that such visions could only be a product of previous indoctrination. And yet, Price has the gall to call them *"demonstrations"* (LM 27; the pompous italics are his), although he then makes the unwittingly embarrassing confession that they began "when I was six years old" (LM 27) —*after* his first exposure to Christianity! The exact nature of these "demonstrations" is (with one exception) by no means clear; all Price says is "Those moments, which recurred at unpredictable and widely spaced intervals till some thirteen years ago, still seem to me undeniable manifestations of the Creator's benign, or patiently watchful, interest in particular stretches of my life, though perhaps not all of it" (LM 27). That final clause is, as we will see, typical of Price's evasiveness, and why these "demonstrations" ceased around 1987 is not apparent. And when Price soberly announces that "the experiences were as real as any car wreck" (LM 29) he betrays his prejudice. *Any* "experience" of this sort— including a madman's unshakable belief that he is the reincarnation of Napoleon—will be real to the person in question; what remains in doubt is the correlation of that experience to the external world.

The one "demonstration" that Price does elaborate upon occurred during his own bout with spinal cancer. Let him tell the story himself:

> In the first weeks of my return from radical surgery and ensuing depression, I experienced what I can only call a vision. It came on a morning just before my five weeks of scalding radiation began, and it took the shape of an utterly real dawn encounter with Jesus on the shore of the Lake of Galilee and then waist-deep in its water. As his disciples lay sleeping around us on the shore, Jesus silently beckoned me into the lake and, with handfuls of water, washed my ugly spinal wound and said "Your sins are forgiven." My own immediate silent response was characteristic of my managerial impatience—"Forgiveness is the last thing I need."

Since I was so obviously in the hands of a known miracle worker, I wanted my ten-inch tumor out of me and gone (surgery had removed only ten percent of its gray entangled mass after chiseling the backs off numerous vertebrae). So I dared to push past forgiveness and to ask Jesus if I were healed—"Am I also cured?" Plainly it hadn't occurred to me to wonder why the Son of God would have chosen to wash my particular wound in a teeming world of dire sickness. But after a pause that signaled reluctance, Jesus said "That too" and walked away from me as the encounter ended. (LM 50–51)

It is remarkable that Price, so adept in his novels at the analysis of character, can be so ignorant of his own. Does it not occur to him to wonder whether his admitted depression had anything to do with the genesis of this "vision"? Has he ever paused to wonder whether a Hindu or a Buddhist, with no knowledge of Chrsitianity, would ever have had such a vision? We need not make much of the fact that Jesus speaks English; the son of God can do anything, I suppose. But in the depths of my ignorance of medicine, I confess to a certain skepticism as to the efficacy of merely *washing* a cancerous tumor with water, even the holy water of the Lake of Galilee.

It would appear that visions of this sort have led to the following corollary: "I'd further claim that he [God] has rescued me since infancy from several life-or-death crises, though occasionally that rescue has come after serious damage was sustained by my body or the body and mind of another creature whom I'd consciously chosen (in fairly normal moments of hunger or malice) to harm" (LM 58). How untimely of God! Maybe he needs an alarm clock.

An elderly friend of Price's remarked to him concerning such "visions" (she calls them "inner events") that "They carry their own authentication" (LM 30): naturally, because they are exactly what the people in question want to believe! Indeed, it becomes evident that Price's belief in God is not a reasoned opinion based upon a study of evidence but a psychological need. The point is made covertly in *A Palpable God*, especially in its long-winded and meandering introduction on "the origins and life of narrative." Price maintains that the true

function of all narrative, and especially sacred narrative, is the "need
. . . for credible news that our lives proceed in order toward a pattern
which, if tragic here and now, is ultimately pleasing in the mind of a
god who sees a totality and *at last* enacts His will" (PG 14). We don't
need to linger over the sophistical use of the word *news*, as if such stories are sober, factual accounts from a CNN reporter. More interesting are the words *ultimately* and (Price's italics again) *at last*. Things
may be bad now, Price implies, but they'll turn out all right later —
maybe only after death (when disproof of the existence of God, the
soul, and the afterlife is conveniently impossible).

Price goes on to say:

> Stories which tell us that the innocent suffer under God's myste-
> rious hand, that our enemies' joints are torn from their sockets, or
> even that uncontrolled monsters patrol the world (most human
> beings assume themselves to be monsters, hence the child's fascina-
> tion with wolves, dinosaurs) — all these can console us in various
> ways, leave us firmed for our public and private lives. Only the story
> which declares our total incurable abandonment is repugnant and
> will not be heard long. (PG 25)

To be sure! (Let us bypass another sophistry: how can we be "abandoned" by a god who never existed?) But *why* are such depressing stories not heard for long? It is because most human beings believe that
"they are false" (PG 25; yes, those are Price's italics again). And why
not? Who would want to hear such a depressing story? But wait a
minute . . . maybe such a depressing story might actually be *true*. The
logical extension of Price's theory is that all unpleasant stories (conceding for the sake of argument — and it is a big concession — that such
a story of our "abandonment" is indeed unpleasant) are false and that
all pleasant stories are true. I suppose, therefore, that Hitler never
really existed: being so unpleasant, this must be just a false story!

Price's final comment on this point is as follows: "The worst of all
events that can befall our selves, our loved ones, or our people are the
appalling if not killing stretches of our lives in which God is silent
and, in that silence, appears to torment us or someone near to us for

no reason discernible by the human mind" (LM 52). But this is tor-
menting only to those who hope or expect to hear the voice of God
and are disappointed when they encounter silence in its stead. Price
cannot bring himself even to consider the possibility that he may be
straining his ears for a voice that is not there.

In both *A Palpable God* and *Letter to a Man in the Fire* Price openly
and brazenly admits that he has been more influenced by artists than
by philosophers and scientists in the formation of his religious views.
Consider his discussion of Genesis 32, the grotesque story of Jacob's
wrestling with God. Price asserts: "The fact that Jacob's tale has been
believed by sizable portions of the human race for thousands of years,
and is still believed and acted on by millions, is the great reward of his
narrative success. No other narrator, except Abraham, has succeeded
longer or deeper in the first—and final—aim of narrative: compulsion
of belief in an ordered world" (PG 34). What exactly does "narrative
success" mean here? Once again, does the mere fact that a lot of credulous and brainwashed people have believed the tale mean that it is
true? Price is too cagey to come out and say so, but surely this is the
implication in a later remark concerning other Bible stories: "I, like
millions, am convinced and have always been by the stories themselves—their narrative perfection, the speed and economy with which
they offer all the heart's last craving in shapes as credible as any
friend's tale of a morning walk" (PG 41). If there is any clearer indication that Price has been led by *aesthetics* (the admiration for "narrative perfection") into a *metaphysical* belief, I hardly know what it could
be. Price concludes with the resounding utterance: "Sacred story is
the perfect answer given by the world to the hunger of that species for
true consolation" (PG 46). Of course it is!—because it tells us (or, at
any rate, those of us who, like Price, "hunger" for "true consolation")
exactly what we want to hear!

The influence of artists and composers upon Price's thought is
made abundantly evident in *Letter to a Man in the Fire:* "I've been sup-
ported by the manifest convictions of the world's supreme artists—the
classic Buddhist and Hindu scriptures, sculptures, and sacred music;
the cathedrals of medieval Europe; and the painting, poetry, and

music of burdened but staunch believers such as Dante, Michelangelo, Donne, Milton, Bach, Handel, and W. H. Auden" (LM 32). No doubt this list is not meant to be exhaustive, but it contains a number of curious inclusions—and exclusions. Indeed, much later Price is sheepishly forced to admit that not all his beloved artists were quite as orthodox as he himself is: "Beethoven was a Christian-reared deist and Verdi and [Wallace] Stevens were at most agnostic" (LM 82)— but they produced pious works anyway! But what value do the beliefs, or even the works, of these great masters have to the central questions of religion? My admiration for Handel's *Messiah* borders upon idolatry; it is my favorite single work of music, and I still sing the tenor parts of all the choruses as lustily as my croaking throat will allow. But I would as readily seek from Handel an authoritative opinion on religion as I would seek from William Faulkner an authoritative opinion on differential calculus.

And, of course, Price's omissions are as interesting as his inclusions. Why do we not hear of such skeptical, agnostic, or even openly atheistic artists as Lucretius, Hobbes, Voltaire, Hume, Shelley (need we recall *The Necessity of Atheism?*), Stendhal, Swinburne, Sinclair Lewis, Virginia Woolf, Gore Vidal, and countless others? Does Price deny that these figures are genuine artists? Does he not read them for fear of disturbing his piety? The day Price curls up in his recliner with Vidal's *Messiah* or *Live from Golgotha* is the day I become a Jehovah's Witness.

The remarks I have already quoted make abundantly clear how abject is Price's adherence to the democratic fallacy—i.e., the notion that what "millions" of people believe must be true, regardless of their overall intelligence or of how they came by the belief. It is a leitmotif in Price's work: "the majority opinion of Homo sapiens throughout our known history is worth, at a minimum, initial respect" (LM 26). I regret to say that the long history of almost universal human folly and error does not incline me to share Price's naive confidence on this point. Given that (to choose only one example among many) 47 percent of the American public believes that human beings were created, pretty much in their present form, a few thousand years ago—an opinion from which Price himself boldly dissents, actually acknowledging that the emergence of the human species may date to as early as four million years ago (PG 9)—Price's confidence in the intelligence of the masses does not appear warranted. And yet, the final sentence of *Letter to a Man in the Fire* repeats the dogma once again: "the proportional number of Homo sapiens who doubt the existence of a conscious Creator—the source of all good if nothing more—is likely no greater than it's ever been" (LM 108). This is fallacious on three separate grounds: first, the notion that truth is determined by a vote of the majority; second, the fact that outside of the pious United States, and especially in Europe, both the number and the proportion of those who call themselves atheists or agnostics has indeed risen markedly in the last hundred years; and third, the plain fact that during the past two centuries the *intellectual elite* (i.e., those who actually have some claim to expertise on matters of religion, philosophy, and science) have indeed become overwhelmingly skeptical in regard to the existence of a "conscious Creator."

The bulk of *Letter to a Man in the Fire* deals with two queries put to Price by his young friend Jim Fox:

1. Was our universe created by an intelligent power; and if so, is the Creator conscious of its creatures and benignly concerned for their lives?
2. If the answer to both halves of that question is Yes, how can a gifted young human being be tormented and perhaps killed early? (LM 25)

Price answers a "troubled Yes" (LM 25) to the first query, although he is aware that the two-part question could be answered in a number of ways. It is scarcely surprising that the most obvious answer—"There is no Creator and there never was. The universe is pure unillumined matter where senseless atoms and vicious creatures stage the awful pageants of their wills" (LM 54)—is one Price rejects out of hand: "A creation without a Creator [is] even more unimaginable than the mind and intentions of a single such Maker" (LM 54). What could be more obvious than that Price has duped himself by a fixation on a mere *word?* If the *word* "creation" implies a Creator, the simple and unambiguous solution is to refer to the universe by some other word or phrase — say, "conglomeration of variegated entities." There is now no *logical* difficulty in regarding such a thing as being self-generated; and scientists of all stripes have been pretty diligent in tracing the precise origin and evolution of every such entity to its current state.

The crux of the matter really rests upon the belief that God is both omnipotent and benevolent. As Walter Kaufmann noted, it is this conjunction of attributes that makes the theist writhe so torturously over the "problem of evil" or suffering (why bad things happen to good people, or indeed to anyone):

> The problem arises when monotheism is enriched with — or impoverished by — two assumptions: that God is omnipotent and that God is just. In fact, popular theism goes beyond merely asserting God's justice and claims that God is "good," that he is morally perfect, that he hates suffering, that he loves man, and that he is infinitely merciful, far transcending all human mercy, love, and perfection. Once these assumptions are granted, the problem arises: why, then, is there all the suffering we know? And as long as these assumptions are granted, this question cannot be answered.[1]

Price does not wish to acknowledge the validity of Kaufmann's conclusion, but he ties himself into knots in the process. In particular, he cannot bring himself to contemplate the pseudopolytheistic solution of a countervailing force of evil in the world ("there seems to me no necessity for Satan or any other demonic power — not immensely powerful demons, in any case — in the workings of our world" [LM 55]), even though this would also be a logically consistent (if, perhaps, not a very scientifically plausible) solution of the difficulty. Evidently Price, although wedded to the belief that the gospels and even many parts of the Old Testament are eyewitness accounts of actual events, does not want to believe the plain evidence of Matthew ("Then was Jesus led up of the spirit into the wilderness to be tempted of the devil" [Matt. 4:1]) or of Revelation ("And the devil that deceived them was cast into the lake of fire and brimstone, where the beast and the false prophet are, and shall be tormented day and

night for ever and ever" [Rev. 20:10]). Another solution — that God is
not benevolent, or at least not consistently so — is also something Price
is most reluctant to acknowledge; as he pungently puts it, "I suspect
that very few human creatures would confess to believing that we're
made and managed by a psychopath of universal proportions" (LM
85), even though this view, too, is rather more logically unassailable
than the one Price evidently holds.

So what, in the end, is Price left with? How can he justify a loving
and all-powerful God with the existence of pain and suffering? One
solution Price cannot adopt is the notion that C. S. Lewis arrived at:
that all pain and suffering is deserved — that those who suffer it are
somehow wicked and evil. Even though such a conception is
embodied in that celebrated couplet from the *New England Primer* ("In
Adam's fall / We sinned all"), it so obviously flies in the face of
common human experience (and, in any case, would not be especially
comforting to Price's young friend, who presumably did not "deserve"
to contract cancer) that it collapses of its own absurdity. But Price
adopts a variant of the idea, suggesting that God's wrath may fall
upon the innocent as a kind of byproduct of his punishment of sinners: "I have no reluctance in believing that a just God who chooses
to survey the human spectacle will find sources of outrage so flagrant
as to warrant his responding with a ferocity that may consume
bystanders who are more or less innocent" (LM 49). I don't think
Price realizes what he is saying here. Can an omnipotent God be so
careless, clumsy, and heedless as to injure innocent "bystanders" in
the process of taking out his vengeance upon the guilty? Who could
possibly love or worship such an entity? When, in war, an army mows
down civilians as well as enemy troops, are they not habitually, and
rightly, considered to be guilty of "crimes against humanity"? Can
Price really acknowledge with insouciance a god who commits such
acts with regularity?

Another device that Price uses with great frequency — one that we
have already seen in a number of other contexts — is simple evasion,
especially in his use of language. We are now asked to believe that "a
fathering God . . . may be all things, creative and destructive, to his

creatures and that each of these things is *good*, whatever our immediate evaluation of it, and good precisely because it is the will of that
Father and in some way fulfills the intent of his ongoing care for all
that exists" (LM 76–77). Does this not rob the word *good* of all
meaning? To say that anything God does is good merely because he
does it is not only to argue in circles but could justify even the most
appalling and sadistic behavior on the part of a deity; after all, it must
"in some way" be fulfilling his aims, whatever they may be. Similarly,
Price states, "I know I believe that God loves his creation, whatever
his kind of *love* means for you and me" (LM 84). If the "love" shown
by God is equivalent to what in every other context would have to be
termed hatred or indifference, what kind of love is it? Price is really
reverting to a very old dodge—the "God works in mysterious ways"
trope. He is quite unashamed in stating it bluntly: "I even suspect that
God is more of an enigma than he's capable of telling us, given the fact
that he made us with such limited instruments of perception" (LM
81). Price doesn't have the faintest realization of what he is letting
himself in for. The difference between saying "I believe in God but
know nothing about his nature, attributes, or intentions" and saying
"I don't know whether there is a God or not" is, to put it mildly, not
immediately apparent. I am reminded of A. J. Ayer's bland delin-
eation of the conventional attributes of God:

> Those who believe that there is just one God are in general agree-
> ment that he is an intelligent person, or something like one, that he
> feels emotions such as love or moral indignation, that he is incorpo-
> real, except in the case of the Christian God, when, for a period of
> about thirty years, if one assumes the identity of the Son and the
> Father, he had what are ordinarily supposed to be the incompatible
> properties of being both corporeal and incorporeal, that, again with
> this exception, he is not located in space, though capable of acting in
> space, that he is either eternal or with the same exception not located
> in time, though capable of acting in time, that he created the world
> and continues to oversee it, that he is not subject to change, that he
> is all-powerful and all-knowing, that he is morally perfect and conse-
> quently supremely benevolent, and that he necessarily exists.

To which Ayer, with a dry understatement only the British can manage, adds: "There may be some doubt whether the predicates that are ascribed to this one God are all of them meaningful or mutually consistent."[2]

But Price's ventures into buffoonery have not yet reached their pinnacle. They do so in a memorable passage in which he takes the Panglossian view that but for the intervention of God things in this world might be even worse than they are: "Yet God appears often to lean in unpredictably to alter physical laws and to balk the power of his Satan and then to tilt the board of the universe in a direction which God desires" (LM 55). Are there any instances of such tilting? Price thinks he has found one: "A plague mysteriously burns itself out" (LM 55). Ah! so we are now to be grateful that when the Black Death killed one-quarter or one-third of the European population, it did not kill half or two-thirds! Very kind of God to have intervened before more serfs and villeins were carted off to mass graves. Does Price have any other instances up his sleeve? Be assured, he does: "a nuclear standoff on the order of the Cuban missile crisis of 1962 dissolves in a matter of hours" (LM 55). Read that carefully, my friends. Let it not be thought that anything so vulgar as political or military expediency inspired the Catholic John F. Kennedy and the atheist Krushchev not to blow up the world—it was really God at work. How exactly God altered "physical laws" to bring about the resolution of the Cuban missile crisis is not entirely evident to my hard-headed cranium, but no doubt Price can tell us if he chooses.

I don't believe I need say any more. Let us leave this dunce cap on Reynolds Price's head and move on.

Annie Dillard is, if possible, even more moony and muddle-headed than Price, which is only fitting for a poet—or what passes for a poet in this most unpoetical age. Dillard (b. 1945) is a respected poet, novelist, essayist, memoirist, editor, and what-have-you, and her work is filled with earnest and bombastic reflections about God. In *An American Childhood* (1987) she seems to me a bit cagey about her religious indoctrination, but finally admits that she grew up as a Protestant (AC 33) and went to a Presbyterian church camp for four summers in her childhood; at this time, she confesses: "I had a head for religious ideas. They were the first ideas I ever encountered. They made other ideas seem mean" (AC 133). Much later she acknowledges, not surprisingly, that "I had got religion at summer camp" (AC 195). She is now, however, a Roman Catholic, but she also exhibits considerable sympathy toward Judaism.

It is a bit odd that Dillard's nail-biting monograph on the problem of evil, *For the Time Being* (1999), appeared within a few months of Reynolds Price's *Letter to a Man in the Fire*, but her concerns on this subject far antedate this silly book. Consider *Holy the Firm* (1977), whose opening sentence—"Every day is a god, each day is a god, and holiness holds forth in time" (HF 11)—perfectly captures the intellectual murkiness of this windy essay. In large part a rather pitiable attempt to imitate Thoreau's appreciation of natural beauty, the essay also features some religious maunderings inspired by a plane crash that resulted in a seven-year-old girl receiving severe burns over much of her body. Her random utterance that "we do need reminding, not of what God can do, but of what he cannot do, or will not" (HF 61) points to the solution Dillard reaches in *For the Time Being*: the renunciation of God's omnipotence. We have seen that Price cannot bring himself to go this far, and that he accordingly ties himself in knots in his attempt to assert both God's omnipotence and his benevolence. Dillard is quite content to retain only the latter, even though it means jettisoning the former. "For I know it as a given that God is all good" (HF 47), she opines, although how this magisterial utterance is to be reconciled with one on the very previous page ("Knowledge is impossible" [HF 46]) is anyone's guess. Indeed, Dillard is perfectly happy to worship a god of whom she admits she knows very little: "I know only enough of God to want to worship him, by any means ready to hand" (HF 55).

The renunciation of God's omnipotence is a common feature among liberal theologians of the past half-century and does not call for specific comment. Dillard's *For the Time Being* is explicit on the issue. I have no particular interest in studying the bulk of this dismally meandering treatise: its back-patting author's note ("This is a nonfiction first-person narrative, but it is not intimate, and its narratives keep breaking. Its form is unusual, its scenes are remote, its focus wide, and its tone austere. Its pleasures are almost purely mental" [FT ix]); its utterances ranging from the inane ("Judaism and Christianity, like other great religions, have irreconcilable doctrinal differences, both within and without" [FT 27]) to the opaque ("We are earth's organs and limbs; we are syllables God utters from his mouth" [FT 133]); its fragmentary presentation of a multiplicity of narratives—on birth defects, on Teilhard de Chardin's travels in China in 1923, on Dillard's own trip to Israel, on sand, clouds, and the like—that have not the faintest thematic relationship to one another and which Dillard herself makes no attempt to link into any kind of unity. What is of minimal interest is how resolutely Dillard proclaims that God is not all-powerful:

> It is "fatal," Teilhard said of the old belief that we suffer at the hands of God omnipotent. It is fatal to reason. It does not work. The omnipotence of God makes no sense if it requires the all-causingness of God. Good people quit God altogether at this point, and throw out the baby with the bath, perhaps because they last looked into God in their childhoods, and have not changed their views of divinity since. It is not the tooth fairy. In fact, even Aquinas dissolved the fatal problem of natural, physical evil by tinkering with God's omnipotence. As Baron von Hügel noted, Aquinas said that "the Divine Omnipotence must not be taken as the power to effect any imaginable thing, but only the power to effect what is within the nature of things." (FT 84–85)

Dillard, moreover, does not wish to adopt the view of the ancient Jewish theologian Rabbi Akiva that "God punishes the good . . . in this short life, for their few sins, and rewards them eternally in the world to come. Similarly, God rewards the evildoers in this short life for their few good deeds, and punishes them eternally in the world to come." Although this is an entirely consistent (if unprovable) thesis, Dillard regards it as a "harsh" (FT 30) doctrine.

It need hardly be pointed out that in making these assertions

Dillard is flatly contradicting the Old Testament, which plainly admits that God is omnipotent but not necessarily (in spite of routine and mechanical mentions of God's "mercy") benevolent. On the very page where she reiterates her idea of "the old fatal-to-reason belief that we suffer at the hands of God omnipotent" (FT 117) she quotes the celebrated passage in Isaiah 45:7 that says exactly the opposite: "I [God] form the light, and create darkness: I make peace, and create evil: I the Lord do all these things."

That God is not omnipotent is, indeed, a way out of the logical difficulties presented by the problem of evil, and Dillard does not much concern herself with whether her notions of the very existence of God are well founded or not. Although she boldly proclaims that "We agree that we want to think straight" (FT 130), she does not deliver on the promise. It is no surprise that she reveals a quick and irrational prejudice against science: "What use is material science as a philosophy or world view if it cannot explain our intelligence and our consciousness?" (FT 93). Here is a prototypical instance of an author assuming that his or her own ignorance is coterminous with the ignorance of the entire human race. Dillard is evidently unaware that "material science" has gone a pretty long way in explaining our intelligence and our consciousness in terms that do not require the assumption of a deity. All Dillard can do to justify her own beliefs is to engage in a series of intellectual dodges: "And 'faith,' crucially, is not assenting intellectually to a series of doctrinal propositions; it is living in conscious and rededicated relationship with God" (FT 147). This is the old "religion as a way of life" smoke screen, but its very formulation conceals a question-begging "doctrinal proposition"—the proposition of God's very existence, which Dillard has accepted as the starting point rather than as the end result of intellectual inquiry.

What solution, then, does Dillard offer? What is God's function in the universe if he is not to be held responsible for either the natural or the moral evils that plague this earth? Dillard asks the question herself: "Then what, if anything, does he do? If God does not cause everything that happens, does God cause anything that happens? Is God completely out of the loop?" (FT 167). Her solutions are worse than useless. Here is one: "God . . . shows an edge of himself to souls who seek him" (FT 167)—of course he does! Who else but one seeking God would find him? How about this? "God participates in bad conditions here by including them in his being and ultimately overcoming them" (FT 169). If any intelligible idea can be squeezed out of that sentence, I would be grateful to be informed what it is. I suppose we are to thank God for "ultimately" getting rid of Hitler, Stalin, Pol Pot, and all the other human horrors in the history of humankind before they killed even more people than they did.

Dillard's final solution is something she calls pan-entheism:

> Rabbi Menachem Nahum of Chernobyl: "All being itself is derived from God and the presence of the Creator is in each created thing." This double notion is pan-entheism—a word to which I add a hyphen to emphasize its difference from pantheism. Pan-entheism, according to David Tracy, theologian at the University of Chicago, is the private view of most Christian intellectuals today. Not only is God immanent in everything, as plain pantheists hold, but more profoundly everything is simultaneously in God, within God the transcendent. There is a divine, not just bushes. (FT 176–77)

Aside from the fact that all this is nothing but a series of unsupported assertions, I again fail to find anything coherent or intelligible in any of it. Of course, the notion that "everything is . . . God" relieves one of the burden of proving that God actually exists: all you do is point to any object in the universe and say, "God is in there somewhere!" But how meaningful is it to say that a bush or a tree or a human being or a cockroach or a spiral nebula is "within God the transcendent" without making even a makeshift attempt to indicate what *difference* God makes by his immanence? What *use* is such a worldview? How does it account for anything? If God is everywhere, God is nowhere.

❆   ❆   ❆

Reynolds Price and Annie Dillard are by no means alone in committing follies on the subject of religion; an entire treatise could be written on the vacuous, nonsensical, meaningless, fallacious, and simply erroneous religious opinions of some of the greatest figures in Western literature. To choose only a handful of American writers of the past century and a half, here is an amusing sampler of fatuity:

Henry David Thoreau in his journals (1852): "The bigoted and sectarian forget that without religion or devotion of some kind nothing great was ever accomplished."[3] I would like Mr. Thoreau to inform me how, on this principle, the collected writings of Bertrand Russell could have come into existence. Or is Russell's achievement not "great"? Or perhaps Thoreau is allowing himself enough wiggle room in his "devotion of some kind" comment to suggest that non-religious figures accomplish great things by some ill-defined pseudo-religious means?

Ralph Waldo Emerson:

> I am ready to give, as often before, the first simple foundation of my belief, that the Author of Nature has not left himself without a witness in any sane mind: that the moral sentiment speaks to every man the law after which the Universe was made; that we find parity, identity of design, through Nature, and benefit to be the uniform aim: that there is a force always at work to make the best better and the worst good.[4]

The upshot of the first part of this remark is that all atheists or even agnostics are lunatics, and as for the grotesquely naive optimism of the last part, no comment is necessary.

Here is a bit of gibberish from Robert Frost:

> As we are driven in flight by those behind us, so we drive others in front of us and then others in front of them. All is flight from fright and force behind. Progress is escape. Civilization [is] sublimation emerging in terrified flight from someone emerging in terrified flight from someone emerging in terrified flight from God. So we find God again. He is the primordial fear that started all this escaping. He started the drive of existence. No one gets anywhere except from the fear of God.[5]

If anyone can attach a coherent meaning to this utterance, he is doing better than I.

Listen now to the sage wisdom of the Catholic Flannery O'Connor on religious censorship:

> The business of protecting souls from dangerous literature belongs properly to the Church. All fiction, even when it satisfies the requirements of art, will not turn out to be suitable for everyone's consumption, and if in some instance, the Church sees fit to forbid the faithful to read a work without permission, the author, if he is a Catholic, will be thankful that the Church is willing to perform this service for him. It means that he can limit himself to the demands of art.[6]

So now we are to believe that not only is the Catholic Church to decide what is "dangerous" and what isn't but that authors are to express gratitude for being censored! I regret to say, however, that what authors under this schema are "limited" to are not the demands of art but the demands of the Church.

The Catholic Mary McCarthy is just as scintillating: "I don't believe in God—that's just a fact, it's not an act of will; I can't even conceive of God, so there it is. But ethics came to me in the frame of Christian teaching, and even though I don't believe in an after-life I'm still concerned with the salvation of my soul. I'm quite incapable of switching to an atheist's ethics, if there is such a thing."[7] How a Catholic can fail to believe in God or the afterlife, and yet still be concerned about the salvation of the soul, is something only she can answer. And I'm mighty grateful for that thundering vote of confidence as to the mere existence of atheist ethics.

I had better stop; it is all too painful and ridiculous. The next time a novelist, poet, composer, painter, sculptor, filmmaker, or any other such person takes it into his or her mind to pontificate on God, my only response will be: Please don't.

NOTES

References to Reynolds Price's works occur in the text as follows: LM = *Letter to a Man in the Fire: Does God Exist and Does He Care?* (New York: Scribner's, 1999); PG = *A Palpable God: Thirty Stories Translated from the Bible with an Essay on the Origins and Life of Narrative* (New York: Atheneum, 1978). References to Annie Dillard's works occur in the text as follows: AC = *An American Childhood* (New York: Harper & Row, 1987); FT = *For the Time Being* (New York: Knopf, 1999); HF = *Holy the Firm* (New York: Harper & Row, 1977).

1. Walter Kaufmann, *The Faith of a Heretic* (Garden City, N.Y.: Doubleday, 1961), p. 151.

2. A. J. Ayer, *The Central Questions of Philosophy* (1973; reprint, New York: William Morrow, 1975), p. 212.

3. Henry David Thoreau, *Journal* (July 27, 1852), in *The Writings of Henry David Thoreau: Journal,* ed. Bradford Torrey (Boston: Houghton Mifflin, 1906), vol. 4, p. 262.

4. Ralph Waldo Emerson, "Speech at Second Annual Meeting of the Free Religious Association" (1869), in *Miscellanies,* vol. 11 of *The Complete Works of Ralph Waldo Emerson* (Boston: Houghton Mifflin, 1904), p. 486.

5. Quoted in Robert Faggen, *Robert Frost and the Challenge of Darwin* (Ann Arbor: University of Michigan Press, 1997), p. 261. The document quoted is an unpublished (and evidently undated) manuscript at Dartmouth.

6. Flannery O'Connor, "The Church and the Fiction Writer" (1957), *Collected Works* (New York: Library of America, 1988), p. 810.

7. Mary McCarthy, "A World out of Joint" (interview with Miriam Gross, *Observer,* October 14, 1979), in *Conversations with Mary McCarthy,* ed. Carol Gelderman (Jackson: University of Mississippi Press, 1991), p. 172.

8.

BEAUTIFUL SOULS

Elisabeth Kübler-Ross

The existence of the "soul" and its survival after death are the most irresponsible and preposterous conceptions in the entire range of theistic thought. They are the least justified by scientific evidence and are overwhelmingly refuted by a titanically immense body of evidence to the contrary. At the same time, these conceptions are among the hoariest and most persistent idées fixes of the common people, and anthropology has traced their origin to the farthest reaches of prehistory. To anyone aware of the democratic fallacy, this persistence need cause no surprise, for it is exactly in this domain of life after death that Ambrose Bierce's definition of religion ("a daughter of Hope and Fear, explaining to Ignorance the nature of the Unknowable")[1] comes into play. Few of us want to die; few of us can even envision utter non-existence and absence of consciousness; but since no one can fail to acknowledge the reality of death, the next best thing is to fancy that some nebulous part of us escapes the dissolution of our physical bodies and lives on somewhere or other, retaining consciousness without bodily functions. And, as Antony Flew points out, the matter will forever lack definitive proof one way or the other (in spite of the overwhelming probability of one view over the other): "If . . . it is the believers who are mistaken, then they will never be embarrassed by a posthumous awareness of their error, any more than we can expect to enjoy the satisfaction of saying to them, 'We told you so!'"[2]

In the late nineteenth and early twentieth centuries, it was thought that experiments by the Society for Psychical Research and other spiritualists would supply definitive evidence of the existence of wandering "souls" separated from their bodies either by death or in some kind of trance state (the "astral body"). Not many sane people accept such "evidence" today. All sorts of troublesome queries emerge from this issue: If *all* human souls (whether they are headed for the northward or the southward destination) survive their bodily deaths, how is it that out of the billions of people who have lived and died on the earth only a tiny fraction of them have purportedly made their presence known to the living? Why is it that such souls reveal themselves only to those who, whether from grief or wishful thinking, most want to hear from them? Why do these souls not tell us anything interesting about life and the cosmos? Have they learned nothing after crossing the Great Divide? These and other irritating queries make us ruefully admit the truth of H. L. Mencken's pronouncement: "I believe that the evidence for immortality is no better than the evidence for witches, and deserves no more respect."[3]

What, after all, is the soul? What place, if any, does it occupy in the body? What is its function? Can it survive outside the body? Is it, indeed, immortal? These questions have vexed the pious from the dawn of history, but their answers are today becoming increasingly hedged with doubts and equivocations as knowledge relentlessly advances and suggests strongly that the soul has no existence whatever, and that the very word is merely a clumsy makeshift term for a wide variety of mental, emotional, and psychological functions in the human body whose workings are becoming increasingly and embarrassingly well known.

If the soul has any existence at all, where is it in the body? Why have such pestiferous nuisances as physicians, biologists, and anatomists not been able to find it and attach a suitable Latin name to it? Virtually all ancient thinkers, including the devout Augustine, believed the soul to be material, but the claim becomes awkward when every part of the human body can be shown to serve some other function. Is the soul, then, immaterial? If so, then another problem immediately supervenes: How does an immaterial entity interact with a material entity? Surely we are beyond the stage of following Descartes' celebrated venture into fatuity in assuming that the pineal gland acts as the mediator between material body and immaterial soul!

But the key question that concerns the religious is not the existence or nature of the soul—they accept that, as they accept the existence of God and many other implausible and unprovable assertions, as a given, and as something not requiring proof—but its survival after the death of the body, and indeed its actual immortality after it rids itself of its cumbersome material shell. Not a great many philosophers today openly espouse immortality: Richard Swinburne (*The Coherence of Theism*, 1977; *The Evolution of the Soul*, 1986) seems a lonely exception, and his evasions, non sequiturs, and question-beggings have been adequately and amusingly shot down by Antony Flew and others. But the belief appears to persist not only among the great unwashed but among the majority of theologians as well—largely because they realize that several central tenets of their faith are dependent upon it. If the soul does not exist and cannot survive the body, what happens to the notions of heaven and hell (where good and bad souls are supposed to go) and, more generally, to the notion that God, in his infinite wisdom and power, has managed to arrange things so that the injustice so obtrusively evident on earth is remedied after our deaths? Why an all-powerful God could not have arranged things so that there is a bit more justice on earth, rendering this kind of posthumous evening-out unnecessary, does not appear to concern the faithful.

The historical arguments for the immortality of the soul are all so palpably absurd that it would appear to be akin to shooting fish in a barrel to mow them down at this late stage of civilization. And yet, one particular argument—intimately related to the redressing of balances discussed above—is worth some attention, because it has had an unusually long life and continues to be voiced in various modified guises even today. It is most coherently found in Marsilio Ficino's *Theologica Platonica de Immortalite Animarum* (1485). I am not sufficiently interested in this issue to care whether Ficino was the first to enunciate this argument; I rather doubt it. In the paraphrase of Ardis B. Collins, the argument proceeds as follows:

> Man, [Ficino] says, suffers from a chronic dissatisfaction with his life on this earth. Restless in soul, weak in body, frustrated by the poverty of all he sees, he continually yearns for something more fulfilling than anything he can find in his earthly environment. If he had no hope of a better life, nothing would be more tragic, more unhappy, more truncated than the life of man. This desire for a better life is the foundation for Ficino's position on human immortality. It is the evidence to which he appeals when he assures us that man, who above all things is the image of God, cannot be doomed to live out his destiny within the limits and frustrations of his earthly existence. His destiny must answer the scope of his yearning. If this mortal existence cannot fill it, then there must be something beyond mortality which does.[4]

The substance of this argument can be broken down into the following syllogism:

1) There is a universal human tendency to believe in a life after death—a life in which the pains and misfortunes of earthly existence would (for a suitably select band of the genuinely "good" and/or pious) be compensated for by the bliss of heaven.
2) God would not have implanted this universal desire in us if it were impossible of fulfillment.
3) Therefore, the belief in an afterlife must have a corresponding reality.

Put this way, it becomes painfully obvious that this formulation is riddled with fallacies and question-beggings. Here are some of them:

1) It assumes, without proof, the existence of God.
2) It assumes, without proof, that God is omnipotent and benevolent.
3) It assumes, without proof, that God, even if omnipotent and benevolent, has the inclination to grant us every wish that we happen to have.
4) It assumes that the desire for immortality is universal, when it is quite obviously not so.
5) It assumes that the belief in immortality, even if universal, is necessarily a true belief rather than merely a universal error, such as (at various times in human history) the belief in witches, or in the flatness of the earth, or in the sun's revolution around the earth.

John Stuart Mill pungently and wittily addresses the second and third of these points in *Three Essays on Religion* (1874):

The benevolence of the divine Being may be perfect, but his power being subject to unknown limitations, we know not that he could have given us what we so confidently assert that he must have given; *could* (that is) without sacrificing something more important. Even his benevolence, however justly inferred, is by no means indicated as the interpretation of his whole purpose, and since we cannot tell how far other purposes may have interfered with the exercise of his benevolence, we know not that he *would*, even if he could have granted us eternal life. With regard to the supposed improbability of his having given the wish without its gratification, the same answer may be made; the scheme which either limitation of power, or conflict of purposes, compelled him to adopt, may have *required* that we should have the wish although it were not destined to be gratified. One thing, however, is quite certain in respect to God's government of the world; that he either could not, or would not, grant to us every thing we wish. We wish for life, and he has granted some life: that we wish (or some of us wish) for a boundless extent of life and that it is not granted, is no exception to the ordinary modes of his government. Many a man would like to be a Croesus or an Augustus Caesar, but has his wishes gratified only to the moderate extent of a pound a week or the Secretaryship of his Trades Union.[5]

Some theists wish to put forward a purely psychological argument for immortality. They assert that without a belief in the afterlife, life on earth would become so meaningless and futile (ending, as it does, in the utter finality of death) that it would induce appalling and possibly suicidal despair in a great majority of human beings, so that the belief, even if false or unprovable, is useful to maintain for purposes of psychological well-being and the preservation of the social fabric. I cannot even begin to understand this conception. No doubt there have been, and continue to be, many people whose lives on earth are so wretched, and so unlikely to be significantly improved, that a belief in some kind of redressing of the balance comes naturally, but whether we are to regard this psychological expedient as in any way intellectually justified is another matter altogether. The very strong possibility that there will never be a redressing of the balance—that in this world the "good" (however defined) will in some, perhaps many, cases suffer and the "bad" (however defined) will in some, perhaps many, cases prosper—may simply be a part of the human condition. That may just be the way things are. And yet, it is quite evident that even if that is how things are there is no necessity for things to be so, and that these injustices are largely a product of social maladjustments that governments and other responsible bodies ought to make a somewhat greater effort to eliminate. Indeed, belief in an afterlife could be said to *hinder* the elimination of these maladjustments by inculcating a fatalism ("things will be all right in the next life") that weakens any incentive toward social reform.

But the whole notion that without an afterlife all one's actions in life are rendered valueless or meaningless is exceptionally bizarre, and can only be the product of a conception of life as a kind of marathon with only a single goal (Heaven) rather than as an ongoing *process* in which pleasure or satisfaction is to be derived from successive experiences—experiences that are open to all, and that can be infused with an intrinsic value all apart from any fancied consummation. I imagine this was what H. P. Lovecraft was getting at when, in one of his noblest utterances, he wrote:

> No change of faith can dull the colours or magic of spring, or dampen the native exuberance of perfect health; and the consolations of taste and intellect are infinite. It is easy to remove the mind from harping on the lost illusion of immortality. The disciplined intellect fears nothing and craves no sugar-plum at the day's end, but is content to accept life and serve society as best it may. Personally I should not care for immortality in the least. There is nothing better than oblivion, since in oblivion there is no wish unfulfilled. We had it before we were born, yet did not complain. Shall we then whine because we know it will return? It is Elysium enough for me, at any rate.[6]

Whether any significant proportion of the human race will ever be sufficiently mature and civilized to adopt this sane outlook is not something that concerns me overly.

There has been a great deal of talk about soul lately, although it is inevitably tainted with vagueness and imprecision. One can point, for example, to Thomas Moore's best-selling *Care of the Soul* (1992), a pop psychology self-help manual that seeks to claim that the great malady of the twentieth century is its "loss of soul."[7] Regrettably, Moore admits at the start that "it is impossible to define precisely what the soul is" (M xi), putting forth the standard mystical argument that "definition is an intellectual enterprise anyway; the soul prefers to imagine" (M xi)—an assertion that makes one wonder how Moore can know what the soul prefers if he is unable to define precisely what the soul is. But this silly book, full of owlish platitudes very similar to those found in the New Thought manuals of the early twentieth century ("Many of us spend time and energy trying to be something we are not" [M 121]), seems to be putting forth nothing more than an elementary adjuration to infuse greater emotional and aesthetic depth into the simple functions of daily life, although why we need someone like Moore to tell us that is beyond my understanding. It is a small mercy, I suppose, that Moore admits the soul has nothing "to do with immortality" (M 5), although he unfortunately follows up this utterance with the perfectly meaningless assertion: "We don't have to take 'immortality' to mean literal life-after-death, but rather the soul's ever-present depth" (M 44).

The psychologist Elisabeth Kübler-Ross (b. 1926) is a more interesting case. She is an excellent example of two traits that lead otherwise intelligent people (many of them scientists) into religious belief—childhood indoctrination and an ignorance of important branches of knowledge (in Kübler-Ross's case, philosophy, anthropology, and the history and psychology of religion) touching upon the sources and continuance of religious belief. This estimable lady has done landmark work on the treatment of dying patients—embodied in the important treatise *On Death and Dying* (1969)—but it appears that her work on this issue gradually warped her mind and led her into beliefs and experiences that only the most egregiously gullible occultist could ever credit.

A good place to start is Kübler-Ross's own autobiography, *The Wheel of Life* (1997), for in this remarkable work she not only reveals, quite unwittingly, her own descent from sober scientist to incorrigible mystic but, just as unwittingly, provides all the ammunition necessary for a refutation of her central contentions regarding the "soul" and life after death. We find in this book that Kübler-Ross has by this time, as she modestly states, found "all the answers to life's big questions" (WL 205). But one would suppose that such all-encompassing wisdom would have led her to come up with something a little less inane and meaningless than "Our todays depend on our yesterdays and our tomorrows depend on our todays" (WL 262), one of the epigrams that persisted in her memory from a journal that was subsequently destroyed. Or how about this?—"you may not get what you want, but God always gives you what you need" (WL 111)—a formulation that could fit every conceivable situation, as could the following: "Life ends when you have learned everything you are supposed to learn" (WL 157). Similarly, pop psychology such as *"Everyone goes through hardship in life. The more you go through, the more you learn and grow"* (WL 18; yes, I regret to say the italics are the author's) is just the sort of thing one is likely to find in an earnest schoolgirl's notebook.

Kübler-Ross makes plain that, in spite of various tussles throughout her life with a succession of odious or small-minded theologians, "as a child I definitely had a spiritual inclination" (WL 41). Christmas, we learn, "was the best time of year" (WL 33) when she was growing up. She married a Jewish man, Emanuel Ross, although she evidently continued practicing the Protestantism in which she was raised. After the first of several miscarriages, we learn, "the only consolation I had was my belief in a higher power" (WL 111). All this puts the lie to Kübler-Ross's contention that prior to her work with dying patients she was a "skeptical semi-believer, to put it mildly, and not interested in issues of life after death" (LD 44). It is clear that her religious orientation was present in her subconscious all along, and only required certain stimuli (themselves produced, in all likelihood, by religious mania) to push her over the edge into full-fledged belief in life after death.

But Kübler-Ross gets into philosophical difficulties in very short order. She wants to maintain that "there are no accidents in life" (WL 16) and that "I was destined to work with dying patients" (WL 16); but only a few pages later she proclaims: "The greatest gift God has granted us is free will" (WL 21). Evidently she is unaware that these statements are philosophically in conflict; the first two espousing determinism and the third free will. If nothing happens by accident, then free will is an impossibility: our apparent "free" choice in taking or not taking certain courses of action is merely a psychological illusion, for that supposed exercise of choice is only one of the steps leading to some "destined" result.

During and after the war, Kübler-Ross worked with Polish refugees, many of them from the concentration camps. She encountered one German woman who was about to be herded into the gas chamber: "By some miracle, by some divine intervention, the door would not close with her in there" (WL 77). This certainly seems to be a miracle—until we read the next sentence: "It was too crowded." Evidently God did not consider all the other millions of victims of

Hitler's gas chambers to be worthy of divine intervention. The woman concludes: "God has chosen her . . . to survive and tell future genera- tions about the barbarity she had witnessed" (WL 77). Kübler-Ross passes no judgment upon this opinion, so presumably she accepts it. As a psychological ploy it is certainly a plausible phenomenon; other survivors have adopted the same strategy to allay their guilt in sur- viving when so many of their relatives and friends perished. But as an account of what actually happened it leaves much to be desired. An omnipotent God could surely have prevented the Holocaust if he had so chosen. One is reminded of what a prisoner whispered into Elie Wiesel's ear after some particularly heinous act in the camps: "Where is God now?"

A turning point in Kübler-Ross's career occurred around 1970, when a hospital patient named Mrs. Schwartz had what is now termed a near-death experience (NDE). Ross was fascinated with this event (or, rather, with Schwartz's account of it) and, in conjunction with a Reverend Gaines, began a systematic investigation of NDEs, eventu- ally collecting information on some 20,000 cases. All this sounds like a model of scientific precision, but there is much reason to think other- wise. Kübler-Ross, along with Raymond A. Moody, who was working on the same subject independently, have certainly been chiefly respon- sible for the popularization of NDEs, but whether her conclusions— "Death does not exist—not in its traditional definition . . . man also had a soul and spirit, a higher reason for life, a poetry, something more than mere existence and survival, something that continued on" (WL 189) — are sound is highly problematical. Another scholar on the subject, Ken- neth Ring—hardly an unsympathetic colleague, as he too, for all the purportedly "scientific" rigor of his research, concludes that "we con- tinue to have a conscious existence after our physical death and that the core experience [of NDE] does represent its beginning, a glimpse to come"[8]—points to the shortcomings of Kübler-Ross's work:

> Neither Kübler-Ross's nor Moody's data have yet been presented in a
> form that renders them susceptible to scientific analysis and evaluation
> . . . although Kübler-Ross has spoken extensively about her findings,
> she has nowhere published them, and thus what the public record con-

sists of are her summary descriptions and illustrative case histories—hardly a solid basis for a scientific judgment of her material.[9]

This was written in 1980; twenty years later Kübler-Ross still has not published her findings but only her own accounts of them. What, exactly, does she have to hide?

Kübler-Ross confidently claims that "in all cases the experiences were so similar that the accounts had to be true" (WL 188). Based upon these accounts, she enumerates five "phases" through which souls pass after death—floating out of their bodies, being "guided by their guardian angel" (WL 191), seeing a bright light, etc.—but it is quite clear from her own account that not all NDEs go through each or all of these phases. Elsewhere, oddly enough, Kübler-Ross specifies only three stages (LD 10). Ring identifies ten stages in the process, although he is a bit more open about the fact that not a single one of his NDEs went through all ten of them. Kübler-Ross dynamites her own case by remarking of one particular phase where "people went through a life review, a process in which they confronted the totality of their lives" (WL 192): "I interpreted this as being heaven or hell. Maybe both" (WL 192). I know of no theology ever devised by human beings that fails to distinguish between heaven and hell.

Kübler-Ross's theory of NDEs is crippled by her ignorance of the psychology of religion. In a lecture she asserts that "this experience is the same for everyone regardless of whether you are an Aboriginal of Australia, a Hindu, a Moslem, a Christian, or an unbeliever" (LD 10), but it is eminently clear that prior religious indoctrination accounts for virtually all the visions, sensations, and emotions experienced by NDEs. Ring's own data show that the orthodoxly religious are vastly more inclined to have such experiences than atheists or agnostics, although he himself fails to draw the obvious conclusion from this, stating preposterously that "religiousness as such plays no determinative role in the core near-death experience."[10] Kübler-Ross makes the same mistake even more egregiously when she states ingenuously: "I never encountered a Protestant child who saw the Virgin Mary in his last minutes, yet she was perceived by many Catholic children" (LD

16). Evidently the Virgin Mary doesn't give a damn about Protestants. But what is Kübler-Ross's interpretation of this bizarre phenomenon? "It is not a matter of discrimination, you are simply received by those who meant the most to you." And elsewhere: "The only difference between people from different religious backgrounds is the presence of certain religious figures" (LD 59). Quite so!

It does not seem to have occurred to Kübler-Ross that her entire work on NDEs—or, rather, the grotesque conclusions that she draws from their supposed uniformity—is fatally vitiated by a very elementary fact: *the people in question were not actually dead.* They were all close to death, and some of them may have been (for brief periods) clinically dead, but they all revived. How, then, can their visions or sensations be included as evidence of what happens to our "souls" after death? Robert Kastenbaum, one of our most respected thanatologists, has recently raised this awkward point:

> Studies have not proven that people were dead at the time the experiences occurred which provided the basis for subsequent NDE reports. There are well studied cases in which it is clear that lives were in great jeopardy and in which the individuals did not seem capable of perception, thought, and response. Later . . . these people reported experiences that were then interpreted as having occurred while they were dead. Not established, however, was (a) convincing evidence that the person was dead; and (b) that the experience actually occurred precisely at the time when the person was out of this life.[11]

Kübler-Ross does in fact approach this vital point tentatively and apprehensively, only to shy away from it. "What I need to say before I end is that Moody's first book, *Life after Life,* which is the only one that is correct [!], is helpful, but it will not tell you what death is all about, because those are all *near*-death experiences." But then, as if this token expression of skepticism is sufficient, she proceeds dogmatically:

> *After* we shed our physical body, which is *physical* energy, we create a secondary, perfect body—meaning without blindness, without amputations, without mastectomies, without defects—with *psychic*

energy, which is man-created and manipulated by man, by our mind.

When we are permanently dead, if I can use such horrible language, irreversibly dead, then we will take on a different form that is the form that we have before birth and after death. And that is when we, in Moody's language, go through the tunnel toward the light. That light is pure *spiritual* energy. Spiritual energy is the only energy form in this Universe that cannot be manipulated by man. (DV 74)

On what evidence Kübler-Ross can justify or validate this series of preposterous utterances, *even granting the soundness of her own interpretation of NDEs,* is beyond my understanding. And that note about the purportedly "horrible" nature of irreversible death is yet another telltale sign of her own anxieties and fears.

Of the obvious claim that a great deal of what is experienced by NDEs—particularly in regard to meeting loved ones (alive or dead), coming face to face with God or Jesus or Buddha, and the like—is nothing more than a succession of wish-fulfillment fantasies, Kübler-Ross is equally dismissive:

Number one: half of our cases have been sudden, unexpected accidents or near-death experiences where people were unable to foresee what was going to hit them, as in the case of a hit-and-run driver who amputated the legs of one of our patients. And yet, when he was out of his physical body, he saw his amputated leg on the highway and at the same time was fully aware of having both of his legs on his ethereal, perfect and whole body. So we cannot assume that he had previous knowledge of the loss of his legs and would therefore project, in his own wishful thinking, that he was able to walk again.

Number two: there is also a much simpler way to rule out the projection of wishful thinking. That is to ask blind people who do not even have light perception to share with us what it was like when they had this near death experience. If it were just a dream fulfillment those people would not be able to give accurate details of their surroundings.

> We have questioned several totally blind people who were able to share with us in their near death experience and they were not only able to tell us who came into the room first, who worked on the resuscitation, but they were also able to give minute details of the attire and the clothing of all the people present, something a totally blind person, the victim of wishful thinking, would never be able to do. (DV 72)

Kübler-Ross puts great stock in these two cases, since she repeats them over and over in book after book, but as we have only her own testimony for them, analysis is difficult. In the first case, I think we can appeal to Kastenbaum's distinction between the actual NDE and the person's (later) *account* of it; it is quite likely that the person in question knew or suspected that he had lost his legs, so his "vision" of it on the highway is easily accounted for. And the cases of the blind people are in all likelihood analogous to the cases of recovered memory that caused such a ruckus several years ago, when it became quite evident that the "memories" were either knowingly or unwittingly induced by the psychiatrists themselves.

On the whole issue of NDEs, Kastenbaum's pronouncement cuts through all the nonsense of Kübler-Ross and her cohorts: "Do NDEs prove survival of death? No."[12]

As it is, Kübler-Ross has destroyed her own credibility by an amalgam of incompetence and credulousness. Her ignorance of all the sciences except that of psychiatry is painfully evident throughout her work. Consider this bit of wisdom on the history of religious belief:

> A long time ago, people were much more in touch with the issue of death and believed in heaven or life after death. It is only in the last hundred years, perhaps, that fewer and fewer people truly know that life exists after the physical body dies. We are now in a new age, and hopefully we have made a transition from an age of science and technology and materialism to a new age of genuine and authentic spirituality. (LD 42)

Let us pass over that sophistical "know"; what is more significant is Kübler-Ross's refusal to accept the plain fact that belief in life after death has declined because the authority of religion has been systematically overthrown by the advance of knowledge. It is clear that her own knowledge of, say, anthropology leaves quite a bit to be desired, as in this gem: "Man has existed for forty-seven million years and has been in its present existence, which includes the facet of divinity, for seven million years" (LD 44). Yes, folks, that is a direct quotation. Does it matter that no anthropologist dates the emergence of *Homo sapiens* earlier than one and a half to two million years ago? And where has she come up with that figure of forty-seven million years? This, in fact, is the date at which *primates* were once thought to have emerged as a distinct order of mammals, although now the date has been pushed back to as far as seventy-five million years. And yet, let us imagine that her figures are sound; what is the upshot? Why was "man" not given that "facet of divinity" (presumably the soul) in the first forty million years of his existence? Was he somehow not worthy of it? If not, why not? And how or why did God suddenly bestow this precious boon upon us? Eighty years ago H. P. Lovecraft amused himself on these points:

> One might ask, to the confounding of those who aver that men have "souls" whilst beasts have not, . . . just how the evolving organism began to acquire "spirit" after it crossed the boundary betwixt advanced ape and primitive human? It is rather hard to believe in "soul" when one has not a jot of evidence for its existence; when all the psychic life of man is demonstrated to be precisely analogous to that of other animals—presumably "soulless."[13]

But wait—it gets better. Ten months after the death of Mrs. Schwartz, the lady who had raised the whole issue of NDEs to her, Kübler-Ross actually saw the ghost of this redoubtable creature walking calmly along a hospital corridor. Not surprisingly, no one else saw her. Kübler-Ross momentarily doubted her own sanity ("Was I having a psychotic episode?" [WL 177]), but quickly came to the conclusion that the event was real. She actually admits that "I had been under some stress," but then adds: "but certainly not enough to be seeing ghosts" (WL 177)—to which the only response would seem to be, "Oh, yeah?" But let her tell it in her own words: "'Dr. Ross, I had to come back for two reasons,' she said clearly. 'Number one is to thank you and the Reverend Gaines for all you have done for me.' I touched my pen, papers and coffee cup to make sure they were real. Yes, as real as the sound of her voice. 'However, the second reason I came back is to tell you not to give up your work on death and dying . . . not yet'" (WL 177). With affecting naïveté, Kübler-Ross actually says: "How did she know I was planning to quit?"—as if a "ghost" created out of her own imagination would not know all the contents of her own mind! But for Kübler-Ross, there is only one possible interpretation: "If you are not ready for mystical experiences, you will never believe them. But if you are open, then you not only have them, and believe in them; people can hang you by your thumbnails and you will know that the experiences are absolutely real" (WL 177). Exactly. Anyone who yearns passionately—I may say neurotically— for confirmation of the existence of souls and life after death is very likely to receive it in the course of time. Is Kübler-Ross ignorant of the notorious case of Whitley Strieber, who passed lie-detector tests when asked whether he had been abducted by extraterrestrial aliens? It would be too mundane and "negative" to believe that Strieber (and Kübler-Ross) were so totally convinced of the reality of their experience that they wholeheartedly believed it. No—we must instead believe that the (psychological) reality of the experience unequivocally points to its *metaphysical* reality.

From this point on Kübler-Ross descended increasingly into more and more grotesque forms of spiritualism and mysticism. On one occasion she saw a photograph that purportedly depicted a tiny "fairy" sitting in a flower. Again she dynamites her own case by the comment "At this point in my life, I was open to anything and everything" (WL 197). Instead of expressing skepticism, she concluded: "This was proof" (WL 197). Proof of what, exactly? Kübler-Ross is not entirely clear on the matter, but evidently it ties in with her ideas on "guides" or "guardian angels," a point on which she is monotonously insistent: "I believe every person has a guardian spirit or angel" (WL 23). As if this isn't bad enough, she goes on to say that this wondrous entity actually helps pick out our parents before we are born! Once again, she unwittingly betrays the religious origin of this notion by her remark "What the church tells little children about guardian angels is based on fact" (LD 15). But let's get back to those fairies. At a later date Kübler-Ross actually took a picture of one; regrettably, the photograph was destroyed when her Virginia farm was torched by ignorant bigots who resented her taking in AIDS babies, so the "proof" is now lost. Evidently she is unaware that Arthur Conan Doyle beat her to the punch by three-quarters of a century. Devastated by the First World War (in which he lost his own son), Conan Doyle turned desperately to spiritualism and, in the process, became obsessed with the idea of photographing fairies and spirits. He published numerous books on the subject, including the priceless *The Case for Spirit Photography* (1922). Let us hear what a modern biographer of the estimable Sir Arthur has to say on the issue:

> Conan Doyle had become deeply interested in the practice of spirit photography, a form of mediumship he defined as the "remarkable power of producing extra faces, figures or objects upon photographic plates." The process was simple: a subject would pose for a photograph taken by a so-called psychic sensitive. When developed, these images were likely to display some unexpected extra element—such as a ghostly form or a disembodied head—which was said to be the work of spirit forces. Often these blurry, half-formed manifestations resembled a departed relative or a prominent figure from history. Abraham Lincoln turned up regularly. . . . the bulk of these images appear crude and unconvincing to modern eyes. Nevertheless, one can only imagine the reaction of a bereaved widow or heartsick mother as the face of a dead loved one loomed up in the shadows.
>
> Conan Doyle displayed many such photographs in his spirit lectures. One in particular showed a crowd of mourners at the London Cenotaph on Armistice Day. The image, taken during two minutes of silent prayer, showed a great fog of spirit beings hovering above the crowd—the solemn and purposeful faces of fallen war heroes. The image invariably brought audience members to tears when it was flashed on the overhead screen. Unfortunately, some of the faces were later identified as those of living football players.[14]

Still later, Kübler-Ross got involved with some spiritualists, whom she identifies only as Mr. and Mrs. B. In spite of later evidence that they were frauds, possibly engaging in sexual abuse of their charges and clearly faking several "spirits" who appeared to both Kübler-Ross and others, she desperately maintains that other "spirits" were real. I have no doubt that the B.'s were adept hypnotists who induced all these visions into Kübler-Ross and others, and that she later was able to hypnotize herself so that the "spirits" appeared to her. It is rather charming to see her affectionately taking to calling them her "spooks."

During one of these sessions one of her "spooks," Salem by name, told her a remarkable story: "Warning me that he was about to take me on a special journey, Salem explained that in another lifetime, the time of Jesus, I had been a wise and respected teacher named Isabel. Together, we traveled back to a pleasant afternoon when I had sat on a hillside, listening to Jesus preach to a group of people" (WL 203). Kübler-Ross does not elaborate upon this touching scene, but I have no doubt that Jesus appeared to her as the blond-haired Aryan of her Swiss Bible, rather than the dark-haired, olive-complexioned Jew that he probably was (assuming he existed at all). Then, around 1984, Kübler-Ross saw Jesus himself appearing on the wall of her farm-house: "He gave his blessings and disappeared. He came back again, left and then returned once more and asked me to name the farm Healing Waters Farm. 'It is a new beginning, Isabel'" (WL 243–44). I assume that last sentence was uttered by Jesus himself, so it appears that he has learned English during his long years in heaven.

At the end of *The Wheel of Life* Kübler-Ross, acting as a modern Jeremiah (although sounding more like a fifth-rate Nostradamus), warns of what can only be called the Apocalypse of Elisabeth:

> The whole planet is in trouble. This is a very tenuous time in history. Earth has been abused for too long without regard for any serious consequences. Mankind has wreaked havoc with the bounty of God's garden. Weapons, greed, materialism, destructiveness. They have become the catechism of life, the mantra of generations whose meditations on the meaning of life have gone dangerously awry.

I believe Earth will soon correct these misdeeds. Because of what mankind has done, there will be tremendous earthquakes, floods, volcanic eruptions and other natural disasters on a scale never before witnessed. Because of what mankind has forgotten, there will be enormous casualties suffered. I know this. My spooks have told me to expect upheavals and seizures of biblical proportions. How else can people be awakened? What other way is there to teach respect for nature and the necessity of spirituality? (WL 284)

There is no point in going on; it is all too pitiable. Kübler-Ross is not fazed by any of the bizarre experiences she has undergone; she swallows them all, one after the other. Even the fact that her own husband left her because of her increasing obsession with spiritualism does little to make her question her own beliefs. What is so transparently obvious to any objective observer—that Kübler-Ross's own fixation with death and dying has led to a desperate fantasy about the survival of the "soul" and its encounter with God—is entirely unperceived by Kübler-Ross herself. Her tendentious use of the "evidence" of NDEs to prove just the points she wants to prove only confirms that she has descended from a sober scientist to an hysterical special pleader. Kübler-Ross warns her skeptical colleagues that "from the scientists, humility is demanded!" (LD 12), but such humility is, for her, clearly unnecessary—*she knows!* She has all the answers to life's big questions. So her ex cathedra utterances must be accepted as the gospel truth, no matter how absurd and unscientific they appear. The fact that millions of people listen hopefully to the ravings of this absurd woman, regarding her as a prophet revealing portentous secrets from the Other Side, only proves how rarely diffused is genuine intelligence in our age.

NOTES

References to Elisabeth Kübler-Ross's works occur in the text as follows: DV = *Death Is of Vital Importance: On Life, Death and Life After Death*, ed. Göran Grip, M.D. (Barrytown, N.Y.: Station Hill Press, 1995); LD = *On Life After*

Death (Berkeley: Celestial Arts, 1991); WL = *The Wheel of Life: A Memoir of Living and Dying* (New York: Scribner, 1997).

1. Ambrose Bierce, *The Unabridged Devil's Dictionary*, ed. David E. Schultz and S. T. Joshi (Athens: University of Georgia Press, 2000), p. 196.

2. Antony Flew, *Atheistic Humanism* (Amherst, N.Y.: Prometheus Books, 1993), pp. 88–89.

3. H. L. Mencken, "What I Believe," *Forum* 84, no. 3 (September 1930): 139.

4. Ardis B. Collins, *The Secular Is Sacred: Platonism and Thomism in Marsilio Ficino's* Platonic Theology (The Hague: Martinus Nijhoff, 1974), pp. 3–4.

5. John Stuart Mill, "Immortality," in *Three Essays on Religion* (London: Longmans, Green, Reader & Dyer, 1874), pp. 209–10.

6. H. P. Lovecraft, "The Defence Remains Open!" (1921), in *Miscellaneous Writings*, ed. S. T. Joshi (Sauk City, Wisc.: Arkham House, 1995), pp. 166–67.

7. Thomas Moore, *Care of the Soul: A Guide for Cultivating Depth and Sacredness in Everyday Life* (New York: HarperCollins, 1992), p. xi. Further references will occur in the text as M.

8. Kenneth Ring, *Life at Death: A Scientific Investigation of the Near-Death Experience* (1980; reprint New York: Quill, 1982), p. 254.

9. Ibid., pp. 19–20.

10. Ibid., p. 135.

11. Robert Kastenbaum, "Near-Death Reports: Evidence for Survival After Death?" in *The Near-Death Experience: A Reader*, ed. Lee W. Bailey and Jenny Yates (New York: Routledge, 1996), p. 258.

12. Ibid., p. 247.

13. H. P. Lovecraft, "Final Words" (1921), in *Miscellaneous Writings*, ed. S. T. Joshi (Sauk City, Wisc.: Arkham House, 1995), pp. 170–71.

14. Daniel Stashower, *Teller of Tales: The Life of Sir Arthur Conan Doyle* (New York: Henry Holt, 1999), pp. 358–59.

9.

CHATTING
WITH THE
BIG GUY

Neale Donald Walsch

I n the spring of 1992 one Neale Donald Walsch had a remarkable experience: he began to have a conversation with God. The result was a book completed almost a year later, *Conversations with God: Book 1* (1995). Walsch continued to have chats with the Big Guy over the next several years, with the result that he produced two more volumes of *Conversations with God* (1997, 1998), then *Friendship with God* (1999), and finally *Communion with God* (2000). All these books became best-sellers, and Walsch has enterprisingly produced a variety of spin-off volumes to capitalize on his newfound celebrity as a divine chan-neler—such things as *Meditations from Conversations with God, Questions and Answers on Conversations with God, Neale Donald Walsch on Relation-ships, Neale Donald Walsch on Abundance and Right Livelihood, Neale Donald*

Walsch on Holistic Living, and *The Wedding Vows from Conversations with God,* written with his fourth wife, Nancy Fleming-Walsch. Walsch has also formed several organizations to promote his vision, chief among which is the ReCreation Foundation, whose function is to "give people back to themselves," whatever that means.

Walsch's agenda, in his first three books, is certainly ambitious; as he himself states in the introduction to book 3,

> Taken together, the trilogy covers an amazing range of topics, from how to make relationships work to the nature of ultimate reality and the cosmology of the universe, and includes observations on life, death, romance, marriage, sex, parenting, health, education, economics, politics, spirituality and religion, life work and right livelihood, physics, time, social mores and customs, the process of creation, our relationship with God, ecology, crime and punishment, life in highly evolved societies of the cosmos, right and wrong, cultural myths and cultural ethics, the soul, soul partners, the nature of genuine love, and the way to glorious expression of the part of ourselves that knows Divinity as our natural heritage. (3.x–xi)

Got all that? And yet, in spite of the supposedly wide range of topics to be covered, Walsch's five primary volumes are massively, almost maddeningly repetitious, as if God is trying to hammer his message home to his millions of recalcitrant readers. Even Walsch, in his own voice, once tells God, "I sometimes feel like I'm hearing the same things, over and over again" (3.106).

In the introduction to the first book of *Conversations with God* Walsch claims to address the natural skepticism with which even the pious would greet his claim. "Yes, yes. I know . . . that's not possible. One can talk *to* God, sure, but not *with* God. I mean, God is not going to *talk back,* right?" (1.ix). Walsch dispenses with these doubts summarily, and he denies that he is a "blasphemer, a fraud, a hypocrite" (1.ix) for having these conversations with God and for setting them down in books. As a rhetorical ploy, this seems superficially clever: exactly like C. S. Lewis with his celebrated "Lord-or-lunatic" dichotomy in regard to Jesus, Walsch is outlining a set of alternatives that appear to exhaust all the possibilities (either he is actually talking with God or he is a blasphemer, a fraud, and a hypocrite). But he is quietly shoving the most obvious alternative under the rug: the alternative, to wit, that he is simply deluded. I am entirely willing to believe that Walsch is totally sincere in his belief that he has written down God's answers to his various questions as they were dictated to him; it is simply that Walsch is wrong. He thinks he is talking with God when in fact he is talking with himself.

Walsch actually does face up to this prospect in the early part of his book, only to dismiss it in the most cavalier way. God has told him that *"Feeling is the language of the soul"* (1.3), and so, when Walsch asks pleadingly, "How can I know this communication is from God? How do I know this is not my own imagination?" God replies with the following remarkable assertion:

> *What would be the difference?* Do you not see that I could just as easily work through your imagination as anything else? I will bring you the *exact* right thoughts, words or feelings, at any given moment, suited precisely to the purpose at hand, using one device, or several.
>
> You will know these words are from Me because you, of your own accord, have never spoken so clearly. Had you already spoken so clearly on these questions, you would not be asking them. (1.6)

So it appears that the clarity of Walsch's feelings—or, more specifically, the clarity of the answers that "God" has provided to Walsch in response to questions that Walsch's conscious mind claims to be unable to answer—is a guarantee that the answers in question actually are from God.

We have already seen, in our examination of William James, that this "argument from feelings" is a very poor one. Many people have had extraordinarily clear and overwhelming feelings or experiences that to their minds irrefutably attest to God's existence or his communication with them. But how is *someone else* to gauge the nature and intensity of these feelings? Suppose I claimed to have a conversation with a God who told me that the human race was so irremediably corrupt and evil that it was my divinely appointed task in life to annihilate as many of them as possible. This would be a very different kind of God from the genial, friendly, nonjudgmental, wisecracking God whose stenographer Walsch purports to be, but he has no way of proving—or even of making a plausible argument—that his God is real and mine isn't. My "feelings" are surely as clear and intense as his; the "answers" that my God has given to my questions are as much beyond the fabrication of my conscious intellect as his. So who is right and who is wrong? Who (if anyone) is speaking to the real God (if there is one) and who isn't? More importantly, how is anyone to decide the matter based solely on "feelings"?

Walsch then resorts to a kind of pragmatic/utilitarian argument for the soundness of his views: "I gave this material to a few people to read while it was still in manuscript form. They were moved. And they cried. And they laughed for the joy and the humor of it. And their lives, they said, changed. They were transfixed. They were empowered" (1.ix). I myself have felt these identical emotions from reading Homer's *Iliad* in Greek, but I wouldn't claim that that fact alone verifies the existence of the Greek pantheon. In later books Walsch expands on the utilitarian argument; as his God states, with a liberal dose of self-congratulation, "Look, even if it really is just Neale Donald Walsch doing the talking in all these books, you could hardly find better advice to follow, on any of the subjects covered" (3.111–12).

This, it seems to me, is a fatal admission. Leave aside the self-con-gratulatory back-patting of this assertion: if Walsch cannot present plausible evidence that the words he attributes to God actually come from him, there is no reason why we should pay any more attention to him than to any other preacher or moralist who has written on these same issues over the past three thousand years of human his-tory. Whether one finds the "advice" offered by Walsch's God good or useful is entirely a matter of temperament; in any event, it is obviously the kind of advice that Walsch himself (subconsciously) hoped to receive, as he himself comes close to admitting in an unguarded moment: "What actually happened is that I allowed myself to believe what I always knew in my heart, and *wanted to believe* [my emphasis], about God" (FG 104). Moreover, there are in these books, beyond mere "advice," a variety of startling assertions about the nature of the universe that could only be swallowed if they were actually thought to come from God. Otherwise, we would be well within our rights to regard Walsch not as God's secretary but as some kind of lunatic.

It also seems troubling that God happens to speak in a succession of solecisms and grammatical blunders, such as "thusly" (1.11), "Alright" (1.23), and "more perfect" (1.43). Strange to say, Walsch himself, when speaking in his own voice, makes these same mistakes. . . . Can it be that Walsch, in these instances, is merely translating into his own shaky English the ineffable utterances of his God? He never says so, but it would seem that this is the only defense he could make; but should he make it, he has opened a dangerous cavern for himself, for how then can we trust anything else that his God says? Perhaps (as certain foolish Christians have stated in order to bypass numerous factual and moral difficulties in the Gospels) there has been some kind of "error in transmission"; but if so, how can we know that even the more sensible parts of Walsch's dictation have been transmitted correctly? Walsch himself actually declares, in a sheepish afterword to the third book, that he may not have been a "perfect filter" and that "some of what has come through me is no doubt distorted" (3.369)— another well-nigh catastrophic admission. (Another theory—that God has to speak in this ignorant and illiterate way in order to reach the mentalities of the millions of ignorant and illiterate people who will read this series of books—is one that never occurs to Walsch.)

One would suppose that if we could catch God making some kind of factual error, we would be justified in casting grave doubts as to whether Walsch's pipeline to the Big Guy were really on the up-and-up. Are there any instances where God is caught with his pants down? Yes, I think so. In one passage, where God is going on about the "Triune Truth" (1.30) that underlies all reality—that is, how "the three-in-one is found in the realms of the sublime"—we learn that scientists also have grasped this truth without realizing its significance. "Some of your scientists see energy, matter, ether" (1.31; see also 2.62). Ether? This can only be a reference to the so-called luminiferous ether, a phantasm of nineteenth-century scientists who, influenced by Aristotle, were unable to conceive how light could travel through "empty" space. The notion of the ether was shattered by Einstein's theory of relativity, and no serious physicist has embraced it since about 1920. How could God make such a ridiculous error? Or dare we speculate that it is actually Walsch—whose knowledge of science is, understandably, rather weak—who is nearly a century behind the times in his grasp of astrophysics?

Consider, too, God's interesting account of human anthropology as found in book 2. Here, in discussing how women came to be subjected to men, God maintains that "in an earlier part of your history, you lived on this planet in a matriarchal society" (2.40). But eventually the men overthrew the matriarchy and established a patriarchy instead. Regrettably, this fashionable theory, popular a few decades ago, has now been entirely discredited by more recent study. No genuinely matriarchal society can be said to have existed in any of the early human civilizations of which we have any knowledge; the whole notion was a tendentious fantasy of ill-informed feminists.

Plainly, a psychoanalysis of Walsch—who seems one of the most unreflective and nonintrospective persons I have ever come upon—would be most useful, for these "answers" from God seem manifestly to have been produced by certain unconscious facets of his mind at a time when he himself admits he was "very unhappy" (1.1); later he says he was "deeply depressed" (3.ix), and still later he expatiates at length:

> That process [that led to his "hearing" from God] began on a night in February of 1992 when I was on the verge of falling into chronic depression. Nothing had been going right in my life. My relationship with my significant other was kaput, my career had hit a dead end, and even my health was failing.
>
> Usually in my life it had been one thing or another, but now it was everything at once. The whole construction was collapsing, and I couldn't seem to do anything to stop it. . . .
>
> I was becoming very angry about my inability to hold a relationship together, my apparent total lack of understanding about

what it takes to do that, and the fact that nothing I tried seemed to work.

    I was coming to feel that I had simply not been given the equipment to play the game of Life, and I was furious. (FG 68–69)

In particular, it would be most instructive to know something of Walsch's previous religious upbringing. In *Friendship with God* he provides numerous details, including a number of points that prove highly illuminating.

    Walsch was raised Catholic. He openly states that his mother was Catholic (2.vii) and his books are full of quotations or paraphrases from the Bible; at one point he anxiously asks God, "Is there such a thing as the Second Coming?" (1.72). At some later date, however, he rejected this and other doctrinaire religions because of their emphasis on the sinfulness of the unregenerate. Walsch's God delivers a most entertaining fulmination on the notion of original sin:

> You were told from your earliest days that you're "bad." You accept that you were born in "sin." Feeling guilty is a *learned response.* You've been told to feel guilty about yourself for things you did before you could even do anything. You have been taught to feel shame for being born less than perfect.
>
>   This alleged state of imperfection in which you are said to have come into this world is what your religionists have the gall to call original sin. And it *is* original sin—but not yours. It is the first sin to be perpetuated upon you by a world which knows nothing of God if it thinks that God would—or *could*—create *anything* imperfect. (1.119)

To such a degree does this God manifest an animus toward this kind of Calvinist doctrine that Walsch, in his own voice, actually upbraids God for "launch[ing] a frontal attack on fundamentalist Christianity" (1.137). Walsch's God also denies that the Bible is an "authoritative source" (1.8), questions whether Jesus was "perfect" (1.192), and maintains that there were no such things as the Ten Commandments (1.95)—although he does so only so that he can spew forth a succession of fatuous New Age rewritings of the Ten Commandments that have nothing to do with either the letter or the spirit of the biblical text, e.g., "You shall remember to keep a day for Me, and you shall call it holy. This, so that you do not long stay in your illusion, but cause yourself to remember who and what you are. And then shall you soon call *every* day the Sabbath, and *every* moment holy" (1.96).

But God is not content to pick apart individual strands of religious doctrine. Throughout the three books he engages in a remarkably broad and thoroughgoing abuse of the very foundations of all conventional religions, which he maintains are "religions of fear." Indeed, in one long passage (2.43–47) Walsch and God lay bare the multitudinous absurdities of Catholic doctrine in a tone of sustained sarcasm that could not have pleased Walsch's pious mother. Manifestly, this is Walsch speaking again, as he admits in *Friendship with God* that throughout his life he was "searching for a God of whom I did not have to be afraid" (FG 276). How uncanny that, at the most stressful moment of his life, he began hearing from just such a God!

There is, however, an enormous logical problem with this trashing of orthodox religion—a problem of which Walsch is utterly and blithely unaware. For if (as the standard mystical party line has it) "We are All One" (3.250)—if there is in fact only one soul, and all entity is linked to God and comes from God and in fact *is* God—then how is it possible for God to repudiate the sacred texts or the religious practices he doesn't like? When Walsch, in his own voice, confronts him with the biblical utterance "Vengeance is mine, saith the Lord," God replies: "I never said that" (3.274–75). But how could he *not* have? How, in other words, could he not have uttered these words (or any other words ever uttered or written by anyone in the universe)? Surely the words could not have been spoken in defiance of God's will; as God rightly points out, "nothing happens against the will of God" (3.248). So how can God refuse to acknowledge the validity of the numerous statements in the Bible or other scriptures of which he manifestly disapproves?

At the same time, God explicitly states that he *did* "inspire" a number of other individuals whose work he approves of. He uses that very word in describing the work of Elisabeth Kübler-Ross, Deepak Chopra (who, along with Dinesh D'Souza, makes me ashamed to be an Indian), John Gray, Ken Keyes, and a number of others. Strange to say, most of these good folk are those whom Walsch himself acknowledges as his models and inspirations. He had even studied for some years with Kübler-Ross (FG 268), from whom he no doubt inherited her quaint idea that "Death does not exist." Even George Lucas's *Star Wars* was divinely inspired, it appears (FG 229), as was the U.S. Constitution (2.205), in spite of the fact that it neglects to mention God anywhere.

I have mentioned New Age influence on Walsch advisedly, for Walsch mentions it himself. When he notes casually that he has had "a dozen New Age teachers" (1.160), one begins to suspect the evolution of his religiosity. It seems highly likely that Walsch's subconscious mind has rejected the dogmatic Christianity he was taught and (acting as the mouthpiece of the "real" God) has chosen to express a relatively conventional mysticism—there is no such thing as time, all entity is one, etc., etc.—generally reminiscent of Eastern religion. This phase of his thought betrays itself especially in his advocacy of reincarnation. In an unwontedly irritated moment, Walsch's God expresses impatience at the thickheadedness of those who still deny this doctrine:

> It is difficult to believe there is still a question about this. I find it hard to imagine. There have been so many reports from thoroughly reliable sources of past life experiences. Some of these people have brought back strikingly detailed descriptions of events, and such completely verifiable data as to eliminate any possibility that they were making it up or had contrived to somehow deceive researchers and loved ones. (1.204)

No wonder Walsch, in his second book, acknowledges the wholesome influence upon his life of Shirley MacLaine, "who has demonstrated that intellect [*sic!*] and entertainment are not mutually exclusive" (2.x). But I regret to say that cocksure pronouncements like the above, in the absence of evidence and of any serious examination of the serious logical and empirical difficulties involved in the notion of reincarnation, are not likely to convince us hardheaded cynics that transmigration of souls is any less preposterous than it is usually assumed to be. And yet, Walsch's God soberly informs him that "you have had 647 past lives" (1.204)!

Certain other passages reveal, rather embarrassingly, that Walsch's God is only telling him what he (subconsciously) wants to hear. Raised as he was as a strict Catholic, Walsch has developed highly ambiguous feelings toward sex: on the one hand he enjoys it tremendously, but on the other hand he feels profound guilt over this very enjoyment. One of his most frequent and insistent questions to God takes this form: "Is sex okay? C'mon—what is the real story behind this human experience? Is sex purely for procreation, as some religions say? Is true holiness and enlightenment achieved through denial—or transmutation—of the sexual energy? Is it okay to have sex without love? Is just the physical sensation of it okay enough as a reason?" (1.205). Walsch's God comes to his rescue, reassuring him that "of course sex is 'okay,'" and going on to say: "*Play* with sex. *Play* with it! It's *wonderful* fun. Why, it's just about the most fun you can *have* with your body, if you're talking of strictly physical experiences alone" (1.205).

Another issue that gnaws at Walsch is money. He appears never to have had enough of it. (This issue has mercifully been put to rest by his best-selling books.) He has always had to scrimp and save, and finally expels the pitiable whine, "Why can't I ever seem to attract enough money in my life?" (1.71). But there is a broader point. Walsch asks: "Is it okay to take money for doing good? If I choose to do healing work in the world—God's work—can I do that and become financially abundant, too? Or are the two mutually exclusive?" (1.72). Now, now, Neale, take it easy. Since "*Everything* is 'acceptable' in the sight of God, for how can God not accept that which is?" (1.61), God concludes as follows:

> Every time in your life that you have had lots and lots of money, you have felt great. You felt great receiving it, and you felt great

spending it. There was nothing bad about it, nothing evil, nothing inherently "wrong." Yet you have so deeply ingrained within you the teachings of *others* on this subject that you have *rejected* your experience in favor of "truth." (1.63)

Whew! No doubt Walsch is glad those days of frugality and guilt are over!

The unfortunate aspect of all this is that whenever God is not uttering utterly inane platitudes ("Thought and feelings are not the same" [1.3]) or incomprehensible mysticism ("I am what I *am not*" [1.9]), some of his recommendations, especially in the political and social sphere, are not lacking in sense. God emphasizes the need for human beings to take responsibility for the state of the world (1.49–50), and goes on to condemn humanity for a mass of environmental and other sins that has caused the near-destruction of the planet. Many of these flaws are a product of the relentless money-grubbing of the race, which God (in book 2) now condemns mercilessly. God, therefore, pragmatically endorses a one-world government (2.141) and the development of an international monetary system (2.186). God, indeed, proves to be quite learned in matters of economics, discussing the United States' GNP (2.138) and such topics as soil erosion (2.182). He becomes almost a cynic when speaking of politicians ("There are few governments which do not deliberately mislead their people" [2.133]). He also has perceptive things to say on human relationships ("Most people enter into relationships with an eye toward what they can get out of them, rather than what they can put into them" [1.122]) and on the raising of children ("You are teaching your children what to think instead of how to think" [2.111]). God in fact recommends a kind of communal raising of children, like that advocated in Plato's *Republic* (3.33).

But these pieces of advice—none of which are beyond the capacity of any tolerably well-informed and unprejudiced person to formulate—are so buried in a mass of imbecility and gibberish that it becomes difficult to pluck the pearls from the mud. Take God's notions on sickness and disease. Instead of maintaining, sanely, that one's mental and psychological state has an important bearing on the course of physical diseases, God becomes a Christian Scientist and claims that "all illness is self-created" (1.187). It is a mercy that we don't actually hear about Malicious Animal Magnetism. But we do learn that people die of AIDS only because they want to (1.188). It would be interesting to know what kind of death-wish Arthur Ashe had when he received the blood transfusion that gave him AIDS. God then turns around and recommends "regular check-ups, once-a-year physicals, and the use of therapies and medicine you've been given" (1.190) to cure disease! Again, God recognizes that we ingest a variety of substances that are probably not good for us and which probably shorten our lives, but he distorts this idea out of all recognition by maintaining that "I designed your magnificent body to last *forever!*" (1.194).

God also engages repeatedly in irritating doublespeak. He tells Walsch, "Follow your feelings" (2.14), but immediately qualifies this by maintaining that some feelings "are *true feelings*—that is, feelings born in the soul—and some feelings are counterfeit feelings. They are constructed in your mind" (2.17). But God does not supply any means of distinguishing the "true" feelings from the "counterfeit" ones. In any case, if everything comes from God, how can *any* feelings be other than "true"? God is also addicted to formulations that are impervious to refutation—but Walsch doesn't realize that this makes them incapable of proof also. For example, his God repeatedly states that we have the power to do anything—*anything*—we wish, so long as we think we can do it. Walsch, in his own voice, expresses a proper skepticism, saying that we can't just fly through the air if we jump off the Empire State Building. God says, Certainly you can—but you have to be "in a state of total awareness" (3.84). So anyone who jumps off the Empire State Building and falls to the ground must not, of course, have been in a state of total awareness. Even if every person in the world jumps off the Empire State Building and falls to his or her death, then it only shows that *no one* was in a state of total awareness. Similarly, in endorsing psychic abilities, God maintains that "when you think of someone, if that person is sensitive enough, he or she can *feel* it" (2.82). Naturally, if such a person does *not* feel it, then clearly he or she was not "sensitive" enough!

Then there is the repeated claim that everyone is "perfect." The notion seems to have been evolved in order to protect God—himself a "perfect" entity—from having created anything imperfect, a conception that Walsch sees as an apparent oxymoron (*"anything I conceive . . . is perfect,"* his God proclaims [1.119]). But if everything is perfect, what would be the point of improving? Clearly, God sees much that is wrong with the world, otherwise he would not have come to the conclusion that the world is in imminent threat of destruction from the foolish actions of us perfect human beings. Walsch himself seems to realize the paradox, so he begins to weasel out of the difficulty. He says in his own voice: "Every soul is perfect, pure, and beautiful. In the state of forgetfulness in which they reside here on Earth, God's perfect beings may do imperfect things—or what we would *call* imperfect things—yet everything that occurs in life occurs for a perfect reason" (FG 47). This passage seems to me void of meaning.

It is, however, in book 3 that Walsch leaves sanity entirely behind. At the end of book 2 he had tantalizingly noted that there are indeed extraterrestrial civilizations all across the universe; we are later told that there are "thousands" (3.271). Indeed, the evidence for the existence of these entities is so "obvious" (3.262)—like that for reincarnation, apparently—that it becomes folly to doubt it. What is more, some of these entities "look exactly like you [i.e., like human beings]—given minor variations" (3.308). So naturally, a few of them are among us as we speak (2.239). And they have lent us some valuable assistance:

> Oh, they give a boost now and then. For instance, surely you're aware that you've made more technological progress in the past 75 years than in *all of human history before that.* . . .
>
> Do you imagine that everything from CAT scans to supersonic flight to computer chips you embed in your body to regulate your heart all came from the mind of man? . . .
>
> You don't find it strange that in this billion-year process of evolution, somewhere around 75 to 100 years ago there was a huge "comprehension explosion"?

You don't see it as *outside the pattern* that many people now on the planet have seen the development of everything from radio to radar to radionics *in their lifetime?*

You don't get that what has happened here represents a quantum leap? A step forward of such magnitude and such proportion as to defy any progression of logic? (2.237–38)

I *knew* we couldn't have developed TVs, VCRs, Stealth bombers, and Viagra on our own! Some of the extraterrestrials in the universe are, however, malevolent, but we are thankfully being "protected" (2.240) by others: "You are being given the opportunity to live out your own destiny. Your own consciousness will create the result" (2.240). What a relief!

Book 3 elaborates at great length on these alien species, many of whom are far more advanced, in every way, than human beings: "I said, in every way. Technologically. Politically. Socially. Spiritually. Physically. Psychologically" (3.265). (How this is meant to square with God's earlier declaration that the human race is "the most magnificent, the most remarkable, the most splendid being God has ever created" [1.16] is anyone's guess.) But it becomes rapidly obvious that these extraterrestrials—whose exact location God neglects to specify and whose actual attributes, aside from their ability to control the weather on their planets (3.267), God fails to elucidate—merely serve as models for all the behavioral changes that God wishes the human race to make. Still more remarkably, God informs us that there was a previous human civilization that destroyed itself because of its unwise use of technology:

> I am saying that once before on your planet you had reached the heights—beyond the heights, really—to which you now are slowly climbing. You had a civilization on Earth more advanced than the one now existing. And it destroyed itself.
>
> Not only did it destroy itself, it nearly destroyed everything else as well.
>
> It did this because it did not know how to deal with the very technologies it had developed. Its technological evolution was so far

ahead of its spiritual evolution that it wound up making technology its God. The people worshipped technology, and all that it could create and bring. And so they got all that their unbridled technology brought—which was unbridled disaster.

They literally brought their world to an end. (3.269–70)

Whether we call this civilization Atlantis, Mu, or Lemuria hardly matters (3.270). It is, however, a bit puzzling that it has not left a single verifiable trace on the earth. It must have destroyed itself with great thoroughness, indeed!

After writing the three *Conversations with God* books, Walsch discovered that his God couldn't shut up. Actually, in *Friendship with God* Walsch speaks largely in his own voice, providing more information than anyone could possibly want on his boring and tiresome life. But some parts are amusing in spite of themselves. Walsch, it transpires, as an adolescent wished to be a "professional" pianist. A pianist like Horowitz, Serkin, or Ashkenazy? No—"like Liberace" (FG 40)! Unfortunately, the dream went up in smoke when Walsch's father destroyed the family's $25 upright piano with a hatchet. (Parenthetically, it may be worth noting how resolutely lowbrow Walsch's tastes are, as his repeated "thanks" to such luminaries as Neil Diamond, Oprah, Steven Spielberg, John Denver, Richard Bach, Barbra Streisand, Dolly Parton, and the like attest. I suppose God's stenographer doesn't have to be an aesthetic elitist, but can't he at least show a liking for, say, the Beatles?)

Walsch is certainly not shy about the impact of his work: "These books will be read and studied for decades, even for generations. Perhaps, for centuries" (3.x). Elsewhere he says: "I believe this to be sacred spiritual material" (3.x). Indeed, God reassures Walsch that it is entirely acceptable for him to maintain that he is a "great teacher" (3.186). After all, haven't his books been read by millions and translated into twenty-four languages (3.185)? (No—make that twenty-seven [CG 215].) In one final attempt to dispense with readers' skepticism, God declares: "Either I am God talking, or this Neale fellow is a pretty bright guy" (3.112). In the afterword to book 2 Walsch states that he wishes to hold a symposium in 1999 on his foundation, ReCreation, to discuss the issues raised by his books. Did this symposium ever occur? Did anyone care? What about the "international forum on using spirituality to end conflict, in Seoul, Korea, in June 2001" that Walsch announces as forthcoming in *Communion with God* (CG 218)? Once again, I regret to say that even I, devoted reader of the *New York Times* that I am, failed to hear a peep about this grand event, and I am writing only two months after its supposed occurrence.

Another disturbing trend—disturbing for Walsch, at any rate, and his dreams of being a new messiah who will usher in an age of peace and unity and guilt-free sex—is the fact that his books are not being read with quite the avidity they once were. *Conversations with God: Book 1* remained on the *New York Times* best-seller list for an astounding 130 weeks (although not always for consecutive weeks), but book 2 lasted only 19 weeks, and book 3 only 16 weeks. I cannot see that *Friendship with God* or *Communion with God* made the best-seller list at all. Can it be that those who gawked at Walsch's initial chats with the Man Upstairs are becoming weary of the plodding monotony of his hectoring message? Walsch may tickle his fancy in assuming that his "scriptures" will be read and studied for centuries, but there is every reason to believe that their popularity, and still more their all-but-imperceptible "influence" upon society and culture, will be of the most transient sort.

What, then, do we make of Neale Donald Walsch? How is it possible not to conclude that this poor deluded fellow is only hearing what he wants to hear, and is trying to cleanse his mind of the frightening, judgmental God of his upbringing and find a more forgiving, welcoming, charitable God? I repeat that a number of his remarks on relationships, politics, and society are eminently sensible, if shorn of their moony mysticism and their preposterous claim of coming direct from the Big Guy. But if he had presented these views sanely and nondivinely, would he have attracted the millions of readers who, whether from curiosity or desperation, wanted to hear the very word of Gawd (but who, it is quite obvious, do not care to follow many of God's more radical precepts)? And more, would Walsch not have had to make at least the rudiments of a reasoned argument to defend some of his more outlandish claims and assertions—a task from which he is now absolved because he can merely point to them as the infallible dicta of the Creator? After all, it is this God who says, "this book has come to bring the truth" (3.289–90) and again, "I have explained to you the mechanics of the universe, the secret of all life" (3.361). Since he is God, no proof is presumably necessary.

But perhaps another statement of God applies a bit more accurately to Neale Donald Walsch and his entire enterprise: "Then there appear to be those who do not know, but who *think that they know.* They are dangerous. Avoid them" (FG 289). For once, God seems on target.

NOTES

References to Neale Donald Walsch's books occur in the text as follows: *Conversations with God: Book 1* (Charlottesville, Va.: Hampton Roads Publishing Co., 1995), *Conversations with God: Book 2* (Charlottesville, Va.: Hampton Roads Publishing Co., 1997), *Conversations with God: Book 3* (Charlottesville, Va.: Hampton Roads Publishing Co., 1998), by volume and page number (e.g., 1.324); CG = *Communion with God* (New York: G. P. Putnam's Sons, 2000); FG = *Friendship with God* (New York: G. P. Putnam's Sons, 1999).

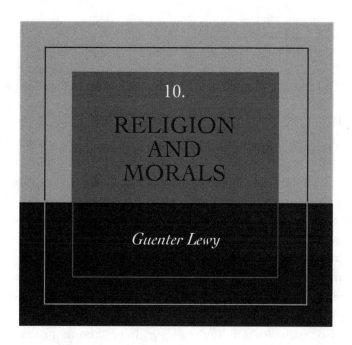

10.

RELIGION AND MORALS

Guenter Lewy

The idea still seems prevalent among the general public that religion is essential to good morals. Oddly enough, professional philosophers have, in the course of the twentieth century, almost unanimously rejected such an idea, and for two very plausible reasons: (1) the difficulty of establishing the existence of God; and (2) the difficulty, even if the existence of God is accepted, of knowing clearly what ethical precepts are or are not sanctioned by God. Since the claims to *metaphysical* truth on the part of religion in general, and any given religion in particular, have now been so vigorously challenged, it would appear inevitable that a religious foundation for morals would be equally problematical. If religion is false in regard to its assertions about the nature of the universe, why should its ethical precepts—manifestly based upon those assertions—be granted any special respect beyond that shown to any other system of ethics, secular or otherwise? These complexities rarely trouble the common people, among whom the great majority of our political and social leaders can be included. And so we have the comical spectacle of the hapless Democratic vice-presidential candidate Joseph Lieberman, an Orthodox Jew, causing embarrassment to himself by remarking: "George Washington warned us never to indulge the supposition 'that morality can be maintained without religion.'"[1] He was quickly challenged on this claim, so that two days later he was forced to eat his words in one great swallow: "Religion in my opinion can be, and in my opinion usually is, a source of good behavior. But two things: I know religious people who I consider not to be moral, and I also know people who are not religious who I consider to be extremely moral. So, you know, I'm talking here about probabilities." Leiberman was even so magnanimous as to say, when asked if he would object to an atheist being president: "Personally, no, if I thought it [*sic*] was a good person."[2] The controversy died out shortly thereafter, producing only a flicker of heat and no light to speak of. It is, of course, only to be expected that the current resident of the White House would quote Martin Luther King's remark: "The church must be reminded that it is not the master or the servant of the state, but rather the conscience of the state."[3]

My own judgment is that religion continues to stake a claim to ethical supremacy by an appeal to what might be called the ghost of its former metaphysical supremacy; that is, even those theists who are no longer particularly vocal about the metaphysical truth of the central tenets of their religion (the existence, omnipotence, and benevolence of God; the existence and nature of the soul and the afterlife; the divinity of Jesus Christ) still rely upon the *prior* acceptance of these tenets as a purely rhetorical means of vaunting their own moral systems over those of such horrible people as "secular humanists" or (still worse) "moral relativists." I will go further and say that with the demise of the metaphysical claims of religion and, in the last two centuries, its ejection from political and military power in most of the

Western nations, the coopting of morals is the only function left to religion if it is not to be entirely irrelevant to present-day concerns, regardless of whether it has any legitimate claim to this office or whether its prior conduct warrants it; so that it is understandable that religions cling to their role as moral guardians with the tenacity of desperation.

Secularists are in part to blame for allowing religion to dominate the moral sphere. In the course of the twentieth century, the most acute philosophers abandoned the practice of evolving viable ethical systems and chose to focus their attention on increasingly picayune and esoteric logic-chopping, chiefly in regard to the language of morals. To a certain extent this kind of analysis was beneficial, for as a result it became evident that the language of moral discourse utilized by almost every philosopher from Plato onward was fatally vitiated by question-beggings, non sequiturs, and, most important of all, a failure to come to grips with the metaphysical basis—or lack of basis—of moral axioms. But the consequence was a kind of moral void—a void filled, inevitably, by intellectual amateurs: theologians, politicians (that self-appointed czar of morals, William J. Bennett, being a shining example), talk-show hosts, and the like.

The views I will propound in this chapter are quite simple, and some of them have been expressed in fragmentary form in earlier sections of this book: (1) religion is not necessary to morals; (2) religion does not, on the whole, make people "better"; (3) the actual morals advocated by most religions are dreadful and appalling. Simple as these tenets are, they require fairly exhaustive exposition and elucidation, and the philosophical issues involved are considerably more complex than those we have faced in earlier parts of this book.

Guenter Lewy (b. 1923) is a useful springboard for this discussion. Lewy is the author of several impressive scholarly volumes on modern history, including *The Catholic Church and Nazi Germany* (1964), in which he takes an unfavorable view of the church's dealings with Hitler during World War II, and *Religion and Revolution* (1974), a study of the role of religion in social and political revolt. He began laying his conservative credentials with *America in Vietnam*

(1978), in which he defended America's role in that conflict, and *The Cause That Failed: Communism in American Political Life* (1990). At the moment I am interested only in Lewy's recent volume, *Why America Needs Religion: Secular Modernity and Its Discontents* (1996). This little book does not appear to have garnered much attention, nor does it deserve to, for it is, almost beyond belief and tolerance, superficial, prejudiced, tendentious, and simply foolish. It is obvious that Lewy himself is one of those secular "discontents": even though he purports to present a balanced view of both the positive and negative sides of religion (he is concerned almost exclusively with Christianity), it becomes quite clear which side he is on. He states that he himself was a kind of secularist at one time:

> For most of my adult life, I had lived with the view that ethical beliefs are a matter of personal commitment and cannot be regarded as true or false. . . . The diversity of moral beliefs and ways of life seemed to me to require acceptance of the idea of ethical and cultural relativism; the impossibility of adjudicating between these diverse practices dictated a noncognitivist approach to ethics—that is, it implied the impossibility of knowing what constituted moral truth. . . . An admirer of the Enlightenment and Freud, I regarded religion not only as an arbitrary invention born out of human weakness but also as unnecessary for leading a moral life. (W ix–x)

His pious publisher was no doubt delighted to gain a convert to the side of the angels. Strangely enough, Lewy does not provide any refutation of the secularist position he has just outlined, although he clearly no longer believes in it. It appears that he has simply been offended by certain bizarre utterances by random secular humanists—one of whom, for example, defends the practice of sex with animals—and has now come to believe that all secularists have gone off the deep end. He also doesn't like some recent secularists' derision and ridicule of religion (he has clearly not read Ambrose Bierce or H. L. Mencken, who showered more virulent abuse on religion and the religious than almost any modern commentator, with the exception of Gore Vidal, dares to do). Of course, Lewy is silent on the still more bizarre utterances of some of his new religious friends, some of which we have already encountered: the belief that Pope Paul II's emergence was an "evidently supernatural" event; that AIDS is God's punishment of homosexuals; that God intervened in the Cuban missile crisis; *und so weiter.* Lewy's sense of outrage is a bit one-sided, it appears.

The overriding issue that Lewy deliberately avoids in his entire tract is the basis of morals. Are moral stances subject to truth or falsity? Can they be objectively verified? Does it make any sense to say that one moral position is (objectively) "right" and another (objectively) "wrong"? There appear to be only two ways in which this can be so: (1) there must be something built into the fabric of the universe that makes some moral values right and others wrong; or (2) a god or gods must dictate a code of morals to human beings. Option 1 is so obviously false that its mere utterance is sufficient to refute it, and I know of no one today who believes it. Option 2 apparently still has some adherents, although even religious leaders are apparently becoming wary of stating it bluntly.

The reasons for this are quite obvious. If God has dictated morals to us, then he must have done so by some means or other. He might have done so by inspiring some prophet, but it is not obvious how we are to distinguish between the truly divine inspiration of a genuine prophet and the ravings of some lunatic who only thinks he is a prophet. Even Jesus said, "Beware of false prophets" (Matt. 7:15), but regrettably failed to provide a formula for detecting them. Otherwise, we are forced to assume that God laid down his moral (and other) commands by means of a sacred text. Now virtually all religions have a sacred text, and virtually all claim that that text was divinely inspired; but all these texts are very different in both the metaphysics and the morals they embody, so that no more than one of them (and perhaps none) can actually be the word of God. I have already shown that Christianity, Judaism, and Islam, to name only three religions, unequivocally assert their possession of the exclusive truth, but this means that at least two (and perhaps three) are wrong in making such an assertion. Let me emphasize this point: *In making an exclusive claim to truth, no more than one religion can be right, but all reli-*

gions may be wrong. In our age of religious tolerance, only fanatical fundamentalists are so tactless as to assert that only they are right and all other religions are wrong, even though the logic of each of these religions requires just such an assertion.

It is often feared that the rejection of some kind of divine — or, at any rate, objective — basis for morals will inevitably lead to "moral relativism," or the belief that all moral systems are all "equal." I am not certain that this characterization of moral relativism is even intelligible — it would seem analogous to saying that an apple is equal to an orange — and I myself would state that the real alternative for "moral objectivism" is its obvious opposite, "moral subjectivism." There might be a third option, which might be called "moral provisionalism," although it is considerably closer to subjectivism than to objectivism. I will have occasion to discuss it later. Obviously, moral subjectivism ("one man's meat is another man's poison") is as repugnant to moral absolutists as moral relativism, but to say that a given conception is repugnant (assuming, for the sake of argument, that it actually is so) is hardly equivalent to saying that it is false. If it were, then all truths would be pleasant. On occasion disasteful truths must be faced. Mencken, in fact, once defined truth as "something somehow discreditable to someone."[4]

In this case, I see no answer to moral subjectivism. The logical positivist A. J. Ayer enunciated this view as pungently as any, in *Language, Truth and Logic* (1936):

> The presence of an ethical symbol in a proposition adds nothing to its factual content. Thus if I say to someone, "You acted wrongly in stealing that money," I am not stating anything more than if I had simply said, "You stole that money." In adding that this action is wrong I am not making any further statement about it. I am simply evincing my moral disapproval of it. It is as if I had said, "You stole that money," in a peculiar tone of horror, or written it with the addition of some special exclamation marks. The tone, or the exclamation marks, adds nothing to the literal meaning of the sentence. It merely serves to show that the expression of it is attended by certain feelings in the speaker.

> If now I generalise my previous statement and say, "Stealing money is wrong," I produce a sentence which has no factual meaning—that is, expresses no proposition which can be either true or false. It is as if I had written "Stealing money!!"—where the shape and thickness of the exclamation marks show, by a suitable convention, that a special sort of moral disapproval is the feeling which is being expressed. It is clear that there is nothing said here which can be true or false.[5]

In spite of the mountains of outraged abuse this conception has received in the decades following its enunciation, it seems to me irrefutable. In essence, Ayer is saying that a moral statement is not a *fact* but an *emotional response to a fact*. In the above instance, the fact in question is the existence of a phenomenon called stealing; the emotional response is the emotion of disapproval of the phenomenon of stealing. There is no physical, moral, political, or social necessity for anyone to have that particular emotion in relation to the fact in question as opposed to some other emotion; the mere fact that a great majority of people do have the emotion in question does not confer any truth-value to it.

The controversial Catholic theologian Hans Küng has attempted to add to this discussion, but I fear his contribution is no more satisfactory:

> Nowadays—after Nietzsche's glorification of "beyond good and evil"—we can no longer count on a "categorical imperative" which is quasi-innate in all, and make the wellbeing of all human beings the criterion for our own action. No, the categorical quality of ethical demand, the unconditioned nature of the ought, cannot be grounded by human beings, who are conditioned in many ways, but only by that which is unconditional: by an Absolute which can provide an over-arching meaning and which embraces and permeates individual, human nature and indeed the whole of human society. That can only be the ultimate, supreme reality, which while it cannot be proved rationally, can be accepted in a rational trust—regardless of how it is named, understood and interpreted in the different religions.
>
> At least for the prophetic religions—Judaism, Christianity and

Islam—it is the one unconditional in all that is conditioned that can provide a basis for the absoluteness and universality of ethical demands, that primal ground, primal support, primal goal of human beings and the world that we call God.[6]

Recognizing the absence of a categorical imperative in moral inquiry, Küng dredges up a mythical "Absolute" merely for the purpose of providing moral objectivity where none exists, presumably because the alternative (moral relativism or subjectivism) is too dreadful for him to contemplate; but far from being a "rational trust" (whatever that may mean), this whole procedure strikes me as supremely irrational.

Lewy, however, along with numerous of his conservative cohorts, would like to believe that—even without appealing to religious ethics—there are a certain core group of moral beliefs that everyone can affirm. It would be nice to think so. Lewy states with touching confidence that "there are *some* moral truths" (W 139), but unfortunately neglects to specify what these are. Lewy's new friend William J. Bennett is a little clearer on the point, asserting that "values such as courage, kindness, honesty, and discipline are common to almost all religious traditions"—and, presumably, to societies at large.[7] The remark is itself questionable in its details—the well-known utterance attributed to Jesus, "Blessed are the meek: for they shall inherit the earth" (Matt. 5:5), does not seem to me an especially thunderous endorsement of the moral rectitude of courage—but let that pass. I maintain, however, that even if it could be established that all societies—indeed, all human beings who have ever lived and who ever will live—have exactly the same moral values, this would still not provide proof of the objectivity of values. Without some additional evidence for the actual (i.e., external) existence of objective values, this uniformity of belief might be nothing more than a universal human error or prejudice. It is conceivable, for example, that the human race, so long as it exists, could be under the impression that the sun revolves around the earth, and that no one would ever suspect the truth of the converse. Mere uniformity of opinion on this point would not in itself establish its truth. We are once more heading toward the democratic fallacy.

Nontheistic moral philosophers have denied moral objectivism on the facts, well known to historians and sociologists, that moral standards vary (a) from one culture to another, (b) within a single culture over time, and (c) (the phenomenon that most troubles our conservative moralists today) from individual to individual, or from subclass to subclass, within a given culture. However, this argument by itself is not sufficient to demolish the claim of moral objectivity, for it could be maintained (although to my mind not plausibly) that one culture, or even one single individual, is still (objectively) "right" in regard to morals and everyone else wrong. What we need is a more thoroughgoing examination of the origin and purpose of ethical systems.

It seems to me manifestly obvious that, barring the extremely unlikely possibility of a fiat from God, every system of ethics had its origin in social organization. In the "state of nature" (the hypothetical condition of prehistory whereby individuals operated as isolated individuals) there can be no morals; or rather, the only morals are self-preservation. Even if it is asserted that the "state of nature" never had any actual existence and that human beings from the very beginning organized themselves into social groups, the emergence of ethical systems is clearly a product of the need to regulate human behavior within these groups. Every ethical system ever devised by human beings (with two exceptions that I shall examine presently) has as its ultimate purpose the preservation or perpetuation of human *society* — not the individual as such; and the variations in ethical systems are simply variations in what different cultures or different thinkers have deemed the appropriate manner of preserving or perpetuating human society. But it becomes immediately evident that when stated in this way all these ethical systems rest upon an unquestioned assumption, i.e., that human society should in fact be preserved. This is, however, not a fact, much less a moral imperative, but merely a prejudice — or, to be a bit more charitable, a preference. There is no necessity, either physical or moral, for the human race to continue its existence. Of course, to assert the reverse — that the human race ought *not* to exist — is equally a prejudice (or preference), but no more so than the other. Lovecraft wrote rather piquantly: "May not all mankind be a mistake—an abnormal growth—a disease in the system of Nature—an excrescence on the body of infinite progression like a wart on the human hand? Might not the total destruction of humanity, as well as of all animate creation, be a positive *boon* to Nature as a whole?"[8]

It may be amusing to see if some plausible justifications for the extirpation of the human race could be provided. I can think of five off the top of my head:

1) THE ENVIRONMENTAL ARGUMENT

This is the assertion that human beings have made such a botch of their planet, especially in their treatment of other living creatures and of the natural world as a whole, that they have forfeited the right to live on the earth. It would seem difficult to deny the basic facts upon which this argument is based, for surely the human race has indeed done great harm to the planet, and the environmental movement of the last few decades has only minimally affected such things as the pollution of the air and water, the destruction of the ozone layer (a destruction that may ultimately lead to the extirpation of the human race whether anyone desires that outcome or not), and the forced extinction of thousands, perhaps hundreds of thousands, of animal species as a direct result of human action.

2) THE MOZART-HITLER ARGUMENT

This argument takes Wolfgang Amadeus Mozart and Adolf Hitler as exemplars of the best and the worst in humanity, and goes on to ask: Are human beings more similar to the one or to the other? If the great majority of human beings are—morally, intellectually, socially, politically—closer to Hitler than to Mozart, then their extirpation might be morally justified. I think a good case could be made that most human beings are indeed considerably closer to Hitler than to Mozart. There may be some difficulty in comparing these two figures, since the one is a representative of aesthetic genius and the other a representative of moral and political evil. It may be a bit easier to use intellectual achievement as a criterion, with Einstein or Bertrand Russell as the best and Ronald Reagan or George W. Bush as the worst. Here it becomes immediately evident that the overwhelming mass of humanity is far closer to Reagan or Bush than they are to Einstein or Russell. Whether the mere existence of a few luminaries in the intellectual, aesthetic, or other spheres justifies the existence of the *entire* human race is a separate enquiry; to me it seems a trifle wasteful to have to generate so many billions of stupid, mediocre human beings merely to produce a handful of geniuses.

3) THE PLEASURE-PAIN ARGUMENT

This argument, of course, is most closely associated with Arthur Schopenhauer, who asserted that the amount of pain in human existence overwhelmingly outweighs the amount of pleasure. This led him to conclude:

> Human life must be some kind of mistake. The truth of this will be sufficiently obvious if we only remember that man is a compound of needs and necessities hard to satisfy; and that even when they are satisfied, all he obtains is a state of painlessness, where nothing remains to him but abandonment to boredom. This is direct proof that existence has no real value in itself; for what is boredom but the feeling of the emptiness of life?[9]

It is not entirely clear what corollary Schopenhauer wishes to draw from this argument; or, rather, what actions he thinks it is appropriate for the human race to take. It might be thought that he would recommend universal suicide, but he does not quite do so; all he does, in the essay "On Suicide," is to recommend the moral right of the *individual* to commit suicide in order to be released from the tedium of life. Elsewhere he actually asserts, rather touchingly: "The conviction that the world and man is something that had better not have been, is of a kind to fill us with indulgence towards one another."[10]

4) THE SINFULNESS ARGUMENT

In a sense this argument is a variant of 1, and asserts that human beings are so generally and irremediably depraved that they forfeit the right to exist. Oddly enough, this argument was enunciated by that tortured Christian, Leo Tolstoy. In a posthumously published work, *The Pathway of Life* (1919), Tolstoy, following Paul, found himself so horrified by the sinfulness of sexual intercourse, even between married people, that he unhesitatingly recommended universal chastity, with the result that the human race would gradually cease to exist as no new generation would emerge to supplant the old. In his argument for chastity Tolstoy draws explicitly upon Paul: "I say therefore to the unmarried and widows, It is good for them if they abide even as I. But if they cannot contain, let them marry: for it is better to marry than to burn. . . . he that giveth her in marriage doeth well; but he that giveth her not in marriage doeth better" (1 Cor. 7:8–9, 38). Tolstoy is unflinching in facing the inevitable conclusion of his recommendation:

> Some say that if all were chaste the human species would cease to exist. But does not the church teach that the end of the world is bound to come? And science equally shows that some day man's life upon earth, and earth itself, must cease; why then does the idea that the end of the human species might come as the result of good and righteous living arouse so much indignation? . . . If man attained perfection and lived in chastity, mankind would cease to exist, and why, indeed, should it then live on earth, for they would become like angels who neither marry nor are given in marriage, as is told in the New Testament.[11]

I do not know how a Christian could deny the force of this argument.

5) THE INSIGNIFICANCE ARGUMENT

This argument asserts that, given the spatial and temporal vastness of the universe, the human race is of such inconsequence that its continued existence is of no importance in the cosmic scheme of things. The only way in which humanity could be seen as intrinsically significant is upon the assumption that it was the special favorite of a god. Lovecraft destroys this argument wittily:

> What am I? What is the nature of the energy about me, and how does it affect me? So far I have seen nothing which could possibly give me the notion that cosmic force is the manifestation of a mind and will like my own infinitely magnified; a potent and purposeful consciousness which deals individually and directly with the miserable denizens of a wretched little flyspeck on the back door of a microscopic universe, and which singles this putrid excrescence out as the one spot whereto to send an onlie-begotten Son, whose mission is to redeem these accursed flyspeck-inhabiting lice which we call human beings—bah!! Pardon the "bah!" I feel several "bahs!", but out of courtesy I only say one. But it is all so very childish. I cannot help taking exception to a philosophy which would force this rubbish down my throat.[12]

This argument is perhaps the weakest of the five, for there is of course no reason why the fate of humanity should be considered from a cosmic perspective: human beings are obviously important to themselves, and the adoption of this human perspective is no less valid than the adoption of the cosmic perspective. But the mere fact that (as Tolstoy also affirmed) the human race is without question a temporary phenomenon in cosmic history—here today, gone tomorrow—could, at a minimum, provide a counterargument for any fancied moral imperative for the continuance of humanity. As it is a high probability that the human race will indeed cease to exist at some future point in time, any rationale for preserving the race will eventually come to naught merely by the passage of time.

In presenting these five arguments I again assert that none of them need be conclusive—only *plausible*. And I repeat that these arguments merely seek to provide some justification for what remains a prejudice—that the human race *ought* to be extirpated. But the notion that the human race *ought* to continue existence is just as much of a prejudice. No one could possibly be deemed (factually) "right" or (factually) "wrong" in asserting the one or the other. (The notion, propounded by certain evolutionary biologists, that the preservation of self, and even of society as a whole, is some kind of built-in instinct in humanity, is too preposterous to require refutation. At a minimum, on such a view suicide would become a physical impossibility.) The great majority of ethical disputes ultimately reach an impasse over just such prejudices and unsupported assumptions, which is why very few such disputes are resolvable. What we are dealing with, again, are not *facts* but *emotional responses to facts.*

I may have strayed far from Guenter Lewy, but I hope I have established that the attempt to establish an objective basis for morals is doomed. Certainly religion cannot provide that basis; or rather, the only way it could is if it could be proved that a given religion were metaphysically *true.* And yet, Lewy in an unguarded moment confesses that "the truth or falsity of a particular religious creed is not the issue before us" (W 81). This is a catastrophic admission. For Lewy, only the *results* of a moral stance are of importance; it makes no difference *why* someone takes that stance. But surely it does make a difference. Consider three persons, each of whom refrains from indiscriminate killing. Person A does so because he believes it would not be conducive to the functioning of a civilized society; person B does so because he believes it would place his own life and comforts in jeopardy; person C does so because a little green man from Jupiter has told him so. How are we to assess the ethical stances of these three individuals? Even though the *effects* of their moral stances (refraining from indiscriminate killing) are identical, surely A is most worthy of praise; B less so, because his motive is manifestly self-serving; and C least so, because his motive is absurd and overwhelmingly likely to be false. It would seem that religious ethics are very much of this third sort. Lewy, in failing to probe the *sources* of religious ethics, unwittingly arrives at the conclusion that a religiously based morality is worth promoting *whether it is based upon a valid motive or not.* Remember that I am not making a claim for the "truth" or "falsity" of the moral principle itself ("Indiscriminate killing is bad"); this is, and can be, neither true nor false. But the motivations that lead to it *can* be assessed in varying degrees of truth or falsehood, probability or improbability.

In spite of himself, therefore, Lewy ends up arguing that religiously based morals have a purely social utility. He explicitly rejects this notion—"the fact that I strongly affirm some of the most basic moral precepts of the Judeo-Christian tradition will hopefully dispel any notion that I appreciate religion only because of its social utility" (W 146)—but the course of his argument inevitably leads to that conclusion.

What is even more unfortunate, Lewy does not even prove his case that religion *is* socially useful—that it actually encourages "moral" (i.e., socially acceptable) behavior. One long chapter of his book is a lugubrious disquisition on the moral failings of the past two or three decades; predictably, the 1960s are the customary whipping boy, from which all horrors appear to have sprung. But the very next chapter seeks to refute the notion that the United States is a radically more secular society than it used to be decades ago. Lewy trumpets the fact that in the United States the levels of belief in God have remained remarkably uniform throughout the twentieth century, hovering between 90 and 95 percent; this allows him to proclaim proudly, "Religion is alive and well and shows no signs of disappearing from the scene" (W 65). I am entirely in agreement with him here. But Lewy does not appear to grasp a fundamental paradox in his argument: if the religious beliefs of average Americans have not been much affected by secularism, how is secularism to blame for rising crime rates, out-of-wedlock births, and other supposed moral and social evils? In particular, Lewy goes on and on about the social and moral evils afflicting African Americans, even though he is fully cognizant of the fact that African Americans are on the whole more religious than other Americans.

Consider Lewy's statement that "the percentage of Americans who condemned premarital sex as wrong declined from 68 percent in 1969 to 39 percent in 1985" (W 46). But if approximately 95 percent percent of Americans still believe in God, then a fair proportion of them must be among those who now no longer condemn premarital sex. What this indicates is not the decline of moral standards caused by increasing secularism (since Lewy has already established that religion is not in fact in decline in the United States), but an explicit or tacit disconnect between the religious beliefs people purport to hold and the moral beliefs they actually espouse. In other words, people claim to be religious but no longer believe everything that their sacred texts or their clerics tell them to believe in regard to important issues of social and moral behavior.

One possible indicator of the beneficial role of religion in regard to morals is its influence as a deterrent to crime; and one possible means for ascertaining this influence would be the relative degrees of religiosity found among the prison population as opposed to the population as a whole. If religion really deterred antisocial behavior, one would expect the prison population to be substantially, or at least minimally, less religious than the population at large, thereby establishing that the religious do not commit as many crimes as the nonreligious. This does not, however, seem to be the case. Lewy ridicules Paul Kurtz's assertion that "reseach studies have shown that the lowest percentage of inmates in prisons are freethinkers and unbelievers or individuals from such backgrounds, and that the highest percentage are from religious backgrounds," referring to this as "one of the most egregious misunderstandings of statistical data." I fear it is Lewy who has egregiously misunderstood the matter. As he states: "Since 89.4 precent of Americans are Christians, Jews, Muslims, or belong to other religions that practice prayer, and since freethinkers constitute no more than a tiny segment of the American population (less than 1 percent [*sic!*]), Kurtz's finding was, of course, hardly surprising" (W 89). But it *is*—or ought to be—surprising to those who believe in some kind of correlation between religion and antisocial behavior. In fact, the results are even more disconcerting to the pious than this. Citing a study from the 1950s, Walter Kaufmann notes: "The percentage of theists in our prisons is much higher than outside. The percentage of men who believe in hell is much higher in the prisons than outside. A much higher percentage of Roman Catholics than of Unitarians or Reform Jews, agnostics or atheists, commit murder."[13] This study was conducted at a time when religious conformity was far greater than it is now, so that we would expect the prison population to be markedly less religious than the general public. Kaufmann does not, however, wish to draw an antireligious message from this study: "This does not mean that Catholicism predisposes men toward murder, but that more crimes are committed by the poor, the uneducated, and the underprivileged; and a greater percentage of the members of the Catholic faith are in this category. For the same reason, Baptists have more than their share of the worst crimes."[14]

Lewy makes a great show of citing a variety of psychological studies that reveal some minimal correlation between religiosity and abstention from antisocial behavior, while at the same time relentlessly criticizing other studies whose results deny any such correlation. The differences between the behavior of the religious and the nonreligious cited in the former studies seem to me so slight as to be more plausibly explicable on other grounds—socioeconomic status being chief among them. I do not wish to pursue the matter here further; let me simply quote the findings of a team of well-respected sociologists who have themselves surveyed a great many such studies:

> Since most research on religion and morality has been associational in nature, the issue of the causes of the observed relationships has not been addressed. Strictly speaking, we cannot conclude that religious groups and degrees of activity have produced differences in moral behavior. People might simply affiliate with groups, the members of which behave as they do. In all probability, we feel that the groups and the extent of commitment probably are responsible for what has been found.[15]

And yet, I cannot forbear commenting on one especially succulent piece of fatuity on Lewy's part. He remarks in passing that "Western Europe appears to be dominated by a secular impulse" (W 82), going on to note the substantially lower levels of belief in God in Europe than in the United States. But he does not go on to pursue the obvious follow-up to this scenario—the relative degrees of criminal behavior in Western Europe and the United States—perhaps because he knows it will be utterly devastating to his entire argument. Where

Lewy is silent, I shall be happy to step in. A publication by the United Nations Office for Drug Control and Crime Prevention contains the following statistics of crime rates per million population for the year 1994 in various parts of the world; it is most illuminating. In North America, rapes averaged nearly 400 per million; in Western Europe, about 80. Assaults averaged nearly 8,000 per million; in Western Europe, about 1,500. Homicides averaged about 100 per million; in Western Europe, about 40. Robberies averaged more than 1,500 per million; in Western Europe, less than 500.[16] The extraordinarily high level of difference in these rates between the pious Americans and the secular Europeans entirely destroys any correlation between religious belief and socially acceptable behavior. If it is argued that it is misleading to compare different cultures in this manner, one can simply reply that (a) the cultures of Western Europeans and Americans are not so markedly different as to invalidate any such comparisons, and (b) if these differences in crime rates can be accounted for culturally, then that itself is an argument that religion does not enter greatly into the equation.

Lewy seems particularly exercised, as many of his conservative cohorts are, about alterations in regard to "traditional values concerning family ties and attitudes toward sex" (W 32). It is a bugaboo that haunts his entire volume. He notes, in tones of appropriate ominousness: "By considering the traditional sexual norms as just one of many different bases for forming various kinds of partnerships, they [the secular humanists] give respectability to lifestyles that often have damaging consequences" (W 31). Lewy does not explain this forbidding utterance, so it is not entirely clear what he means by it. Can he possibly be referring to homosexuality, a subject he rarely discusses in his tract? If so, he would be on the far right end even of the religious spectrum, for a number of the more liberal churches have given up the notion of homosexuality as "deviant" behavior, much less that it is somehow forbidden by God. More likely the reference is merely to alternative living arrangements evolved by heterosexual couples who eschew traditional marriage. Lewy betrays his prejudice in making anguished references to "the decline of the family" (W 43), when in fact it is only *his conception* of the family that is in decline. Consider the following remarkable set of assertions: "The symptoms of family decline are manifold and striking. The number of cohabiting unmarried couples in the United States tripled during the 1970s and nearly doubled again during the 1980s. In today's society, divorce is available upon request and carries no social stigma. The religious and moral bonds that hold families together have been loosened" (W 43). Another self-appointed Jeremiah from the political right, Gertrude Himmelfarb, has made a similarly fatuous utterance on this issue: "Those who seldom or never attend church have seven times the cohabitation rate of those who do."[17]

Exactly why cohabitation—people living together without marriage—should be so frightening to our friends on the right is something they never bother to explain; they must feel it is self-evident. But surely it is abundantly self-evident that an increasing number of individuals are rebelling at the stifling control of social practices that both religion and government have always sought to maintain. Religion in particular, even after it was expelled from the government, still sought (and continues to this day to seek) to supervise, or place its imprimatur, upon as many aspects of social and individual existence as it can—birth, sex, marriage, recreation (remember Sunday laws?), and death. It claims to do so in order to "sanctify" these critical stages of life, but it is really a grab for power, and religions have bitterly and furiously resisted any diminution or rejection of their power in these and other areas. As late as 1907, a papal decree declared civil marriage to be null and void. What is happening now is that more and more people are realizing that a loving relationship does not require the validation of some cleric mumbling words in front of an altar, or even a piece of paper issued by the government. Even in the bearing of children, couples are no longer seeking religious or governmental sanction. The number of married people with children in the United States actually *declined* slightly in absolute numbers from 1970 to 1998, in spite of a population increase of 66 million in that period. The number of children living with unmarried couples increased 665 percent in that same period.[18] Marriage, it is abundantly clear, is a purely artificial social arrangement fostered by religion and government because it is more convenient for religion and government that people be neatly paired up rather than being dangerously free individuals.

At the same time that Lewy is wringing his hands over what he perceives to be sexual laxity and the decline of the family, he (in tune with his conservative friends) pays no attention whatever to other societal tendencies that clearly do violate Christian teachings — or, more precisely, the teachings of Christ. Shall I have the temerity, in this new Gilded Age we find ourselves in, to deprecate the pursuit and acquisition of money? Is this not the most widespread contravention of Christ's utterances that present-day society can offer? Do we really need to quote once more all those famous tags: "Blessed are the poor in spirit: for theirs is the kingdom of heaven" (Matt. 5:3); "Lay not up for yourselves treasures upon earth" (Matt. 6:19); "Ye cannot serve God and mammon" (Matt. 6:24); "the deceitfulness of riches" (Matt. 13:22); "If thou wilt be perfect, go and sell that thou hast, and give to the poor, and thou shalt have treasure in heaven" (Matt. 19:21); "Verily I say unto you, That a rich man shall hardly enter into the kingdom of heaven" (Matt. 19:23)? And yet, Lewy maintains a stony silence about the appalling money-grubbing that has characterized American "civilization" from its inception. As I write these words, I note the wild popularity of the best-selling religious tract, *The Prayer of Jabez*, by Bruce H. Wilkinson, which preaches that it is entirely acceptable to ask God for assistance in securing large amounts of cash and property, "as long as that success has a godly purpose," whatever that may mean.[19] More than four million copies of this pint-size book have been sold in a few months.

It is worth pausing on this whole notion of "traditional values." Predictably, Lewy fails to define, except by implication, what he means by it. The great majority of conservative and religious critics seem to believe the phrase is self-evident, but in reality it rarely means anything except the morals the critics themselves grew up with and with which they, by the accident of their birth, feel comfortable. This seems a trifle myopic. What they fail to grasp is that morals have been evolving ever since human society was formed tens or hundreds of thousands of years ago. The morals dictated by any of the chief religions of humanity were simply the morals to which that particular society happened to grant its credence at that particular point in history. Even religious morals have evolved, as Lewy would be the first to admit. But neither he nor other religious critics have any understanding of the stupendous implications of *any* "evolution" or revision of the morals (or, indeed, of any other element) found in a sacred text: *it automatically renders it instantly unlikely that that sacred text could have been written under the inspiration of a deity.*

The point would be obvious if religionists were not as self-blinded as they are. Consider the matter of religious coercion. This was a commonly accepted, and indeed universally approved, practice of the Christian religion for nearly two millennia; only in the last century have reservations been made against it. It has abundant scriptural support (Jesus himself purportedly said, "Compel them to come in, that my house may be filled" [Luke 14:23]), and indeed the logic of Christianity requires it. If Christianity is the one true religion, the possibility that anyone could die outside its fold, and thereby go to hell, must be acutely painful to the pious, so that they are under an obligation to force all individuals to become Christians. This is, if anything is, a "traditional value"; and yet, it is a value no longer espoused except by extreme fundamentalists, and I imagine Lewy is not one of these. What of the persecution of witches? What of the condoning of slavery? What of the suppression of women's rights? All these things similarly have definitive scriptural support and have been practiced by Christians for centuries or millennia; they, too, must be "traditional values." Why are they not so recognized today?

Can it be that the actual morals recommended by the Bible do not in fact accord with the morals of a modern civilized society? Can it be that, in attempting to salvage what can be salvaged out of this morass of barbarism and intolerance, the Christian Church and such of its supporters as Guenter Lewy are presenting a kind of whitewashed Christianity in order for it to be acceptable to present-day citizens who are not religious bigots, slave owners, and misogynists?

What is more, is it not obvious that every departure from these teachings casts doubt upon the inerrancy and divine inspiration of the Bible? The only recourse left to the devout is the desperate expedient of assuming that there has been some sort of faulty "transmission" of the divine text. We have already seen—in the case of William F. Buckley, who tentatively makes this argument—how ridiculous are the consequences of this stance. Would it not, indeed, be an astounding coincidence if exactly those portions of the Bible that have now become an embarrassment—whether it be moral/social doctrines such as those listed above, or physical doctrines such as the geocentric theory or the flatness of the earth,[20] also stated or implied in numerous biblical passages—were "faultily" transmitted? How can one pick and choose, as from a smorgasbord, what one wishes to believe in a text that is purportedly the word of God? If it is *not* the word of God, why should we accord it any greater respect than any other ethical theory that has been propounded in the last three thousand years of human history? Need I repeat Russell Kirk's asseveration on this point? "The Resurrection lacking, what we call Christianity would be a mere congeries of moral exhortations, at best; and exhortations founded upon no more authority than the occasional utterances of an obscure man whose hints of divinity and half-veiled claims of power to judge the quick and the dead might be regarded as manifestations of delusions of grandeur."

Of course, the whole notion that the Bible was inspired by God—although still believed by a third of the American people, as Lewy points out (W 75)—never had much going for it. What is the support for this notion? In large part, the argument appears to run as follows: The Bible is divinely inspired because it says so. This is what I call the argument from assertion: something is true because I say it is. Consider the statement in 2 Timothy 3:16: "All scripture is given by inspiration of God." Well, I myself could write a scripture, consisting of exactly two sentences: "This book is divinely inspired. S. T. Joshi is the son of God." Therefore, on this reasoning, I must *be* the son of God. Some of the other rationales that Christians have supplied over the years—e.g., the belief that various texts in the Old Testament, specifically Isaiah, predicted the birth of Jesus Christ and must therefore have been inspired by God—are not quite as preposterous as this, but they are preposterous enough.

What exactly *are* Christian morals anyway? More specifically, on what basis are they founded? The conventional belief that Christianity is, at least in principle, a religion of love and charity is based on what Jesus calls his two commandments: "The first of all the commandments is, Hear, O Israel; The Lord our God is one Lord: And thou shalt love the Lord thy God with all thy heart, and with all thy soul, and with all thy mind, and with all thy strength: this is the first commandment. And the second is like, namely this, Thou shalt love thy neighbour as thyself. There is none other commandment greater than these" (Matt. 12:29–31). At the moment I am not concerned with the degree to which any Christian has actually observed these commandments; the likelihood that the great majority of Christians have not done so does not in itself detract from the abstract validity (if any) of these principles. But a quandary is immediately evident: If the first commandment is false (i.e., if there is no god to whom we can direct our love), on what (objective) foundation can any Christian base the second? The great majority of Jesus' moral axioms have as their motivation the need for human beings to mimic the unconditional love that God purportedly offers; hence his celebrated utterance, "Love your enemies, bless them that curse you, do good to them that hate you" (Matt. 5:44), because these acts presumably are a dim reflection—the closest that human beings can achieve—to God's own love of sinners and of those who reject him. But if there is no god, then these principles have no metaphysical support. They may still be worthy moral axioms upon which to base a society, but they will no longer have the *authority* that many of the pious desire.

It is a matter of debate, in any event, to what degree either the Christian God or Jesus himself demonstrated this unconditional love. Christians have long been fond of believing that there is a fundamental distinction between the ethics of the Old Testament and the New. One Christian scholar, George F. Thomas, has said of the former: "The primary ethical principle of the Old Testament is that of *obedience to God's will*."[21] There is, indeed, nothing worse in the Old Testament than atheists, heretics, infidels, and unbelievers: "The fool hath said in his heart, There is no God. Corrupt are they, and have done abominable iniquity: there is none that doeth good. God looked down from heaven upon the children of men, to see if there were any that did understand, that did seek God. Every one of them is gone back: they are altogether become filthy; there is none that doeth good, no, not one" (Ps. 53:1–3). But I regret to say that the New Testament is not as much different in this regard as some would like to think; as Thomas himself states in characterizing Jesus' conception of the Kingdom of God: "The most fundamental thing about the Kingdom is that it is the *Reign of God* in the lives of men and rests upon *obedience to God* as the Lord of all life."[22] It would therefore appear that no matter how virtuous one's life is in other regards, a refusal to acknowledge the existence of God, or the divinity of Jesus, would condemn one to hell, as Jesus himself states, "Whosoever shall deny me before men, him will I also deny before my Father which is in heaven" (Matt. 10:33). How this attitude is to be reconciled with "loving your enemies" is beyond my understanding.

It is evident, then, that a multitude of specific moral doctrines propounded by Jesus have been jettisoned, or at least swept under the rug, by modern Christians—chiefly because they have been found to be crude, barbaric, primitive, and wholly unworkable. Consider, for example, the doctrine of hell. It is well known that the notion of hell in early Judaism was similar to that of the Greek Hades, i.e., a place where *all* the souls of the dead, of whatever moral stature, reposed. Only in late Judaism did the notion evolve of hell as a repository for the wicked, and it is this latter conception that Jesus has adopted. Some theologians have sought to distance Jesus himself from an acknowledgment of the literal existence of hell, but this can only be done by a sophistical obfuscation of the plain meaning of numerous passages in the gospels. There are too many mentions of "hell fire" (Matt. 5:22), "eternal damnation" (Mark 3:29), and the like for them all to be later interpolations. What is more, as I have demonstrated earlier, Jesus was quite convinced that only a relatively small proportion of humanity would ever get to heaven, the others being consigned to hell ("For many are called, but few are chosen": Matt. 22:14). Later passages in the Bible make clear that hell is a very real place: "Then he [Jesus] will mete out punishment to those who refuse to acknowledge God and who will not obey the gospel of our Lord Jesus. They shall suffer the penalty of eternal destruction, cut off from the presence of the Lord and the splendour of his might" (2 Thess. 1:8–9 [REB]). This conception endured in Christian thought for the better part of two millennia; as Edward Westermarck has noted, "The immense bulk of Christians have naturally regarded hell and its agonies as material facts."[23]

But in the last two centuries the doctrine of hell has become something of an embarrassment to Christians. Why? In the first place, it has come to seem unjust to condemn certain types of "sinners"—those, for example, who have led exemplary lives but who simply did not "acknowledge God"—to *everlasting damnation.* The crime does not seem commensurate with the penalty. Earlier Christian thinkers made a kind of way station called Limbo for those who, having the misfortune of being born prior to Jesus' revelation, did not have the benefit of his teaching; Plato and Aristotle, those *animae naturaliter Christianae,* were prominent among these. But this exception was not granted for subsequent heretics, infidels, and unbelievers. And yet, the doctrine of hell has surely fallen into disrepute largely because it is simply implausible, unverifiable, and contrary to what we know about the nature of the universe. In other words, there probably is no such place. But stated in this way, it should be clear that the doctrine of hell has lost its credibility *almost exclusively from the influence of secular thinkers.*

Accordingly, many churches (the fundamentalists, as always, excluded) have sought to brush hell under the rug. In 1979 the Sacred Congregation for the Doctrine of the Faith decreed that hell is merely a place where sinners "will be deprived of the sight of God." (This strikes me as a very bizarre kind of punishment, especially for atheists: the one thing an atheist would want, one would suppose, is separation from God, so that this would really be an atheist's heaven.) But we learn further that "the official magisterium . . . does [not] affirm that any individual human person has been condemned to hell"!²⁴ This is all most remarkable. Hell is apparently either a real or a metaphorical place—but no one is there! If some people regard it as a trifle uncivilized to condemn perfectly decent but irreligious people as David Hume and John Stuart Mill to such a place, then surely no one would have any compunction in placing Hitler or Stalin there. So the doctrine of hell seems to be passing away, even though one recent Christian philosopher has stated plainly that "no emancipation from that doctrine is possible without abandoning Christianity itself."²⁵

There is also the issue of whether certain facets of Christian doctrine are so unworkable in the real world as to be morally empty. Jesus' notions of loving your enemies and not resisting evil (see Matt. 5:44, 5:39) seem prime candidates of this sort. It may well be the case that Jesus' Apocalypticism—his assumption of the imminent coming of the Kingdom of God—was the origin of these doctrines, but nevertheless, there they are, and the fact that the overwhelming majority of Christians find it impossible to obey them, and in some cases even to accept their validity, makes one wonder whether the original ethics of Jesus—without the modifications brought on by the development of secular civilization—can be of any practical value. Thomas Paine lashed out against the loving-enemies idea as follows: "Morality is injured by prescribing to it duties that, in the first place, are impossible to be performed, and if they could be would be productive of evil; or, as before said, be premiums for crime. The maxim of *doing as we would be done unto* does not include this strange doctrine of loving enemies; for no man expects to be loved himself for his crime or for his enmity."²⁶

Religions, therefore, have been compelled to "evolve" their doctrines, even if it means departing farther and farther from the letter and even the spirit of their own scriptures, in order not to become entirely irrelevant to the evolving societies in which they find themselves. As Lovecraft put it rather pungently: "Half of what Buddha or Christus or Mahomet said is either simply idiocy or downright destructiveness, as applied to the western world of the twentieth century; whilst virtually *all* of the emotional-imaginative background of assumptions from which they spoke, is now proved to be sheer childish primitiveness."[27] And yet, it seems to me that that evolution is almost always *subsequent* to the evolution of the societies themselves, or at least of the (largely secular) thinkers who have heralded those changes. Where, exactly, does Christianity stand in regard to the evolution of such doctrines (which I assume few would deny are a moral advance) as the liberation of women or the humane treatment of animals? These are only two, but many others could be noted. I regret to say that Christianity has done almost nothing to advance these causes but instead has trailed far behind secular society and secular philosophers in advocating them.

The long history of the subjugation of women need not, at this point, be rehearsed. Along with racism and religious tyranny, it is perhaps the most dismal chapter of human history, and that chapter is by no means over even now. That for millennium after millennium half the human race could be held in effective bondage, their intellectual, economic, political, aesthetic, and other resources only minimally utilized, would seem to make another strong case for the extirpation of the human race as unworthy of bare existence. At this point it is also unnecessary to rehash the degree to which the Bible reinforces this subjugation, from almost the very first chapter of Genesis onward. Some peculiarities, however, may be noted. Exactly why should a woman who bears a female child be regarded as more "unclean" than one who bears a male child, to the extent that she should be set apart from the community for two weeks instead of one (Lev. 12:2–5)? Why should a woman who is not a virgin when she marries a man be stoned to death (Deut. 22:20–21), but no similar penalty meted out to a man who similarly errs? More entertaining material can be found in the epistles of Paul, one of the great misogynists of human history. The following passages are also very well known, but it is difficult to resist quoting them:

> But I would have you know, that the head of every man is Christ; and the head of the woman is the man; and the head of Christ is God. . . . For the man is not of the woman; but the woman of the man. Neither was the man created for the woman; but the woman for the man. . . . Let your women keep silence in the churches: for it

is not permitted unto them to speak; but they are commanded to be under obedience, as also saith the law. And if they will learn any thing, let them ask their husbands at home; for it is a shame for women to speak in the church. (1 Cor. 11:3, 8–9; 14:34–35)

It is no wonder that pioneering feminist Elizabeth Cady Stanton, in her fiery pamphlet *Bible and Church Degrade Woman* (1885), wrote: "the Church has done more to degrade woman than all other adverse influences put together."[28]

Christian misogyny did not, of course, end with Paul. A quite random sampling of opinions over the past two or three centuries, even if restricted to American thinkers, is illuminating. Consider, for example, the seventeenth-century Puritan theologian Cotton Mather, who already showed himself to be a buffoon in his crackpot defense of witchcraft belief in *Wonders of the Invisible World* (1693). Among his hundreds of books and pamphlets is *Ornaments for the Daughters of Zion* (1692), a manual of conduct for the "virtuous woman." Here are some of the duties of the wife:

> Her *Love* to her Husband, will also admit, yea, and produce the *fear* of, *a cautious Diligence never to displease him.* 'Twas this which the Apostle *Peter* meant when he recommends unto the Women, *a chast Conversation coupled with Fear* [1 Pet. 3:2]; and *Paul,* when he requires of the Woman, *to reverence her Husband* [Eph. 5:33]. While she looks upon him as *her Guide,* by the Constitution of God, she will not scruple with *Sarah* to call him *her Lord;* and though she does not *fear* his *Blows,* yet she does *fear* his *Frowns,* being loth in any Way to grieve him, or cause an *Head-ake* in the Family by offending him.[29]

Once again, it is not clear what the husband has done to deserve this wondrously sycophantic treatment. And Mather's allusions to various biblical passages make it quite clear that he is simply following quite literally (or at best drawing out the obvious implications of) the words of a text he regards as sacred and divinely inspired.

Let us move on about a century and a half. Jonathan F. Stearns, pastor of the first Presbyterian Church of Newark, New Jersey, delivered a sermon in 1837 published as *Female Influence, and the True Christian Mode of Its Exercise.* In blandly citing many of the most notoriously misogynist passages in the New Testament, Stearns remarks (quite soundly) that "the apostle speaks in these passages in a tone of authority," and then goes on to say:

> But I apprehend it will not appear difficult, to one who duly considers the nature of the case, as well as the history of the world, to see *reasons* sufficient to establish the wisdom of these precepts, independent of apostolic authority. I am confident no virtuous and delicate female, who rightly appreciates the design of her being, and desires to sustain her own influence and that of her sex, would desire to abate one jot or tittle from the seeming restrictions imposed upon her conduct in these and the like passages. They are designed, not to *degrade*, but to *elevate* her character, — not to cramp, but to afford a *salutary* freedom, and give a useful direction to the energies of the feminine mind. A prominent object of the apostle seems to have been, to protect those peculiar traits of character, which are the chief source of woman's influence over society, from the injury they are likely to sustain from rude exposure in public life. Let woman throw off her feminine character, and her power to benefit society is *lost;* her loveliness, her dignity, her own chief protection is *lost.*[30]

The argument that the various "restrictions" on women's thought and action were designed for their *benefit* is one that was used long after Stearns lived and died.

It is almost painful to quote from *Woman as God Made Her* (1869), by J. D. Fulton, a Baptist clergyman who distinguished himself by writing numerous polemics against the Catholic Church. This fellow actually appeals to science (or what, in his mind, passes for such) in the following bit of erudition:

> Woman's mind is quicker, more flexible, more elastic than man's, though the brain, in weight, is much lighter. Man's brain weighs, on an average, three pounds and eight ounces. Woman's brain weighs, on an average, two pounds and four ounces. The female intellect is impregnated with the qualities of her sensitive nature. It acts rather

through a channel of electricity than of reasoning. Its perceptions of truth come, as it were, by intuition. It is under the influence of the heart, that has deep and unfathomable wells of feeling; and truth is felt in every pulse, rather than reasoned out and demonstrated. You cannot offend a woman so quick, in any way, as to ask her why she wishes to do thus, or why she reaches such a conclusion. Her reply is, invariably, *"Cause!"* And that is nearly all she knows about it; and yet woe be to the man who ignores her intuitions, or treats with disdain her advice. Woman reads character quicker and better than man. Her policy lies in her heart. She feels rather than reasons. Man reasons rather than feels. Hence she is a helpmeet. She fills a lack, and supplies a want.[31]

Fulton's contemporary, Orestes Augustus Brownson, is an interesting case. He was raised in a Calvinist Congregationalist home and was ordained as a Universalist preacher in 1826, then as a Unitarian in 1832. At this time he spoke against organized religion and slavery and endorsed women's rights and education. In 1844, however, he converted to Roman Catholicism and violently repudiated his earlier Protestantism, chiefly on the grounds that it vaunted individualism and was opposed to the organic unity of society that Brownson sought. In an anonymous review of several feminist tracts, published in *Catholic World* for 1869, Brownson declared himself opposed to woman suffrage; amusingly enough, he did so in tones that sound remarkably akin to those of the conservative social critics of today:

The conclusive objection to the political enfranchisement of women is, that it would weaken and finally break up and destroy the Christian family. The social unit is the family, not the individual; and the greatest danger to American society is, that we are rapidly becoming a nation of isolated individuals, without family ties or affections. The family has already been much weakened, and is fast disappearing. We have broken away from the old homestead, have lost the restraining and purifying associations that gathered round it, and live away from home in hotels and boarding-houses. We are daily losing the faith, the virtues, the habits, and the manners without which the family cannot be sustained; and when the family goes, the nation goes too, or ceases to be worth preserving. God made the family the type and basis of society; "male and female made he them." A large and influential class of women not only neglect but disdain the retired and simple domestic virtues, and scorn to be tied down to the modest but essential duties—the drudgery, they call it—of wives and mothers. This, coupled with the separate pecuniary interests of husband and wife secured, and the facility of divorce *a vinculo matrimonii* allowed by the laws of most of the States of the Union, make the family, to a fearful extent, the mere shadow of what it was and of what it should be.[32]

He goes on to picture the horrors that might result if the vote were granted to women:

Extend now to women suffrage and eligibility; give them the political right to vote and to be voted for; render it feasible for them to enter the arena of political strife, to become canvassers in elections and candidates for office, and what remains of family union will soon be dissolved. The wife may espouse one political party, and the husband another, and it may well happen that the husband and wife may be rival candidates for the same office, and one or the other doomed to the mortification of defeat. Will the husband like to see his wife enter the lists against him, and triumph over him? Will the wife, fired with political ambition for place or power, be pleased to see her own husband enter the lists against her, and succeed at her expense? Will political rivalry and the passions it never fails to engender increase the mutual affection of husband and wife for each other, and promote domestic union and peace, or will it not carry into the bosom of the family all the strife, discord, anger, and division of the political canvass?[33]

Another writer in *Catholic World,* John Paul MacCorrie, writes even more heatedly about women's rights:

We contend, and we regret not without some opposition, that in the home and family are concentrated woman's first and highest "rights." "Let her learn first to govern her own house," says St. Paul;

and whatever else she may claim in common with man must be after her duty has been fully acquitted in this respect. For each sex, because it is a sex, has its own specific and peculiar appointments which cannot be delegated to the other, and which being abandoned by those to whose care Providence has entrusted them, must remain for ever unaccomplished.

Say what we will, woman was created to be a wife and a mother; that is, after a special religious calling to the service of God, her highest destiny. To that destiny all her instincts are fashioned and directed; for it she has been endowed with transcendent virtues of endurance, patience, generous sympathies, and indomitable perseverance.[34]

With the turn of the twentieth century and the increasingly vocal demands by feminists for the right to vote, a succession of religiously inclined opponents actually declared suffrage to be anti-Christian. Representative of them is William Parker, who wrote a variety of eccentric treatises including *The Fundamental Error of Woman Suffrage* (1915). In it he declared:

It is a notable fact that women are more easily deceived than men. It largely accounts for the eagerness with which they embrace these false and antichristian teachings. A strategic move was made when this antichristian spirit enlisted so many women in its cause. It accomplishes this by promising them freedom from the bondage and servitude imposed by man, a release from the restraints of that institution called home. No longer hampered by the necessity of motherhood, she can take her place beside man and vie with him in those things that will stultify her God-given nature, debase her womanhood, cause her to deny her Creator, and, in the end, to repudiate her own soul. You can readily see that such doctrines are directly antagonistic to true Christianity. When you consider the indisputable fact, Christianity is the only religion that re-establishes the home, sanctifies motherhood, and glorifies womanhood.[35]

If it be assumed these opinions (which could be replicated almost ad infinitum) are only representative of a benighted era when people didn't know any better, let us turn to some relatively recent documents. John Erskine was a poet, novelist, and critic who taught for nearly thirty years at Columbia (1909–37). In the piquant treatise *The Influence of Women and Its Cure* (1936), Erskine ingeniously argues that women—who have customarily been thought to be, on the whole, more religious than men—are actually causing men to leave the church. How so? Just listen:

> The women are taking the masculine element out of religion, so that the men can't find in the churches what they need. You can state the problem in few words. The male element in religion is positive, the female is passive. You can turn to religion either to give something or to get something. You either are aflame with a vision and wish to utter it, or you are looking for comfort, for a spiritual salve, a bandage or a plaster. The masculine form of religion is aggressive, it would build an empire, it would spread its gospel; the feminine form is introspective, it is occupied with its own sensations in the presence of a ritual or a discipline, it would rather conform than push ahead.[36]

One more item and I am done. The Jesuit Joseph H. Fichter taught at Loyola University for much of the period between 1947 and 1992; late in life he actually advocated marriage for priests and became a member of the National Organization of Women. But early in his career he wrote "The Decline of Femininity" (April 1945), asserting that women should not do men's work and that many women (except for Catholics) are being led by contemporary societal influences into a licentious lifestyle. Fichter's analysis of the cause of this woeful decline in morality is one that would have warmed Guenter Lewy's heart: "Modern civilization has lost its sense of sin and moved away from God."[37]

Conversely, many of the major advocates of women's rights over the past two centuries have been wholly or largely secular. The pioneering writer of them all, Mary Wollstonecraft, wife of the atheist William Godwin and author of *A Vindication of the Rights of Woman* (1792), did have some ecstatic religious experiences in youth, but by the end of her life had adopted a deism similar to Thomas Paine's.[38]

The agnosticism of John Stuart Mill, author of *The Subjection of Women* (1869), is too well known for citation, although he prudently withheld the publication of his *Three Essays on Religion* (1874) during his lifetime. I have already cited the atheist Elizabeth Cady Stanton. Her longtime colleague, Susan B. Anthony, was not quite as hostile to religion; she wavered between the Quakerism of her youth and a vague Unitarianism. As her biographer notes, "Susan never denied the existence of God, but her beliefs were secularized and lodged in the world around her."[39] Another leading feminist of the later nineteenth and early twentieth centuries, Carrie Chapman Catt, read Darwin and Spencer in her youth and was always highly skeptical and critical of religion: "Organized religion held little interest for her and she found the antifeminism of most churches exasperating."[40] The agnosticism of Virginia Woolf, author of *A Room of One's Own* (1929), is also well known. As her nephew and biographer writes, "After a momentary conversion in childhood she lost all faith in revealed religion and, while never committing herself to any positive declaration, she maintained an attitude sometimes of mild, sometimes of aggressive agnosticism."[41] The catalog could be greatly extended down to the present day.

It is clear, then, that religion—specifically the Judeo-Christian religion—has done virtually nothing, in two thousand years, to foster social, political, intellectual, and cultural equality between men and women, and in fact has done everything it possibly could to stand in the way of it. What is more important to note is that the Bible (a divinely inspired text, in the minds of its believers) sanctions this inequality emphatically and repeatedly, and every departure by the religious from its dictates on these issues is a departure from Judeo-Christian belief itself. One cannot be a religious Jew or a Christian and believe in equal rights for women.

As for the evolution of the humane treatment of animals, the record is no better. We have already seen that the claim that Christianity fosters equality among all human beings is a sham; such a claim could not even be plausibly made in regard to animals, as the Bible so unequivocally denies any rights whatever to animals. Can we forget that, in the very first chapter of Genesis, we are told: "And God said,

Let us make man in our image, after our likeness: and let them have *dominion* over the fish of the sea, and over the fowl of the air, and over the cattle, and over all the earth, and over every creeping thing that creepeth upon the earth" (Gen. 1:26). Surely "dominion" here can mean nothing but the power of life and death. The New Testament is no better, as witness Paul's contemptuous remark: "For it is written in the law of Moses, Thou shalt not muzzle the mouth of the ox that treadeth out the corn. Doth God take care for oxen?" (1 Cor. 9:9).

It was the redoubtable Thomas Aquinas who fossilized Christian teaching on the subject, so that only the most minimal advances in the treatment of animals occurred until well into the eighteenth century. In *Summa contra Gentiles* he wrote:

> If in Holy Scripture there are found some injunctions forbidding the infliction of some cruelty towards brute animals . . . this is either for removing a man's mind from exercising cruelty towards other men, lest anyone, from exercising cruelty upon brutes, should go on hence to human beings; or because the injury inflicted on animals turns to a temporal loss for some man, either the person who inflicts the injury or some other.[42]

It appears, therefore, that treating animals in a civilized manner is only of possible benefit to humans—animals have no rights whatever in the matter. Aquinas was, indeed, being quite orthodox, for does not the Bible claim that only human beings have souls? It was on this basis that Descartes devised his notorious theory that animals do not feel pain: since they lack souls, they must also lack consciousness; therefore they are mere "machines." We have already noted the sorry confusion into which C. S. Lewis lapses when attempting to defend a similar notion.

It was only in the eighteenth century that matters began to change, and, once again, the impetus came again largely from secularists. As a leading historian of animal rights asserts, "In the early years of the century, . . . it was secular writers who began to outnumber the theologians in their support for 'brute' nature."[43] A strong impetus came from science, specifically the observations by naturalists of the unnerving similarities between apes and human beings. (As Mencken once wrote, "The important thing is that ape and man are biological cousins and as closely related as duck and canary bird. The anatomical and physiological differences between them are mainly trivial; the likenesses are innumerable and profound. Shave a gorilla and it would be almost impossible, at twenty paces, to distinguish him from a heavyweight champion of the world. Skin a chimpanzee, and it would take an autopsy to prove he was not a theologian."[44])

The record of the Christian religion in regard to the treatment of animals is poor at best. Let not the pious bring forward the case of Francis of Assisi, since it is widely acknowledged that in spite of his preaching to birds and references to "brother Wolf" he "accepted the anthropocentric view that all creation exists for humankind's benefit."[45] While some other religions, ancient and modern—Pythagoreanism, Hinduism, Buddhism, even some aspects of Islam—have promoted respect for animals (although their basis for doing so is the quite nonsensical doctrine of the transmigration of souls), in the West the advance has come largely as a product of the overall moral advance of secular civilization that similarly decreed torture (including torture of witches and heretics), forced conversion, and wars over religious doctrine to be beyond the bounds of civilized society.

Let Ambrose Bierce have the last word on this subject. Responding to a preacher who maintained, "I will quit preaching if any one can give anything new and beneficial to mankind that is not in the New Testament," Bierce replied:

> Very well, Doctor; just have the goodness to point out those passages which command, teach or suggest kindness to dumb animals. It will hardly be denied, I think, that kindness to animals—to domestic ones, at least—is "beneficial to mankind"; and if it is not taught in the New Testament it is "new" in the sense in which you use the word. . . . I do not say that there should be anything in the New Testament about man's duty to the animals; I only say in point of fact there is not. Nor is that the whole truth: there is not anywhere in the whole scheme of Christianity, so far as I know—neither in its prayer books, nor in its catechisms, in the writings of its

Early Fathers, in any of its canonical literature and accepted utterances of its most authoritative expounders up to the present century (perhaps I might say the present quarter century) any hint or intimation that cruelty to the helpless creatures that we hold to the service of our needs and pleasures is incompatible with holiness and the fear of the Lord. So far as concerns Christianity and Christians, justice to animals is very new indeed—so new that it has not yet passed the stage of ridicule.[46]

And yet, in spite of the inconclusiveness of his findings, and in spite of repeated assertions both by himself and by religious leaders that religion is not necessary to good morals, Lewy ends with the following grand peroration:

A society that tries to cut itself off from the religious roots of its moral heritage is doomed to moral decline. . . . Society needs a morality that will curb the antisocial tendencies of human beings, and this morality cannot be taught simply on the rational grounds that it is socially necessary. No society has yet been successful in teaching morality without religion, for morality cannot be created. It requires the support of tradition, and this tradition is generally linked to religious precepts. Certainly in the eyes of the great majority of the American people, morality is inseparably connected to religion—the moral rules are seen as God-given and derived from religion—and this connection yields concrete results. . . . There are nonbelievers who engage in morally praiseworthy deeds, but it should be remembered that their conduct is considered praiseworthy because it is the sort of conduct that has been prescribed by the Judeo-Christian norm that by now is an implicit part of our moral tradition. (W 131–35)

For once I am rendered almost speechless by this excursion into sustained and unadulterated imbecility. Where to begin in shooting down this rubbish?

We've heard this business about "moral decline" before. Earlier, Lewy quoted with approval exactly the same comment by George Washington that got Joe Lieberman into so much trouble: "Whatever may be conceded to the influence of refined education on minds of peculiar structure, reason and experience both forbid us to expect that national morality can prevail in exclusion of religious principle" (W 124). Washington is, in effect, making the claim that religion is "essential" to morals, but if so, then by definition no nonreligious person can be moral. But even a single instance of a nonreligious person who led an upright life—David Hume or John Stuart Mill, for example—is enough to shatter this argument. The best that could then be asserted is that religion is *helpful* to good morals, and even this weaker formulation is, as we have seen, highly questionable.

So "morality cannot be taught simply on the rational grounds that it is socially necessary"? Why not, pray tell? What does it say about the mass of human beings that they cannot, on this hypothesis, behave in a moral manner unless they are duped by fantasies and improbabilities? Is the person who behaves "morally" because he considers it a debt he owes to a society that protects him from murder and robbery and rape and chicanery really worse than the person who behaves "morally" because he thinks a (probably imaginary) God might otherwise send him after death to a (probably imaginary) hell? Are the latter's motivations not merely likely to be false but also contemptible? Does reason count for so little among the general public? If so, why should that state of affairs be blandly tolerated instead of being censured? Has the advance of knowledge and civilization over the past three millennia all gone for naught?

And Lewy also informs us that "no society has yet been successful in teaching morality without religion, for morality cannot be created." In the first place, morality *is* created, as I have already demonstrated. Secondly, the idea that a morally sound secular society has not yet existed says nothing about the possibility that it might not exist in the future. Once again, Lewy's vision is curiously myopic. Secularism as a coherent mode of thought is scarcely more than two or three centuries old, and over much of this period it has had to fend off furious and irrational hostility from orthodoxy; meanwhile, religion has held the field for countless millennia. Even if it is assumed (and I am not yet prepared to make that assumption) that secularism has failed to articulate a morality readily acceptable to a wide spectrum of the populace, the future may be very different. Even Lewy, in hoping against hope for a regeneration of morality as he conceives it, writes, "I am ... enough of an antihistoricist and optimist to believe that we humans make our own history and are not doomed to be prisoners of some inevitable destiny" (W 145). I am myself not so optimistic on the matter — stupidity, fear, wishful thinking, and irrationalism, the great religion-producers, have flourished throughout human history, and I see no indication of their radical or imminent decline — but certainly societies can change radically. Let me repeat what I have stated in an earlier chapter: Two centuries ago it could have been truthfully asserted that no society had ever existed without the institution of slavery; a century and a half ago it could have been truthfully asserted that no society had ever granted women the right to vote. But if Lewy is willing to be an "antihistoricist and optimist" in his way, then I suppose I am permitted to be one in mine.

And as for the contention that unbelievers who behave morally are implicitly adhering to Judeo-Christian standards of morality, Lewy has the matter exactly reversed. It is precisely because Christian ethics have, in the last two centuries, been shorn of their numerous elements of savagery, bigotry, and exclusivity that they are now in approximate conformity with the secular morals that the advance of civilization has engendered; and I repeat that this entire process has only come about because Christians have tacitly or explicitly *rejected* a multitude of moral axioms and adjurations plainly found in their scripture and plainly attributed to God or the son of God. Punishment of unbelievers, forced conversions, hostility to learning, subjugation of women, condoning of slavery — these and other moral principles found in the New Testament have been quietly jettisoned by mainline Christian churches, *and only through relentless criticism from secular thinkers.*

The overriding problem that religiously based morals face is a lack of *authority* if the metaphysical tenets of religion are found to be false or unlikely. Religious morals, qua morals, might be defended independently and could be self-supported as secular morals are, but in that case, they simply take their place as one moral code among many others, with no intrinsic superiority. If there is no God who has commanded human beings to obey a given set of morals, then the *compulsion* to obey these morals suddenly vanishes. I am far from condemning all religious morals in themselves, even if I believe the *bases* for those morals are entirely false. Consider, for example, the Golden Rule ("Therefore all things whatsoever ye would that men should do to you, do ye even so unto them" [Matt. 7:12]). Let it pass that this approximate formulation can be found in Confucius, Aristotle, and perhaps other thinkers before Christ; it strikes me as an eminently sound principle upon which to found a society, and it would certainly be welcome if more people (including more Christians) observed it. But my *reasons* for approving of this dictum are considerably at variance with the reasons by which an orthodox Christian is *obliged* to approve it, i.e., that it is the word of God or the son of God. I regard that as preposterous nonsense, and therefore a flawed *basis* upon which to establish the doctrine.

There is also the danger that religiously based morals will themselves be perceived to be "false" (although, as I have stated earlier, no morals can be "true" or "false" in any meaningful sense) if the metaphysics behind them is shown to be false. Lovecraft pondered this matter long ago:

> The time is coming when the old formulae will cease to enchant, for nothing can last eternally which is not founded on demonstrable truth. And for that future we must provide while there is time. Without attacking religion in any way, let us admit that virtue and honour are possible outside its charmed circle. Let us cultivate morality as an independent principle. Let us cultivate philanthropy for its own sake. True, religion has hitherto done marvels for these things—but religion will some day perish, and these things must never perish.[47]

Whether Lovecraft is correct in believing that "religion will some day perish" is not to the point: what *is* to the point is the widespread conviction among the intelligentsia and even among religious leaders that religion is no longer essential to moral behavior (what the general populace believes hardly matters). The formulation of a secular ethics thereby becomes a necessity if human society is to survive (granting, for the sake of argument, that it actually should survive). If it is really beyond the capacity of average persons to "cultivate morality as an independent principle," then it reveals a dismaying lack of civilization on their part. If one can only be moral because God tells you to be or because you will be rewarded after death, then the foundation of morals is indeed shaky. Ironically, it is not atheists or agnostics (whose belief in the observance of a moral code for the sake of pre-serving a civilized society is impervious to any new findings in science or philosophy, and will endure as long as civilized society itself endures) but religionists who are in danger of falling into the cele-brated Dostoevskian formulation "Without God, everything is per-mitted": if the basis of their morality (commandments from God) is pulled out from under them, where can they stand?

It would therefore seem that a pressing need today is the articulation of a valid set of *secular* morals, based upon a balance between the good of the individual and the good of society. That balance will always be a matter of debate; conservatives will always want society (and its hand-maiden, government) to have more of an upper hand in moral issues than liberals or secularists, either because of some psychological need for an imagined (and imaginary) "stability" in morals or because they wish to turn their brains off and live and behave—and expect others to live and behave—as they always have. Lewy warns us ominously "Secular-ization has created a dangerous uncertainty about morals" (W 135), but that uncertainty was always implicit in moral inquiry, and to blame sec-ularization for pointing it out is to blame the messenger for the message. There has never been a time when morals have been anything but uncer-tain and provisional; all that has changed is the degree of uncertainty and the degree to which some individuals or some segments of the pop-ulation have rebelled against the prevailing moral code. As with sexual morals, we are manifestly in an age of transition, perhaps rapid transi-tion, and the attempts by conservatives to freeze morals at a particular point that they happen to prefer is doomed to failure.

And the overall attempt to base morals upon religion is also doomed. Among the intellectual class, the overwhelming unlikelihood of the metaphysical truth of any specific religion is too well established, so that unless one adopts the stance (which Lewy explicitly rejects) that religion, even if false, is a useful means to rein in the great masses of the ignorant through threats of eternal punishment for bad behavior or enticing rewards of eternal bliss for good behavior, there would seem to be no choice but to establish ethics on some secular basis.

How exactly that is to be done is, indeed, a quandary. One of the most trenchant analyses of the "problem" of morals remains Walter Lippmann's *A Preface to Morals* (1929). His dissection of the downfall of religious authority for morality is unexceptionable, and his depiction of moral flux, even a certain moral confusion, among secularists struggling to found morals upon some other basis is, although a bit exaggerated, not without merit. But Lippmann fails—perhaps inevitably fails—in his solution to the dilemma. All he can recommend is a kind of moral "maturity" and a "religion of the spirit" to lead us out of the labyrinth. I confess to being quite uncertain what this "religion of the spirit" is, and I would be grateful to learn if any intelligible ideas can be derived from the following:

> Since [human beings] are unable to find a principle of order in the authority of a will outside themselves, there is no place they can find it except in an ideal of the human personality. But they do not have to invent such an ideal out of hand. The ideal way of life for men who must make their own terms with experience and find their own happiness has been stated again and again. . . .
>
> It [the religion of the spirit] alone can endure the variety and complexity of things, for the religion of the spirit has no thesis to defend. It seeks excellence wherever it may appear, and finds it in anything which is inwardly understood; its motive is not acquisition but sympathy. Whatever is completely understood with sympathy for its own logic and purposes ceases to be external and stubborn and is wholly tamed. To understand is not only to pardon, but in the end to love. There is no itch in the religion of the spirit to make men good by bearing down upon them with righteousness and making

them conform to a pattern. Its social principle is to live and let live.
It has the only tolerable code of manners for a society in which men
and women have become freely-moving individuals, no longer held
in the grooves of custom by their ancestral ways. It is the only dis-
position of the soul which meets the moral difficulties of an anar-
chical age, for its principle is to civilize the passions, not by regu-
lating them imperiously, but by transforming them with a mature
understanding of their place in an adult environment. It is the only
possible hygiene of the soul for men whose selves have become dis-
jointed by the loss of their central certainties, because it counsels
them to draw the string of possessiveness out of their passions, and
thus by removing anxiety to render them harmonious and serene.[48]

Perhaps Lippmann should not be criticized for the extreme generality
of his remarks, for he is manifestly attempting the broadest of *outlines*
of a moral stance rather than a specific code of morals that can deal
with any given situation that may arise; the very title of his book indicates the preliminary nature of his enterprise. But there are still troubling aspects to his formulation. Surely there are limits to allowing
people to "find their own happiness," for if one person's happiness is
random killing then it causes a certain restriction in other people's
happiness. The seeking of "excellence" also sounds nice, but when one
remembers that Hitler was quite excellent at mass destruction, then
we begin to have reservations.

What, then, is one to do? Is there no moral stance that is unassailable? Is there (and this is the great concern of conservative moralists
today) no way in which we can condemn what we find to be morally
repugnant behavior in other individuals or other cultures? My answer
to the first question is a regretful No; to the second, a conditional Yes.
This is not a contradiction. We must be fully aware that any moral stance
any one of us adopts is "provisional"—provisional to our upbringing,
our socioeconomic class, our national heritage, and our place in human
history. Nevertheless, since human beings must live by some kind of
moral code (assuming, for the nonce, that human beings ought to live at
all), we can simply say that by our moral code (a code that is, and should
be, subject to change, even radical overhauling, if circumstances war-

rant) certain actions are repugnant to us. The one thing we cannot legit-imately do is simply to evade the issue and pretend to a certainty and authority in moral inquiry that does not exist. Lewy states pontifically: "It is difficult to doubt that it is immoral to torture people for the amuse-ment of others or to rape a mentally impaired minor girl. We know these actions to be morally repugnant, monstrous, and unacceptable just as surely as we know anything at all, and this knowledge is neither dependent upon faith in God nor culture-bound" (W 139). This sounds unexceptionable, but I fear that *knowledge* is not by any means involved here. We are free to condemn such actions, but only because we have evolved a moral and social stance that makes these actions incommensu-rate with the kind of society we happen to prefer. And once again, I regret to say that there is simply no argument against the person who maintains that the kind of society *he* prefers would include these actions, or against the person who maintains that he prefers the destruction of all society and all human life. All we can do is to prevent such persons from carrying out these and other actions in our own society.

This is not a solution likely to please many of us, liberal and con-servative alike. But pretending that things are other than they are will only lead to folly and absurdity.

NOTES

References to Guenter Lewy's *Why America Needs Religion: Secular Modernity and Its Discontents* (Grand Rapids, Mich.: William B. Eerdmans, 1996) appear in the text under the abbreviation W.

1. Richard Pérez-Peña, "Lieberman Seeks Greater Role for Religion in Public Life," *New York Times*, August 28, 2000, p. A14.
2. Richard Pérez-Peña, "Lieberman Explains Call for Bigger Role for Religion," *New York Times*, August 30, 2000, p. A21.
3. Quoted in Jim Wallis, "Will Aid Make Churches Docile?" *New York Times*, February 3, 2001, p. A13.
4. H. L. Mencken, *A Little Book in C Major* (New York: John Lane, 1916), p. 24.

5. A. J. Ayer, *Language, Truth and Logic* (1936; rev. ed. London: Victor Gollancz, 1946), p. 107.

6. Hans Küng, *Global Responsibility: In Search of a New Ethic* (New York: Crossroad, 1991), pp. 52–53.

7. William J. Bennett, *Our Children and Our Country: Improving America's Schools and Affirming the Common Culture* (New York: Simon & Schuster, 1988), p. 178.

8. H. P. Lovecraft, letter to the Kleicomolo (August 8, 1916), *Selected Letters 1911–1924*, ed. August Derleth and Donald Wandrei (Sauk City, Wisc.: Arkham House, 1965), p. 24.

9. Arthur Schopenhauer, *Studies in Pessimism*, trans. T. Bailey Saunders (London: Swan Sonnenschein, 1890), pp. 37–38.

10. Ibid., p. 29.

11. Leo Tolstoy, *The Pathway of Life*, trans. Archibald J. Wolfe (New York: International Book Publishing Co., 1919), vol. 1, pp. 128, 137.

12. H. P. Lovecraft, letter to Maurice W. Moe (May 15, 1918), *Selected Letters 1911–1924*, pp. 63–64.

13. Walter Kaufmann, *The Faith of a Heretic* (Garden City, N.Y.: Doubleday, 1961), p. 280.

14. Ibid., pp. 280–81.

15. Bernard Spilka, Ralph W. Wood Jr., and Richard L. Gorsuch, *The Psychology of Religion: An Empirical Approach* (Englewood Cliffs, N.J.: Prentice-Hall, 1985), p. 286.

16. Graeme Newman, ed., *Global Report on Crime and Justice* (New York: Oxford University Press, 1999), p. 53.

17. Gertrude Himmelfarb, *One Nation, Two Cultures* (New York: Knopf, 1999), p. 95.

18. See Andrew Hacker, "The Case against Kids," *New York Review of Books* (November 30, 2000): 14.

19. Laurie Goldstein, "A Book Spreads the Word: Prayer for Prosperity Works," *New York Times*, May 8, 2001, pp. 1, 25.

20. Shortly after writing these words, I was regaled by an obituary of Charles Johnson, president of the International Flat Earth Society. Johnson, it appears, "based his own ideas on the Old Testament references to a flat earth and the New Testament saying that Jesus ascended into heaven. 'If earth were a ball spinning in space, there would be no up or down,' he told Newsweek magazine in 1984." *New York Times*, March 25, 2001, p. 44.

21. George F. Thomas, *Christian Ethics and Moral Philosophy* (New York: Scribner's, 1955), p. 3.

22. Ibid., p. 18.

23. Edward Westermarck, *Christianity and Morals* (New York: Macmillan, 1939), p. 51.

24. Zachary Hayes, "Hell," *The New Dictionary of Theology*, ed. Joseph A. Komonchak, Mary Collins, and Dermot A. Lane (Wilmington, Del.: Michael Glazier, 1987), p. 458.

25. Jonathan L. Kvanvig, *The Problem of Hell* (New York: Oxford University Press, 1993), p. 18.

26. Thomas Paine, *The Age of Reason* (1794–96), in *The Writings of Thomas Paine*, ed. Moncure Daniel Conway (New York: G. P. Putnam's Sons, 1894–96), vol. 4, p. 187.

27. H. P. Lovecraft, letter to James Ferdinand Morton (October 30, 1929), *Selected Letters 1929–1931*, ed. August Derleth and Donald Wandrei (Sauk City, Wisc.: Arkham House, 1971), pp. 47–48.

28. Elizabeth Cady Stanton, *Bible and Church Degrade Woman* (Chicago: H. L. Green, 1885), p. 12.

29. Cotton Mather, *Ornaments for the Daughters of Zion; or, The Character and Happiness of a Virtuous Woman* (1692; reprint Boston: S. Kneeland and T. Green, 1741), p. 89.

30. Jonathan F. Stearns, *Female Influence, and the True Christian Mode of Its Exercise* (Newburyport, Mass.: John G. Tilton, 1837), p. 17.

31. J. D. Fulton, *Woman as God Made Her: The True Woman* (Boston: Lee & Shepard, 1869), pp. 40–41.

32. [Orestes Augustus Brownson], "The Woman Question," *Catholic World* 9, no. 2 (May 1869): 150.

33. Ibid.

34. John Paul MacCorrie, "'The War of the Sexes,'" *Catholic World* 63, no. 5 (August 1896): 605–607, 612–15.

35. William Parker, *The Fundamental Error of Woman Suffrage* (New York: Fleming H. Revell Co., 1915), pp. 107–108.

36. John Erskine, *The Influence of Women and Its Cure* (Indianapolis: Bobbs-Merrill, 1936), pp. 85–86.

37. Joseph H. Fichter, "The Decline of Femininity," *Catholic World* 161, no. 1 (April 1945): 60–63.

38. See Janet Todd, *Mary Wollstonecraft: A Revolutionary Life* (London: Weidenfeld & Nicolson, 2000), pp. 329–30.

39. Kathleen Barry, *Susan B. Anthony: A Biography of a Singular Feminist* (New York: New York University Press, 1988), p. 96.

40. Jacqueline Van Voris, *Carrie Chapman Catt: A Public Life* (New York: Feminist Press, 1987), p. 90.

41. Quentin Bell, *Virginia Woolf: A Biography* (New York: Harcourt Brace Jovanovich, 1972), vol. 2, pp. 135–36.

42. Quoted in Richard D. Ryder, *Animal Revolution: Changing Attitudes towards Speciesism* (Oxford: Basil Blackwell, 1989), p. 33.

43. Ibid., p. 59.

44. H. L. Mencken, "Cousin Jocko," *Chicago Sunday Tribune* (November 8, 1925): part 5, p. 1.

45. Ryder, *Animal Revolution*, p. 33.

46. Ambrose Bierce, "Prattle," *San Francisco Examiner* (March 1, 1891): 6.

47. H. P. Lovecraft, letter to Maurice W. Moe (May 15, 1918), *Selected Letters 1911–1924*, p. 66.

48. Walter Lippmann, *A Preface to Morals* (New York: Macmillan, 1929), pp. 326–27, 328.

CONCLUSION

I contend that religion *is of no value in modern society.* It is of no value to knowledge, to government, to society, or to psychological well-being.

It is customary to regard a stance of this kind as "extreme"— somewhat akin, perhaps, to advocating infanticide as a method of birth control or mandatory ownership of guns. Accordingly, both the religious and the nonreligious tend to search for some kind of middle ground whereby the purportedly "valuable" or "viable" facets of religion can be preserved while the stupid or embarrassing or barbaric facets are jettisoned. But if the claim I have made throughout this book, namely, that religion is *false*—that it is not true to the facts of the universe as we now know them—is sound, what "valuable" or "viable" parts can possibly remain? How can there be a middle ground between the belief that $2 + 2 = 4$ and the belief that $2 + 2 = 5$? Is there any sense in "compromising" and declaring by fiat that $2 + 2 = 4.5$? If religion is true, then it would be little short of insane *not* to use it as an inflexible blueprint for *every* facet of human life, society, government, and thought, for in that case it would be enunciating the most significant and awesome truths about the universe that could possibly be enunciated. But if (as is overwhelmingly likely to be the case) religion is false, then every social, moral, political, or intellectual feature of it must also be, in some measure, false, at least in its basis. Religionists have managed to dodge this fundamental fact only by avoiding critical scrutiny of the truth-value of their doctrines, and by asserting not that religion is *true* (for this flies too much in the face of the mountains of evidence that have been amassed to the contrary) but that *it cannot be definitively proven to be false.* But if any given religion, or religion as a whole, has only a one in a billion chance of being true, why should anyone cling to belief in it except as a desperate psychological defense mechanism?

Secularists are in no small part responsible for this overall state of affairs, for they seem too timid to state their chief objection to religion forthrightly. They have internalized religion's clever suggestion that there is something reprehensible in criticizing religion in any manner; that it is in itself a sign of fanaticism—or, at the very least, of bad taste—even to hint that the metaphysical claims of religion are shaky. But to my mind, this is the critical issue in the entire debate. For all the social and political harm that religions have historically done in the past; for all the fascistic tendencies of the "religious right" and other fundamentalist movements; for all the need, in the United States, to be ever vigilant in protecting the constitutional separation of church and state, the real problem with religion is that it is overwhelmingly likely to be false. H. P. Lovecraft was more honest on this point. Replying to a pious colleague who asked him with all due ingenuousness what he had against religion, Lovecraft replied that his chief objection was very simple: "the Judaeo-Christian mythology is NOT TRUE."[1] He could as easily have cited any other religion.

Surely there is a problem in founding any intellectual, social, political, or moral theory upon a view of the world that is false or, at best, extremely implausible. No doubt a perfectly consistent theory of human behavior could be founded upon the notion that the earth is flat, but the earth is *not* flat, and so such a theory must necessarily be flawed at its very origin.

Even those who admit that religion has some difficulty in justifying its truth-claims often try various end-runs around this uncomfortable idea. Consider Karen Armstrong, who in *The Battle for God* (2000) showed conclusively that the various fundamentalist movements in the twentieth century—Christian, Judaic, and Islamic—have all failed in their chief theological, moral, and political agendas. Nevertheless, her book is full of vague and unsubstantiated claims that "religion gave humanity insights that science could not," and that there is some kind of "higher, 'mystical' truth" in religion.[2] Others maintain that religion is vital to the preservation of morality, but we have just seen what a hollow claim that is. As a final, desperate expedient, the pious assert that the "comforts" provided by religion (a belief in a benevolent God, heaven and hell, and the immortality of the soul), even if they are delusions, are so strong that many people would find it impossible to go on living without them. There would be general social anarchy, and the fabric of civilization would be irremediably torn.

I hardly know how to respond to this argument, given that it is purely hypothetical and, as yet, unverified. There has never been a purely secular society, and accordingly its descent into anarchy has not been witnessed. This argument unwittingly emphasizes exactly the claim I made at the outset—that the great majority of human beings are stupid or, at best, psychologically weak. Since there have been, throughout history, at least a small handful of exceptional individuals who have publicly declared—and have proven by their actions—that they have been able to lead happy and productive lives without subscribing to any religious tenets, and many more who have probably felt the same way but have not had the opportunity of expressing their views in print, it cannot possibly be claimed that religion is necessary to *individual* psychological well-being. We are then faced with an apparently large residue of the ignorant and neurotic who are presumably so wedded to the delusionary comforts of religion that they find life intolerable without them. As it is entirely beyond my powers of imagination to comprehend this mind-set, I am not in a position to pass judgment upon it. But since, as I have indicated, there is strong evidence of widespread skepticism and agnosticism in many European societies, and since these societies do not show any signs of imminent collapse, I do not think that the "social utility" argument in support of religion is a good one.

The adherents of most of the world's religions have unwittingly placed themselves in an intolerable bind. Their scriptures plainly compel them to adopt conceptions of the world, and of the human race, that are entirely at odds with the knowledge gained by patient human labor over the past two or three millennia; but the moment they deviate from those conceptions, they have implicitly underscored the lack of divine authority for the scriptures in which they profess to have faith. (The great majority of believers, of course, are blithely unaware of this dilemma because they are quite ignorant of the doctrines their own scriptures compel them to accept.) The only solutions for the pious are either the ostrich-act of the fundamentalists (who deny, in the face of overwhelming evidence, the absurdities found in their own sacred texts) or the adoption of a deliberate vagueness and imprecision in regard to what they actually believe—hence the popularity of a nebulous, nondoctrinal, nondogmatic "spirituality" or "religious way of life" that could apply just as well to one religion or the other, and that is incapable of disproof or even viable rebuttal because the tenets adopted are so loose and cloudy that intellectual debate becomes all but impossible. But the unwitting effect of this vagueness is a stance that, closely scrutinized, is scarcely distinguishable from agnosticism or even atheism itself.

Will, then, religion ever die out even among the foolish and desperate? I must confess my doubts on the matter. And yet, even H. L. Mencken felt some kind of optimism on this point:

The time must come inevitably when mankind shall surmount the imbecility of religion, as it has surmounted the imbecility of religion's ally, magic. It is impossible to imagine this world being really civilized so long as so much nonsense survives. In even its highest forms religion embraces concepts that run counter to all common sense. It can be defended only by making assumptions and adopting rules of logic that are never heard of in any other field of human thinking.[3]

In fact, conventional religion in the West *has* declined incalculably in stature and prestige over the past five hundred years—as a direct result, I must again state, of the general advance of knowledge and civilization. This is why I am not much concerned about the so-called rise of religious fundamentalism. The plain fact is that it and all other signs of religious "revival" are, in the overall history of the church within Western civilization, precisely analogous to the galvanic twitching of a corpse. Religion is dead as an arbiter of truth, as a dictator of governmental policy, as a societal bond, and even as an infallible guide to morals; and this death applies not merely to the intelligentsia but to the people at large. Consider the following points of interest:

1) There is no Inquisition to enforce orthodoxy and stamp out heresy. Indeed, even though the Christian, Jewish, and Islamic faiths all maintain their possession of the exclusive truth about the nature and attributes of God, they now live in relative peace among themselves, except in places like the Middle East where religion is largely used as a smoke screen for political disputes. Less onerous forms of religious oppression have also been done away with, such as mandatory taxation in support of religion (as was done in some American states even after independence), religious tests for office holding, and the like. The expelling of religion from government in the West has produced the greatest advance in civil liberties in human history.

2) The idea that Sunday is a "day of rest" in which no activity of any kind—whether it be sports (can one imagine Sundays in the fall without the NFL?), mall-roaming, or what have you— is now so quaint as to provoke mirth or bafflement.

3) Do missionaries still exist? It is more than a century since the pestiferous Christian missionaries in China helped to bring about the Boxer Rebellion. The very idea that members of one faith should attempt to convert those of another now elicits outrage; so far as I can tell, only the Mormons continually and unashamedly engage in the enterprise.

4) Are sermons ever published today? Does the average person have any conception of how many volumes of sermons were published in the seventeenth, eighteenth, and nineteenth centuries? Conversely, can one even conceive of the flaccid, platitudinous sermons of today's priests and ministers achieving the dignity of print?

5) Could a preacher who is obviously guilty of adultery or some other sexual peccadillo be found innocent merely because he is a preacher, as happened to Henry Ward Beecher of none too fragrant memory in the celebrated trial of the 1870s? Nowadays, when accusations of priestly shenanigans with women, girls, or boys are made, we assume the poor fellow's guilt without even the formality of a trial.

6) The mere fact that there can even be a debate as to whether homosexuality is a "sin" would have been inconceivable even a half-century ago—perhaps even twenty years ago. Most of the religious sects in this country will inexorably yield on this point as they have yielded on so many others, lest they be deemed (what they in fact are in any case) utterly irrelevant to present-day concerns.

7) When was the last time you heard the word *heathen* used seriously by a religious person? Behind this single word lies such a history of disapproval—indeed, actual persecution—that its current reduction to the level of a joke (for the word can now only be used as a joke) would have astounded our pious forefathers of even a century ago. (The resurrection of the word *infidel* by Osama bin Laden and the Taliban only confirms their benighted medievalism.)

The list could be continued almost indefinitely. To be sure, American Christians still pride themselves on the depth and extent of their piety, but it is plain that the great majority of them conduct almost every single facet of their public and private lives as if no God existed to disapprove of their thirst for money and possessions, their titillation at the middle-class pornography of television sitcoms, and their general lack of interest in converting their Jewish, Islamic, Hindu, Buddhist, or even atheist friends (assuming they have any of these) to their faith, even though their scripture states repeatedly that anyone not so converted is heading straight to hell. Only on Sunday does it occur to them that it might be socially, politically, and economically advantageous to be seen entering a church—any church, it hardly matters which—for an hour or two of mechanical ritual and platitudinous sermonizing.

And yet, the picture is not entirely rosy for the irreligious. Although there is no longer any danger of being burned at the stake, the announcement that one is an atheist remains an embarrassing conversation-stopper—a feeble vestige of the prodigious disapproval of "infidels" and "heretics" during the church's heyday centuries ago. Moreover, there can scarcely be a doubt that specifically atheistic or even agnostic voices have some difficulty in getting a hearing in major organs of public opinion in this country, whether it be newspapers, magazines, television, radio, or films. The reasons for this should be obvious: each of these media, compelled by economic necessity to appeal to as wide a section of the populace as possible, cannot take the risk of offending any large proportion of their readership or viewership by presenting arguments blatantly contrary to their religious prejudices. Accordingly, nearly all discussions of religion in the mass media either are absurdly contentless and nondoctrinal, or treat every religion, no matter how foolish or preposterous, with a studied respect that it does not seem, on purely intellectual grounds, to deserve. All this may come as a surprise to Christian fundamentalists, obsessed as they are with the purported godlessness of the mass media, but the dominance of secularism is really only a function of American religious diversity: the media have found it *safer* to avoid all substantive discussion of religion, much less the advocacy of any one religion or (heaven forfend!) atheism or even agnosticism. If the result is a kind of "agnosticism by default," then that is only a function of the perceived need to avoid giving offense on this hot-button issue. There are, after all, several radio and cable television stations devoted entirely to Christian proselytizing; I don't know of any explicitly atheistic or agnostic radio or television station.

Let me repeat what I stated at the outset: it would be a good idea if atheists, agnostics, and secularists were a bit more forthright in speaking out against the devout and their theological lackeys. Many years ago the poet George Sterling, writing to H. L. Mencken, noted that "we non-believers have been taking it lying down, and what this country needs is a good hot religious war, with the pen, not the sword."[4] More recently, Gore Vidal has called for "an all-out war on the monotheists."[5] I think a little more toughness in combating religious mummery and obscurantism would be welcome.

Religion may never be doomed to utter extinction, but its function as a force that actually affects daily behavior, or broader political, social, and moral tendencies, seems — except in pockets of fanaticism such as Christian and Islamic fundamentalist communities — definitively over. As John Beevers noted long ago, the only problem is how to get rid of the corpse before it begins to smell too much.

NOTES

1. H. P. Lovecraft, letter to Maurice W. Moe (May 15, 1918), *Selected Letters 1911–1924*, p. 60.

2. Karen Armstrong, *The Battle for God* (New York: Knopf, 2000), pp. 158, 367.

3. H. L. Mencken, *Minority Report: H. L. Mencken's Notebooks* (New York: Knopf, 1949), p. 207.

4. George Sterling, letter to H. L. Mencken (May 4, 1926), in *From Baltimore to Bohemia: The Letters of H. L. Mencken and George Sterling*, ed. S. T. Joshi (Rutherford, N.J.: Fairleigh Dickinson University Press, 2001), p. 230.

5. Gore Vidal, "Monotheism and Its Discontents" (1992), in Vidal's *United States: Essays 1952–1992* (New York: Random House, 1993), p. 1051.

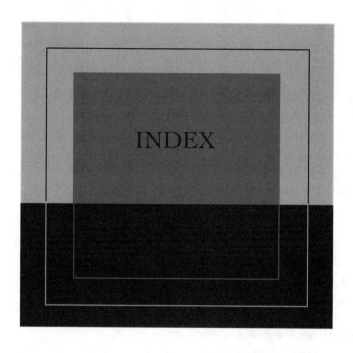

INDEX